Driven to Wonder

Eight years in an RV with two kids: A Memoir

First Edition

by

Michael Boyink

Show Me Your Words, LLC • Ava, Missouri

Copyright © 2022 Michael Boyink

All rights reserved. No portion of this book may be reproduced in any form without permission from the publisher except as permitted by U.S. copyright law. For permissions contact: mike@boyink.com.

ISBN: 978-0-578-29414-8 (Paperback Edition)

Printed and bound in the USA
First printing May 2022

Published by:
Show Me Your Words, LLC
600 East Garfield Avenue
Ava, MO 65608
showmeyourwords.com

Cover illustration copyright © 2022 by Paul Burton of oddburton.com

Disclaimers: Some names have been changed for privacy. Some photos have been edited to remove or obscure trademarks and faces. Any remaining trademarks and copyrights are the property of their respective owners and the author has no affiliation with them. Some locations have been obscured to protect specific places or businesses. Some historic accounts are fictionalized and shouldn't be considered official. Profiles of historic figures are based on public information, aren't official or authorized versions, and - along with the rest of the content in this book - are intended for entertainment or informational purposes only. The author and anyone else associated with this book shall not be held liable for damages incurred through the use of information provided herein. Content in this book isn't intended to be, nor does it constitute, the giving of professional advice. The author and others associated with this book make no representation as to the accuracy, completeness or validity of any information in this book. While every caution has been taken to provide accurate information, please use discretion before making decisions based on the content herein. The author and others associated with this book aren't liable for any errors or omissions nor will provide any form of compensation if you suffer an inconvenience, loss or damages of any kind because of, or by making use of, the information contained herein. Any advice given is the author's own, based on his personal experience. Always seek the advice of a professional before acting on any part of this book. This book contains references and links to third party products and services. These references have been included for the convenience of the readers. They shouldn't be construed as endorsements from these third parties or endorsements of their products or services. These links and references may contain products and opinions expressed by their respective owners. The author does not assume liability or responsibility for any third party material or opinions.

The acknowledgments section at the back of this book has additional copyrights, disclaimers, and permissions.

To Crissa (MsBoyink), Harrison, and Miranda.
Fellow adventurers all.

Contents

Preface

Driven to Wonder. You may think I made a typo. Surely a book about travel should be called *Driven to Wander*?

RVers have a phrase.

The hitch itch.

Hitch itch occurs when the urge to see what's down the road becomes strong enough to justify the work of packing everything up and getting mobile.

The itch is a symptom.

The cause?

Wonder.

Wondering what's up around that bend in the road.

Wondering what there is to see there. Who there is to meet. What new meal might be shared. What new thing could be learned.

Wonder.

There's more to wonder than simple curiosity.

There is astonishment. Admiration. Rapt attention to something new or mysterious.

You can wonder what's around that bend in the road, and then wonder at what you find.

I'm not sure there's a better word to more completely capture our eight years of full-time RV travel as a family in the USA.

The idea had its genesis in wonder.

We were living the ideal American suburban life. We had two children, a ranch house, and a station wagon with wood-grained sides.

I was self-employed. MsBoyink was the homemaker and homeschooler.

The kids were involved in Little League, Girls on the Run, Cadets, GEMS, etc.

Saturdays were spent on house or vehicle projects. On Sunday we went to church.

We'd go camping once or twice a summer. Maybe grab a date night once a month.

We were busy.

And we were restless.

We wondered.

Is this all there was?

Busyness, then an empty nest?

We realized I could work anywhere with an internet connection. We could homeschool anywhere.

An off-the-cuff joke about selling the house and hitting the road in an RV turned serious.

I looked into the finances and calculated we could keep our house and afford to buy a truck and used fifth-wheel.

We decided to go for it.

Traveling in an RV full-time as a family.

But just for a year.

Because we also wondered.

Would we enjoy it? Would we drive each other crazy? Would an RV constructed of furring strips and staples hold up to two kids going through puberty?

We did. We didn't. And miraculously, it did.

We came back after the initial year, sold the house, gave away most of the stuff that was in it, and went all-in on the RV lifestyle.

For another seven years.

Because we had wondered.

We wondered at the sea, at rocks that rang inexplicably when struck, and at colorful boiling natural pools.

We wondered at strangers who took us kayaking, created intricate treasure-seeking games for us, or helped us when we broke down.

And we wondered at the way travel helped us overcome various fears.

The trip that began in wonder was sustained by wonder.

Wandering?

That was just a means to an end.

I wrote *Driven to Wonder* for a few reasons.

One was for me. I often need to write about experiences in order to understand the life lesson they held. Some lessons I need to learn multiple times.

Another was for our kids to share as a scrapbook with their families.

But it's also for anyone considering doing something similar with their own family.

Who might be wondering.

Wondering where you might go. What you might experience. Who you might meet. What you might learn. How you might be changed.

Your trip will be different from ours.

We met other RV familes who liked places we didn't, lived in rigs we couldn't, and went on adventures we wouldn't.

My hope is that the following pages faithfully present one account of family life while RVing full-time - the good and the bad, the experiences we wouldn't

wish on anyone and the moments we'll treasure forever.

May you find the sense of wonder driving you the way it did us.

Photos:

1. Michael and Miranda on the Blue Ridge Parkway in NC.
2. MsBoyink in the Cathedral of Junk in Austin, TX.
3. Harrison feeling a waterfall in Austin, TX.
4. Seashelling on the seashore in NC.
5. Miranda tidepooling in Port Angeles, WA.

How We Did It

In a coronavirus world, RV sales are hitting record highs. More RV owners means more demand for RV content. The market has responded - hardly a day goes by where I don't find a new RV-related blog, podcast, or YouTube channel.

If you want to learn how to shop for, evaluate, finance, use, maintain, repair, or customize an RV, a web search will find multiple, recent, well-constructed answers to those questions.

I set out to write a *why to RV* book more than a *how to RV* book.

Still, you probably have questions about how we managed to RV full-time as a family for eight years.

Here are answers to the most common questions people asked us:

What kind of RV did you buy?

We owned three RVs over the duration of our travels. The first was a used *30*-foot bunkhouse fifth-wheel. We chose it because:

- We liked how fifth-wheel bunkhouse floorplans put bedrooms at opposite ends of the trailer. The bunkhouse motorhomes had adjacent bedrooms at the back of the rig (like, you could touch toes while all in bed. We had teens. Think about it).
- A used truck and used fifth-wheel was the cheapest way we found to get on the road.
- If the truck needed repair our house wasn't in the shop with it.
- A fifth-wheel was easier to hook up and shorter once connected than a bumper-pull RV.
- Once we setup the RV in a campsite, the pickup truck was a perfect exploration rig for the four of us.

After a few years, the kids outgrew their bunks. And the rig needed repairs. We chose to upsize the RV instead.

We knew exactly what we wanted, couldn't find it used, so ordered a new 34-foot bunkhouse fifth-wheel to our specifications (and without stripes).

It wasn't rated for full-time living, but it worked well for us. The rig only needed a few minor repairs over the four years that we owned it (our tactic of visiting the RV factory and bribing the workers with fudge must have worked).

Our final RV was a used Class B campervan.

Our son had moved out. Our daughter was planning to. We were scheming a radical downsize with hopes of doing more remote camping than the fifth-wheels allowed.

Then our trusty truck needed an expensive engine repair and I didn't think it was worth fixing. We sold it and the fifth-wheel as a package and accelerated our move into the campervan.

Overall, each RV worked for what we needed at the time and we'd buy the same rigs if we had it to do over again.

Gas or diesel?

Ah, the age-old question.

I wanted a diesel truck to tow with, but didn't want a payment. I couldn't find a diesel I was happy with for the budget I had.

We found the RV first. Time was running out to find a truck when a super clean, low-mileage Chevy 2500 came along for less than our budget. It had an *8.1* Liter gas engine and an Allison transmission- an excellent drivetrain for towing. I jumped on it.

It wasn't the truck I wanted, but it proved to be a tow monster. The longer I owned it the more I loved it.

I know RVers generally prefer diesels, but it seemed like every diesel owner we talked with had stories of expensive repairs. We put around *110,000* miles on our gasser and the only unexpected repairs were a radiator and an exhaust manifold. It never lacked for power towing up steep grades. Going down steep grades it felt like I had an engine brake. The drivetrain would control our speed and I didn't have to ride the brakes.

It got *7-10* mpg while towing.

How did you get your mail?

We used a mail forwarding service. For a monthly cost, they provided an address for us to have mail sent to.

They'd scan the mail coming into that address and email us the images. We'd let them know whether to trash it or forward it on to us.

However, the mailing address wasn't usable as a residential address. I tried and got a nastygram from the state licensing bureau.

What did you do for a legal residential address?

We bribed family members to let us "live" with them. On paper, anyway. We used their addresses on our driver's licenses, tax returns, etc.

Search "RV domicile" for more information about this issue.

How did you get internet?

Generally speaking there are two sources of internet for RVers - campground wifi and cell-based internet (3G, 4G, 5G, etc).

Cell-based internet required a modem (or hotspot) with a monthly data plan. We bought different modems and monthly plans when better deals came along.

To increase our odds of having coverage, I put the hotspots on Verizon and kept my smartphone on AT&T.

For hardware, I bought external antennas, amplifiers, and routers that could grab either cell internet or campground wifi and repeat it into our RV for sharing to multiple devices.

Overall, campground wifi was unusable. As I bought new hardware I quit worrying about it and focused on getting a usable cell signal.

If you're shopping for internet gear and haven't yet run across Cherie Ve Ard and Chris Dunphy at rvmobileinternet.com, check them out. Buy what they recommend. They've been testing and reviewing mobile internet gear since before we started traveling and remain the industry experts.

Then 12 months after you buy internet gear, start shopping again. What you have is probably obsolete.

How did you decide where to go?

We didn't have a consistent way of choosing our next destination. We based each move on a combination of factors including:

- "Bucket-list" destinations we circled on a map while prepping
- Weather forecasts
- Proximity of friends or family
- Destinations recommended by others
- Available campgrounds
- Internet coverage
- Battery status
- Holding tank status
- Scheduled training classes
- Scheduled work-camping engagements
- Calendar issues (holidays or weekday/weekend)

We used a GPS, smartphones, laptops, and traditional paper atlases to plan our routes.

At times we had to be somewhere on a certain date. We found that stressful. We much preferred to move at our own pace.

We enjoyed the freedom of either traveling randomly or having loose goals like driving the length of the Mississippi River.

Sometimes we wouldn't even choose a destination. We'd just start driving and figure it out on the way. Other moves took three to four hours of research and multiple phone calls before heading out.

How did you finance your travels?

When we first launched I had a web development business and a training business.

I could do the web development anywhere at any time. I'd log hours on client projects then send them an invoice. Clients sent payment to our bank in Michigan and the bank deposited the checks.

Through the training business I sold ebooks and screencasts online. The income came into our Paypal account and we'd transfer it to our bank account. I sold physical books through Amazon, who paid via electronic bank transfer.

We also hosted classroom training events at hotels in different cities as we traveled. The income from these events came to us online or by paper check, which we mailed to our bank (before they had an app for making deposits on our phone).

After a few years on the road most of that income dried up. The product it was all based around was eclipsed by a hot new competitor.

I didn't want to rebuild my business around the new product. After nearly 20 years of building websites, I was ready for something different. I tried and failed to find a remote job. The last option was to pivot our business with new services.

I relaunched as a content studio offering blog posts, ebooks, and social media copy to clients. It took a while to gain traction, but eventually between it and residual web development clients we made a go of it.

The transition was tough. We work-camped to keep our costs down, but also

incurred some credit card debt that took time to pay off.

What did you do for school?

We were homeschoolers before we started traveling. Visiting places rather than just reading about them was a main reason for wanting to RV in the first place.

MsBoyink was the homeschool planner. She was always trying to create a more structured curriculum for the kids. The year before we started traveling she felt she'd finally created a well-organized school year.

Planning for our big RV adventure came at the cost of her school planning time. The week before we were scheduled to leave, she was in a bit of a panic. She hadn't finalized any schooling plans,

purchased any curriculum, or lined up any books.

I recommended the unthinkable.
Let it go.

I didn't want to sit outside of Yosemite waiting for the kids to finish their workbook pages. I hoped the trip itself would provide as many "teachable moments" as we were willing to learn.

That proved true.

In Erie, Pennsylvania we learned about the War of *1812*. In Gettysburg, Pennsylvania we learned about the Civil War. In Philadelphia, Pennsylvania we learned about the founding fathers. In Richmond, Virginia we learned about sundials. In Virginia Beach, Virginia we learned about ocean life. In Upper Black Eddy, Pennsylvania we learned about rocks that ring like bells.

And that was just the first few months.

As we traveled, schooling became a combination of travel experiences and formal curriculum.

Miranda dug into her love for the Sonoran desert. Harrison joined another traveling teen and created Lego stop-motion movies.

Both kids took on new physical challenges including mountain biking, hiking, surfing, snorkeling, and BMX racing.

They both took online classes, meeting kids from all over the world (and remaining friends with some of them). They watched and listened as the House of Representatives discussed and took vote on a bill. Harrison had his first "real job" and Miranda worked with horses, goats, and dogs. They hung out with kids and adults of all ages.

I could go on.

What did we do for school? We went RVing for eight years.

And it all cost less than the average four-year college degree.

What did you do for church?

Hooboy.

I could write a book on this topic alone.

Basically, our physical journey triggered an unexpected spiritual journey. That journey had three phases.

The first was *disillusionment*. Full-time RVing and the traditional model of church in the United States don't mix

well. Finding churches and always being the newcomer wasn't fun.

The second phase was *destruction*. We began to question every aspect of what we knew as church. Why is it mostly indoors? Why is worship mainly communal singing? Why do so many denominations have such similar services? Why do we have paid professional pastors? Why did Jesus only mention church twice in the Bible? And more.

The third phase was *rebuilding*. We put together a new yet biblically-based approach to living our faith. We chose to stop outsourcing our faith journey to professionals and found ways to crowdsource it with other amateurs. We tried to simply love the people God put in our path. We gave up trying to schedule "church" or force an agenda in any situation. We purposed to be around others on the same journey but with no expectations.

Now that we're off the road church looks more traditional again. We're trying to keep the same mindset and not feel guilty for choosing to spend a glorious sunny spring Sunday morning outdoors rather than inside a stuffy building.

How did you find community?

MsBoyink and I are introverts. We're perfectly happy to spend quiet days together in the house, reading, working on projects, and listening to music. We didn't grow up in houses where guests were common. We don't have large networks of friends that we spent time with.

My assumption was that full-time RVing would be like that, just in different places.

I couldn't have been more wrong.

We made more friends while traveling than while living stationary. The friendships were deeper, because they were with people that we had more in common with than simply being the same age or living in the same town.

We had all opted out of the normal suburban workaday worlds, simplified our lives enough to get mobile, and were actively exploring the world.

Having those shared, counter-cultural experiences enabled instant, deep connections.

Social media was the key. We'd watch the blogs and Instagram accounts of other travelers. We'd reach out if they looked nearby, and we'd either stay in place or pull up stakes if it meant we could meet. Other families did the same for us.

We met traveling families all over the country. We caravaned with another family through several states. We had a "planned neighborhood" one winter in Florida.

We miss that community as much as we miss the travel.

How did your kids share a small space?

Our kids - one girl and one boy - were 12 and 13 when we first started traveling.

Society will tell you that kids that age need their own private spaces. We believe that's a privileged modern American view.

Talk to people from earlier generations, from low-income families, or from other countries and you'll find many sto-

DRIVEN TO WONDER

ries of families of all ages sharing small spaces.

Our kids dressed alone either in the RV bathroom, the campground showerhouse, or by negotiating with the other for their bunkroom.

The only minor issue they had was the tidiness of their room. One was a neatnik. The other, not so much.

Were you able to have date nights as parents?

Yes. Both to that question and the one lurking behind it.

Our kids were old enough that we could send them to hang out with friends, go on ranger-led hikes, or just watch a movie while we retired for a "nap."

We could also leave them overnight while we rented a nearby Airbnb.

Other RVing parents we talked with had the same experience. Finding time alone as parents was possible, they just had to get creative.

Did you use any discount campground programs?

Yes. Programs like Passport America or the Good Sam discount were a no-brainer way to save money.

Thousand Trails (TT) was another matter. Many full-time RVers claim buying a TT membership and staying exclusively in TT parks is the only way they can afford the lifestyle.

We bought TT "zone passes" at different times when it made financial sense (like winter in Florida).

But we never went all-in on a full TT membership because we just didn't enjoy staying in the parks. They often felt desolate, run-down, and depressing. We preferred city, county, state, and national park campgrounds instead.

We also noticed that people with a full TT membership tended to only travel to where there was a TT park. There are large areas of the country without TT parks and we wanted to explore those areas too.

Any regrets?

Only that we didn't do it sooner.

Photos:

1. Our first RV was a used *30*-foot ultralight bunkhouse fifth-wheel.
2. Our second RV was a new ultralight *34*-foot bunkhouse fifth-wheel.
3. Our third rig was a *1995* Class B Motorhome/Campervan.
4. Our tow rig was a two-wheel drive *2002* Chevy *2500* with an *8.1* Liter gas engine and Allison transmission.
5. A campsite office in South Carolina.
6. The kids' schooling often included interactive museum exhibits like this one in Mobile, AL.
7. Enjoying a community bike ride with traveling friends in Crater Lake, OR.
8. MsBoyink and I shared this malt while on a date at a classic soda fountain in North Dakota.

1 Delaware, OH

We were almost ready. We'd made room in the house for a new renter. We had forwarded our mail. We'd adjusted our insurance polices.

Our new-used RV was in the driveway. It had new tires, a repainted bumper, and a recaulked roof. We had stocked it with new furniture, freshened-up wardrobes, and wireless internet gear.

We'd lined up sponsors. Scheduled work-related meet-ups. Revised our training materials.

MsBoyink had planned a route. The route had options. The options had options. We had laptops, smartphones, a GPS, and printed road atlases to help us decide.

It was September, and we'd been planning our family adventure since the previous Christmas. We'd checked off a hundred items on a dozen to-do lists.

Then a friend said, "The adventure begins when the plans fail."

Pithy, but we were confident.

We hitched up the RV. We took pictures. Then I drove out while MsBoyink took video of the kids waving from the truck windows.

The plan was to drive out of Michigan and get somewhere we'd never been.

Thirty miles down the road, the "check engine" light came on.

Our plan hadn't lasted an hour.

We spent the first night of our adventure in my in-law's driveway. I had the truck looked at the next morning. A couple hours later we launched again.

Already behind, we drove longer to make up the miles.

It started raining.

We arrived at the campground as darkness fell.

Only there wasn't a campground. I had entered the address wrong on the GPS.

After an hour of backtracking in the dark, we found the actual campground.

We registered and drove to our campsite. I spent another hour backing the RV in and out while MsBoyink and the kids waved flashlights around like airport ground crew members.

We rolled into bed exhausted. We questioned our sanity.

I didn't sleep well. I was up before dawn, worried about how this day was going to go.

The dark sky began to turn blue as dawn approached. I grabbed my camera, headed out, and took what would be the first of *1,000s* of travel photos.

Looking back, God's message that morning is clear:

"Be still. Be calm. Yes, the new day holds adventure. But leave the plan to Me."

Alum Creek State Park is 30 minutes north of Columbus, OH. The park features camping, fishing, biking and more. Visit alum-creek-state-park.org for details.

Photos:

1. Sunrise over Alum Creek Lake at Alum Creek State Park.
2. Miranda skips rocks on the Alum Creek.

2 Erie, PA

There were places we wanted to visit but never made it to - like Glacier National Park, Big Bend National Park, and Acadia National Park.

There were places we did visit but left feeling like we hadn't really seen - like Yosemite, Yellowstone, and Southwest Colorado.

And there were places we'll probably never visit again.

Like Erie, Pennsylvania.

Hold on.

Before you fire up that email.

I'm sure there are wonderful people in Erie. And I'm sure many others have special memories of visiting.

Experiences of one place while on a road trip are multifaceted. The season, the weather, the people you meet, what your interests are, your personality, and any other of a dozen factors may influence what you experience in a given location.

We drove into Erie during our first week on the road.

Honestly?

Erie didn't stand much of a chance.

It had been a stressful week. We had to deal with a "check engine" light on our truck. The weather had been cold, gray, and wet. Our RV had a roof leak I hadn't been able to fix.

We were still exhausted from all the pre-travel preparations. We were stressed from trying to learn how to best navigate using new devices and software. MsBoyink and I hadn't worked out our system for getting the RV into a campsite yet.

And our waste tanks were full. We had yet to practice dumping them under real-life conditions.

So Erie started off in a hole.

And dug itself deeper.

We rolled up in 40 degrees and rain.

The RV park that sounded great online was not all that in person. There were falling-apart seasonal RVs, run-down facilities, and muddy gravel drives.

The camp office said "Back at 3:00." At 3:30 the door finally opened.

But we had reserved three nights, so we checked in, got our site assignment, and got back in the truck.

And found our way blocked by an older gentleman on a golf cart.

Our escort.

DRIVEN TO WONDER

Some RV parks do this. The escort shows you to your campsite. It's always a man. Usually "of a certain age" who needs to be kept busy doing something. They always seem to be wearing a polo shirt and baseball hat.

If the campsite requires you to back in, they like to stand in front of your truck and wave their arms in an attempt to show you how to best turn your steering wheel to get the RV into place.

While he was doing that in front of my truck, MsBoyink was at the rear of the site, standing where I could see her in my mirrors, waving her arms.

He waved one way.

She waved the other.

I couldn't win.

So I made the only choice I could make.

I put the truck in park.

And got out. And thanked escort man for his help.

But also said, "We're just getting started on a long trip and need to prac-

tice backing the RV in. We won't always have you to help us."

He understood and left us to it.

We got the RV parked, setup camp, and put the heaters on full blast trying to dry out and warm up.

We adopted a clothes drying rack as a third child, giving it living room space and a seat at the dining table.

The wifi didn't reach our trailer.

Cell service was one bar.

The showers were coin-operated.

Being too cheap for that, I showered in our rig. Then I saw water dripping from the belly of the RV.

I found a leaking cleanout under the shower.

And broke it trying to stop the leak.

Cold. Wet. Muddy. No internet. Broken pipes. We started to question this whole idea to travel full-time.

Erie is famous for being the location of the Battle of Lake Erie during the War of 1812. Master Commandant Oliver Hazard Perry was in command.

Perry had a flag made to signal the other ships when it was time to engage the enemy. On the flag he had sewn the dying words of a friend.

"Don't give up the ship!"

We took those words to heart.

After changing two letters. "Ship" became "Trip."

We bundled up. Dumped our tanks in a drizzle. Hitched up while dripping. Sloshed through the mud puddles getting out of the RV park.

And headed down the road.

Where I found parts to fix the plumbing. And, eventually, the sun came out again.

Erie, PA is located in the "Erie Triangle," land once claimed simultaneously by New York, Pennsylvania, Connecticut, and Massachusetts. Learn how the dispute was resolved at eriereader.com/article/the-story-of-the-erie-triangle.

Photos:

1. Sunset over Lake Erie in Erie, PA.
2. MsBoyink and the kids learn about the War of 1812 battles fought near Erie, PA.
3. "Don't give up the ship!" became "Don't give up the trip!"

3 Watkins Glen, NY

I've never claimed to be a professional photographer. Yes, I can talk shutter speeds, aperture settings and ISO values.

I've taken the classes. I've proven to myself that I could shoot using manual settings if I wanted to.

I just don't want to.

I enjoy seeing and framing a shot. But I don't enjoy futzing with camera buttons, so I leave the camera set on automatic.

Traveling made taking photos easy. And we had a travel blog that needed photos.

New place? Click. New activity? Click. New experience? Click. Good background for a family photo? Click.

Click. Click. Click.

I clicked at least 15,000 times.

Quality through quantity is my approach. Click enough and odds are you'll get some good shots.

Or maybe an impossible shot.

We were visiting Watkins Glen, New York. We'd driven by the famous racetrack. Then spent a morning hiking in the breathtaking state park, with its 19 waterfalls in two miles.

At lunchtime we parked on the shores of Seneca Lake. We lunched on the tailgate of our truck.

With the seagulls.

Aggressive, annoying, hungry seagulls.

They'd steal the sandwich off your plate if you turned your back.

I bet the kids that they could feed the gulls by hand. The kids didn't dare. But I did.

On a whim, I decided to try taking a picture at the same time.

I held up a cracker in one hand. And my iPhone in the other.

There was no way it should have worked.

I had to watch the gulls. I didn't want to get bitten, pecked or...worse. I couldn't look at my phone to frame the shot.

And it was over in a couple seconds.

A seagull swooped in. I clicked the shutter button with my right hand as the gull snatched the cracker from my left hand.

It flew off.

I gave the kids my best "neener" look.

And then couldn't believe what I saw on my phone.

Two seagulls backlit by the burst of a noonday sun. The holes in the cracker are visible. The seagull is looking right into the camera - face intent on getting that cracker before his buddy does.

It's an impossible, unplanned photo. There's no way it should have turned out.

Life is like that, sometimes. We think the only way to achieve the perfect moment - or the perfect photo - is by having the perfect plan.

"Failure to plan is planning to fail." Right?

But somewhere in all that planning we can find ourselves trying to take God's place.

For me, this photo was a reminder of God's power. He can step into an unplanned moment and pull off something amazing.

And I imagine He's got a pretty good "neener" look as well.

The city and state park of Watkins Glen are located at the southern end of Seneca Lake, the middle and largest of New York's "Finger Lakes." Learn more at watkinsglenchamber.com.

Photos:

1. Possibly my luckiest photo ever - feeding seagulls in Watkins Glen, NY.
2. Watching leaves get carried away by the river current.
3. The Boyink girls take in the view.
4. A view from the hiking trail at Watkins Glen State Park.

4 Cooperstown, NY

Confession: I don't really like baseball. It's not just baseball. I'm not interested in sports, generally.

I didn't grow up in a sports-focused family. We were "gearhead geek readers" with CBs, ham radios, trail bikes, snow-mobiles, dune buggies, and well-worn library cards.

When MsBoyink and I had children, we mostly followed the same path. Home-schooling kept us even further away from team sports.

But my son broke ranks. He became a baseball fan. I blame my father-in-law.

And Harrison wasn't a casual fan. He was a walking statistical baseball archive, striking up passionate conversations with anyone who commented on his Detroit Tigers hat. Or shirt. Or coat.

He created his own baseball fantasy league, filling multiple notebooks with grids of statistics that he somehow generated by rolling dice.

We nicknamed him "Data."

When we asked the kids where they wanted to go on our travels, Harrison's immediate response was "Cooperstown, New York."

He wanted to do two things there. Visit the Baseball Hall of Fame.

And play baseball.

It didn't have to be in an actual game. A simple round of catch would be enough.

But he wanted to stand on an actual Cooperstown baseball field.

We left Michigan in September and headed east. Stopped at Niagara Falls. And the Erie Canal.

Then on to Cooperstown. MsBoyink and Harrison went in to experience the museum.

Miranda and I headed to an apple farm with hundreds of different jams, jellies, salsas, and spreads to sample.

We met back up and looked to check off Harrison's second goal.

Simple, right? Find an empty baseball field and have a game of catch.

Except, not so much.

"Baseball is Cooperstown," says the city website. If baseball wasn't actually invented there, it's where the heart of the game beats strongest. The dream destination for many baseball fans.

Over 30 baseball fields in or close to town.

And all of them gated or locked.

Driving around, I kept looking in the rear-view mirror at Harrison. Sitting in the back seat, ball glove on one hand, watching out the window. Excitement waning.

We came across the local high-school ball field. Not gated. Not fenced in.

But posted: "No Trespassing."

I read the sign.

And looked at my son.

And looked at MsBoyink.

There are moments, as a father. Moments where you have to ask yourself tough questions.

What's the risk? What's my respon-

sibility as a parent? What's the greater good?

I parked the truck.

I put on Harrison's spare glove. Grabbed the ball. Shrugged at him.

"Go deep."

Cooperstown, NY is located roughly halfway between Syracuse and Albany, NY. Learn more at thisiscooperstown.com.

Photos:

1. Scofflaws on the field in Cooperstown, NY.
2. Harrison watches a game next to the Baseball Hall of Fame and Museum.
3. Dear Cooperstown, NY schools: Sorry not sorry. I hope you can forgive us.

TRESPASSING
THIS FIELD IS USED STRICTLY FOR
.C.S. ACTIVITIES OR BY OBTAINING
WRITTEN APPROVAL FROM SCHOOL
ADMINISTRATIO

5 Upper Black Eddy, PA

Going in, it looks like every county park you've been to. There's a small sign partially obscured behind a power pole. There's a circle drive in the forest with about a dozen parking spots. There are picnic tables and a portable outhouse.

But it's what this park didn't have that made it one of our favorite stops in eight years on the road.

There are no on-site rangers. There's no interpretive center or gift shop. No equipment rental booths. No boxes with printed pamphlets. No signs with detailed scientific explanations for what we were about to experience.

And that's because science can't explain it.

A footpath through the woods took us to a clearing large enough to play about five games of football in. The clearing contains a ten-foot-deep tumble of boulders, ranging from footstool to refrigerator-sized.

And these rocks?

They ring.

Strike a ringer with a hammer, and it will produce a resonate metallic sound. It's a bit like hitting a railroad spike with a sledge hammer.

A non-ringer will just thud - like a hammer on cement.

The ringers are easy to spot. Hammer-wielding visitors have been hopping through these rocks for over a hundred years, leaving behind a musical trail of pock marks to follow.

There have even been concerts staged, with multiple "rock musicians" swinging away at the same time.

After rock-hopping and hammering we had a single question. Why do some ring while others don't?

Wikipedia has a page on ringing rocks. It has several paragraphs about the science behind these and other ringing rock fields found in Australia and England.

You can sum up the answer in three words: "We don't know."

I love that.

There's so much we humans do know. At the molecular level we can talk of atoms, bonding, and geometries. At the galactic level we can talk about stars, interstellar gas, and dark matter.

In between those extremes are almost countless areas of discipline that people build entire careers and livelihoods around.

We know so much. Sometimes we think we know it all.

Yet, here's a simple, inexplicable rock.

It's a good reminder that we humans aren't so smart after all. But there is One who is. And He said something that makes me wonder if the ringing rocks aren't a gentle reproof.

"I tell you," he replied, "if they keep quiet, the stones will cry out."

In Upper Black Eddy the rocks are crying out.

Are we being too quiet?

Ringing Rocks County Park is roughly two hours north of Philadelphia, PA. The park doesn't have a street address, so use the GPS coordinates instead: 40.559916, -75.128538. Bring your own hammer.

Photos:

1. MsBoyink takes a turn making a rock ring by striking it with a hammer.
2. Michael strikes a note on a ringing rock.
3. Harrison and Miranda explore the rocks.

6 Gettysburg, PA

Gettysburg. The site of a historic battle that helped turn the tide of the Civil War in favor of the Union.

Also where the "Gettysburg Address" was given at a ceremony to honor the vast number of men who died at the battle of Gettysburg.

But there wasn't just one Gettysburg Address.

There were two.

The first began:

"Standing beneath this serene sky, overlooking these broad fields now reposing from the labors of the waning year, the mighty Alleghenies dimly towering before us, the graves of our brethren beneath our feet, it is with hesitation that I raise my poor voice to break the eloquent silence of God and Nature. But the duty to which you have called me must be performed;– grant me, I pray you, your indulgence and your sympathy."

It goes on from there.

For two hours.

It references Greek mythology. It remembers the Pilgrims. The founders of Boston. President George Washington. It captures the details of the battle.

It praises the North and vilifies the South, while attempting to call for a renewed America.

The speaker was the obvious first choice for the occasion. He was considered America's finest orator. A child prodigy, having graduated Harvard at age *17* - as valedictorian.

He briefly became a pastor at *19*, then went back to Harvard to teach. The position involved study in Europe, where he received the first German PhD awarded to an American.

Back in the States, his resume filled in further. President of Harvard. Ten years in the US Congress. Governor of Massachusetts. Literary magazine editor. Secretary of State.

And he had the voice - described as "the most mellow and beautiful and correct of all instruments of the time."

He spoke without notes, enrapturing the crowd, often moving them to tears.

And when he finished, amidst great applause, he sat down.

After a hymn from the Baltimore Glee Club, the second speaker got up.

This speaker was only invited as a courtesy. As a formality. The event organizers weren't even sure he'd show up.

Born in a cabin to illiterate parents.

No formal education. No high school diploma.

Mostly self taught, his early speeches were filled with backwoods rhetoric, tall tales, rough slang, and working-man grammar.

But he'd learned.

Enough to study law. And enter politics.

His speech was in his coat pocket. He'd worked on it for a couple of weeks, then finalized it in his room the previous night.

He wasn't feeling well, but gathered himself, looked about the crowd, and began to speak.

Two minutes later he finished and sat down.

To an awkward silence.

Then a smattering of polite applause.

Press accounts would label his speech as "silly, flat and dishwatery" and a "ludicrous luckless sally."

But history often uses a different lens than the present.

Edward Everett was the first Gettysburg speaker. He and his address have largely been forgotten in the folds of time.

But the second one, the one that began with:

"Four score and seven years ago our fathers brought forth on this continent, a new nation, conceived in Liberty, and dedicated to the proposition that all men are created equal."

Delivered by President Abraham Lincoln?

That one we remember.

Gettysburg, Pennsylvania is home to Gettysburg National Military Park which features historic structures, battlefields, *interpretive tours, and more. Plan your visit at nps.gov/gett.*

Photos:

1. Walking through the Gettysburg cemetery.
2. A Civil War cannon.
3. A statue of B.G. John Buford surveys the battlefield.
4. The Eisenhower National Historic Site is visible from the Gettysburg battlefield.
5. A battle monument in the fall color.

7 Harpers Ferry, WV

Brown signs. AKA - as we were to learn - tourist signs. Brown signs point the way to parks, zoos, museums, trails and other tourist attractions.

When you live and work in one place, brown signs are often invisible. Maybe you stopped there already. Maybe you will someday when you "get a chance." Or maybe between a full-time job, house, and family you simply don't see them anymore.

For traveling folks, brown signs become important. Brown signs point the way to the thing you came to see. Or they direct you to the spot you'll call home for the next few days.

Or brown signs can take you by surprise.

We were in the middle of a travel day. Gettysburg, Pennsylvania to Greenville, Virginia.

We started driving past brown signs for Harpers Ferry National Park.

It sounded familiar.

But honestly?

We hadn't carefully researched all the National Parks.

We weren't huge history buffs.

We didn't have a set agenda for our travels.

We really didn't know why Harpers Ferry was an important place.

But we were flexible.

And curious.

And connected.

MsBoyink grabbed our smartphone and researched the park while I drove.

She rattled off a bullet-point list of why the location was significant includ-ing Lewis and Clark, the Civil War, and Thomas Jefferson.

All interesting.

Then she mentioned a river confluence. The Potomac and Shenandoah, in this case.

That had me looking for a turn-around spot. It was time for a morning snack-and-potty-break anyway, might as well get some pretty photos at the same time.

We followed the brown signs to the parking lot.

The roadblocks started.

The first was a $6 parking fee.

Just for a quick look?

But we wanted to buy a National Park yearly pass anyway, so $6 became $85.

I parked the rig and we jumped out for a quick break. I looked around for the visitor center, viewing platform, or scenic trail.

Nothing.

Just shuttle buses waiting.

Looking at the map we got along with our pass, the second roadblock became clear.

The parking wasn't by the interesting stuff.

This wasn't going to be the quick stop I had planned.

Plans.

On the one hand, we weren't the sort to create detailed plans for travel days.

We met people who did. Exact departure times set. Routes previewed in Google Street View. Refueling stops already chosen. The next campsite reserved and waiting.

That was all too formalized for us.

But we didn't fly completely by the seat of our pants either.

I knew where I wanted to be by when.

I didn't want to fight 5 p.m. traffic. I didn't want to setup in the dark.

But one of the reasons we started traveling was to visit important and historic places rather than just read about them.

As my GPS would say - *recalculating.*

Worst case, if we stayed too long we could overnight in a local Walmart parking lot and eat the $25 we'd paid to reserve the campsite we were angling for.

Seemed like a small risk.

We grabbed snacks and got on the shuttle.

We explored town. Walked a few steps of the Appalachian Trail. Saw the spot where Abolitionist John Brown raided town in what is now called the "Tragic Prelude" to the Civil War. Saw where Lewis and Clark provisioned for their expedition.

We stood upon Jefferson Rock, and viewed the river confluence in the distance - a sight Jefferson said was "worth a voyage across the Atlantic."

I got the pretty photos that started this whole serendipitous diversion.

We got back to the RV around lunchtime. We heated up canned soup to eat, then pulled out to complete the rest of our travel day.

The research didn't stop once we left the park. MsBoyink grabbed the smart phone again, and kept filling us in on what we had just experienced.

A desire for a pretty spot to rest for a few minutes turned into a homeschool history lesson complete with field trip.

All because of those brown signs.

Learn more about Harpers Ferry National Park at nps.gov/hafe.

Photos:
1. The confluence of the Shenandoah and Potomac Rivers.
2. Main street, Harpers Ferry, WV.
3. Ruins of the *1852* St. John's Episcopal Church.
4. The Winchester and Potomac Railroad Bridge remains open to pedestrian traffic.
5. The St. Peter's Roman Catholic Church was built in *1833.*

8 Waynesboro, VA

A rinse-cycle start. That's how a friend described our first month on the road.

Rain.

Driving in rain.

Setting up camp in rain.

Rain, rain, rain.

Around the one-month mark, three things happened.

First, the weather broke. We finally got to see sunlight on the fall colors that draped the Appalachian Mountains.

Second, it finally sunk in. This wasn't just a long vacation. This was life. No one in a flat-brim hat was going to knock on our door and tell us that we'd had our fun and it was time to go home now.

Third, the plans ran out. Initially we had destinations like Niagara Falls. The Baseball Hall of Fame. Gettysburg.

Those stops were behind us. Now we were winging it.

Many northern campgrounds and RV parks close in October. We were struggling to find places to spend the night.

We did what most RVers do when the season turns. We headed south.

We figured we'd drive till the road ran out then we'd turn right.

We found an open private RV park in the Waynesboro, Virginia area.

I looked at the map and saw that it was close to the northern terminus of the Blue Ridge Parkway, and the southern entrance to the Skyline Trail.

Serendipity strikes.

We got the RV situated in the campground and drove over for our first taste of the Blue Ridge Parkway.

We found the Humpback Rocks area. The grounds included a cabin. We mar-veled at the tenacity of early settlers. Our home on wheels was about the same size, but we still had all the amenities.

We enjoyed a tailgate lunch in the parking lot. While eating we spotted a high-elevation outjutting of rocks off in the distance.

The Humpback Rocks.

A ranger let us know we could park at the base and hike up to them. He said the view was fantastic.

This was turning into the kind of travel day we dreamed about. Nice weather. Pretty views. Unexpected attractions. Outdoor experiences.

A family hike seemed like the right

thing to do. We drove up the road, found parking, and hit the trail.

I'm not sure why it didn't occur to us at first.

Our starting point was low. Our goal was high.

Which meant the entire trail was uphill.

And we were not in shape.

Being naive, we hit the trail anyway.

We stopped to catch our breath. We drank water. We mopped our brows.

A family with young kids was on the trail behind us. Too proud to be passed by six year olds, we'd start walking again just before they caught up with us.

We made it to the top.

There was no observation deck, no paved path, and no handrails.

Just the large rocks sloping up, then a steep, long drop-off past them.

There are times when one situation makes differences in personality abundantly clear. This was one of them.

I respect heights but am not afraid of them. I crept up to the edge of the slanted rock to enjoy the rewards of that all-uphill hike.

My son also approached the edge, but he has a cautious side. He stopped a couple feet short of where I did.

My daughter crept up to the same spot as her brother, then got overwhelmed. She had to turn away for a few minutes and collect herself.

And MsBoyink? I looked around and didn't see her right away. I spotted her back down the hill several yards.

She waited until the rest of us had enjoyed the view by the edge, and then came down from it. Only then did she creep up for a better look.

Maybe you've heard of parents who won't fly together, taking separate flights to decrease the odds of leaving their children parentless.

My thoughts were on seeing the view. Hers were on the future of the family.

Yes, I married up.

The Humpback Rocks are at milepost 5.8 - 9.3 on the Blue Ridge Parkway. There is a visitor center, exhibits, costumed interpreters, and a gift shop. Check availability at nps.gov/blri/planyourvisit/humpback-rocks-trails.htm.

Photos:

1. A settler's cabin on the Blue Ridge Parkway.
2. Hikers enjoy the fall colors at the top of the trail.
3. The Boyink kids at the Humpback Rocks.
4. Michael in front of the view of the George Washington National Forest.
5. MsBoyink took her turn enjoying the view only after the rest of us backed away from the edge.

9 Chesterfield, VA

We left with grand plans. Plans for where to go. Plans for what to see. For who to visit. For how to eat.

And for getting more exercise.

Hiking and biking, mainly.

There's a backstory here.

MsBoyink has never particularly liked biking.

We bought mountain bikes for each other as wedding gifts. They gathered dust hanging in the garage.

I added a kiddie seat to mine when we started a family. It was only used for "daddy-time" out riding with the kids.

We tried some rails-to-trails parks when the kids got older. It was fun, but required too much planning.

She wanted to like biking. We hoped being on the road and around more bike-friendly places would encourage her to get out pedaling.

I even sprang for a brand new bike with a more comfortable seating position for her.

But from Walmart.

For $88.

My reasoning was if she wore out or broke the cheap bike I could justify buying something more expensive.

We left with bikes for all four of us optimistically strapped to the rear of the trailer.

Between the season and our route it was several weeks before we had a chance to use them.

Pocahontas State Park, just outside of Richmond, Virginia features over 60 miles of bike trails. The park had available camping and the weather forecast was favorable.

A family bike ride happened. All four of us, on bikes, on a relatively flat wooded trail, all at the same time.

I have video proof.

Keeping the bikes with us wasn't easy. The rack on the back of the trailer broke. I fixed it. It broke again. I added reinforcements. They broke. I added better reinforcements. They also broke.

I worried about the bikes falling off and into traffic, so I bought a rack to carry them on the roof of the truck. They rode better up there, but getting them up and down was a two-person affair.

Looking back through my photo archive, I find photos of us biking in

South Carolina, Texas, New Mexico, Utah, Michigan, Arizona, Colorado, Oregon, Georgia, and Washington. Not that we ever became hardcore bikers, but we did enjoy them when we had the chance.

"We" being the kids and I.

I have evidence of just one more family bike ride with MsBoyink on that Walmart bike - in Wallace, Idaho. It had a rails-to-trails path that we enjoyed.

In South Dakota, after nearly making a complete lap around the United States riding on the roof of the truck, I found the Walmart bike wasn't holding up well. It was rusting out. It wasn't shifting well. It had a flat tire. The repairs would cost more than the bike did.

And I realized the biggest exercise benefit anyone was getting from that bike was putting it up on the truck roof and getting it down again.

I left it by the dumpster in a Wall, South Dakota campground.

A couple years later, I tried again. I bought MsBoyink a pretty blue vintage Schwinn with chrome fenders.

I don't even remember what happened to that one.

Near as I can tell, it's been seven years since I've had MsBoyink on a bike.

But I have a new grand plan.

Here in our empty-nest, have-a-house-again years.

I'm going to buy a tandem.

I just hope she pedals.

Located 20 miles from Richmond, VA, Pocahontas State Park offers camping, fishing, hiking, biking, and entertainment venues. Learn more at dcr.virginia.gov/state-parks/pocahontas.

Photos:

1. The Boyink girls push bikes up a hill on the trail during a ride at Pocahontas State Park in Chester, VA.
2. A view from the bike trail.
3. Sunset after our big family ride.

10 Chesterfield, VA

You might say it was ironic. But don't go there. Especially if you are telling the story to someone picky about words.

It was probably just coincidence.

But that doesn't sound as interesting.

Let's call it a poetic coincidence.

We were at Pocahontas State Park just outside of Richmond, Virginia.

Pocahontas. A young Native American woman.

Who, according to one report, saved English settler John Smith from a beheading by placing her head on his.

Two cultures intersect. One saves the other.

Pocahontas State Park is known for its mountain bike trails.

My son and I were exploring them. It was a perfect crisp fall day with the sun streaming through the trees. The paths were littered with brown fallen leaves that crunched against our tires as we rode.

We pedaled past a lake with geese floating on it. We rode next to streams dribbling through dappled sunlight. We talked about the trail. We talked about

our experiences on the road so far, and where we might head to next.

And in all of our talking, lost track of where we were.

We had a map. And we certainly hadn't left the park boundaries. We were in no real danger.

But we didn't know where we were.

Or which way to go to get back to the RV.

While we were looking over the map, we heard the crunch of leaves and the snapping of twigs.

Virgina is bear country.

Several "fight or flight" thoughts ran through my mind.

Mainly I wondered if bears could run faster than we could pedal our bikes. I probably worried more because a race between my son and I probably wouldn't end in my favor.

More leaves crunched. Branches parted.

And out stepped our knight in shining armor.

No.

Really.

What stepped out onto the trail by us was a man in his late 20s or early 30s.

Dressed as a medieval knight.

No, not a full-on clanking suit of armor.

But wearing a cape, chain-mail hood, raised shoulder guards, apron, boots.

And yes, holding a sword.

I don't often use the word gob-smacked.

But we were just that.

To this day I'm frustrated that I was so shocked at the sight that I forgot I was holding a camera.

I don't remember our knight saying anything.

He just raised his sword.

Pointing the way.

We nodded, jumped on our bikes, and headed down the trail.

Saved by a knight in shining armor.

Two cultures intersect. One saves the other.

Pocahontas would approve.

Pocahontas State Park is located approximately 20 miles from Richmond, VA. The park offers camping, hiking, biking, fishing, boating, and hunting. And the occasional knight in shining armor. Learn more at dcr.virginia.gov/state-parks/pocahontas

Photos:

1. Harrison consults a trail map while riding the trails at Pocahontas State Park in Chesterfield, VA.
2. A stream on the trails.
3. A tiny toad we found on the trail.
4. Sunset casts a pink hue over the park and our truck.

11 Bucks County, PA

"Mr. Ferguson!"

Travel days bring their own routines. Hitching tow vehicles to RVs. Checking lights. Locking doors. Gathering snacks and drinks.

When all of that was done, MsBoyink (our navigator) would call out: "Mr. Ferguson!"

We had a fancy voice-activated GPS. Much like Siri or Amazon's Alexa, we had to call out the device name to wake it up.

Why Mr. Ferguson?

Because I'm a fan of Mark Twain.

In *1869* he published *The Innocents Abroad*, about his travels to Europe and the Holy Lands. In the book, Twain describes how he would hire local tour guides at every stop. But he didn't want to remember each new guide's name, so he just called them all Ferguson.

The GPS was our guide, so - like Twain - we named it Ferguson.

Turns out, to a fancy voice-activated GPS, "Ferguson!" and a sneeze are the same sound. This made for interesting drives during allergy season, so we had to make the relationship more formal.

Once we had the attention of Mr. Ferguson, MsBoyink would ask for directions to our next destination. Mr. Ferguson would return options, and MsBoyink would make a choice. And off we'd go.

Trusting.

Trusting the route would be a good one for us.

When all hitched up we were 55 feet long and just under 12 feet tall. We needed a large space to turn around. Backing up was difficult.

Recovering from a routing mistake could be more than just an inconvenience. It could be costly.

Our destination in Bucks County, Pennsylvania was a campground next to a covered bridge. The interior height of the bridge was one foot lower than the exterior height of our RV.

Mr. Ferguson's route took us across that bridge.

Luckily, MsBoyink had also looked at the campground's website. Their directions warned about the low-clearance bridge. We chose to override Mr Fergu-

DRIVEN TO WONDER

son's opinion on the matter and come in another way.

Once at the campground, the owner regaled us with stories of RV roofs and AC units peeled off by that bridge.

Those RVers had trusted their GPS units too much. It cost them thousands of dollars in repairs.

We started questioning Mr. Ferguson's routes more often. We'd scan RV forums and campground review websites. We'd ask our community of traveling friends.

Rather than blindly trust what our technology recommended, we sought wisdom based on experience.

It's not just when we're driving that we need help navigating. Jobs. Spouses. Kids. Habits.

We're learning to apply the same lesson we learned from Mr. Ferguson.

Seek wisdom based on experience.

The Sheard's Mill covered bridge is one of 12 in Bucks County, PA. Learn more about them at buckscountycbs.org.

Photos:
1. Built in *1873*, the Sheard's Mill Covered Bridge crosses the Tohickon Creek in Bucks County, PA.
2. Geese swimming upstream of the bridge.
3. Evidence of frustrated fishermen.
4. The resplendent fall colors.

12 Virginia Beach, VA

We were scheduled to leave the next morning. Then they showed up.

Those people.

You know those people, right?

They arrived in a monster truck pulling a travel trailer. Truck bed heaping over with gear and surrounded by multiple full-sized flags on poles. Exhaust volume level topped only by the music coming from the open truck windows.

The beer cooler was on the picnic table before the trailer was parked in the campsite.

MsBoyink and I didn't need to say anything. A traded glance was enough.

We'd have to endure the night, but could be rolling early in the morning.

Then a knock sounded at the door.

It was the monster truck driver.

Tall. Long hair. No stranger to the gym. Add a cape and he'd be a professional wrestler.

And holding a beer.

"Excuse me, do you have an extra plug adapter we could borrow?"

OK. So at least polite. And willing to come over himself rather than sending his wife or kid.

I had what he needed.

He followed me back to a rear storage compartment. He noticed the decals we had on the RV, saying that we were on a one-year family RV roadtrip.

A conversation started.

Wives were brought in. A campfire started. Chairs setup.

Their friends - with another monster truck, travel trailer, and beer cooler - joined in.

The men were "Coasties" - Coast Guardsmen.

The conversation flowed easily. They talked about weekend camping experiences and asked us about full-time RVing.

Our kids asked if it was OK if they went down to the beach with the "coastie kids." They took flashlights, made sea urchin discoveries, and played games of manhunt and pickle.

They made a late night of it. Then came home with that whole "we just had a great time but now we have to leave in the morning" angst.

We realized it had been a while since our kids had been around other kids.

And they were nice kids.

And we weren't on a hard schedule.

So in the morning, MsBoyink visited the park office and extended our stay another night.

Telling the neighbors "we just met you and unexpectedly liked you so much we booked another night to be next to you" was a bit awkward.

But we got over it.

The next day the kids all played on the beachfront again while the parents hung out in the campground.

We shared a meal at their picnic table.

They brought out games.

We introduced them to geocaching.

As evening fell, they brought out their camping pièce de résistance.

Karaoke.

Battery-powered and portable, even.

And so it was that for one night, on the shores of Chesapeake Bay, well after the posted quiet hours of *10* p.m. at First Landing State Park...we sang karaoke at full volume.

Which meant.

We had become *those people*.

First Landing State Park is on Cape Henry in North Virginia Beach, VA, near where the American Colonists first came ashore in 1607, before establishing themselves at Jamestown. Learn more at first-landing-state-park.org.

Photos:

1. Heading down the boardwalk to do some beachcombing and ship spotting.
2. Tucked into our campsite at First Landing State Park in Virginia Beach, VA.
3. The Boyink kids play "monkey in the middle" with new friends on the beach.

13 Outer Banks, NC

Yosemite. The Grand Canyon. Niagara Falls. Gettysburg. Washington, D.C.

All places that people purpose to visit on vacations.

All places that, once people learned that we were traveling full-time, said were "must-see" while we were on the road.

The Outer Banks of North Carolina (OBX) were also on that list. Friends had special memories of family summer vacations there.

Researching, we learned the area had 100 miles of ocean-front beaches on thin needle-shaped islands barely visible on the map. Wild horses. Wright Brothers history. Pirate history. Lighthouses. Ferries.

It all sounded awesome.

Our first challenge was finding a place to park the RV. It was November and all of the state parks and national forests were already closed for the winter season.

Which left private RV parks. Which were expensive. Like $80 a night expensive. Too rich for our "not on vacation" mode of travel.

MsBoyink rolled up her sleeves, pulled out her "full-time RVer and cheapskate" bag of tricks and found us options for $30 per night instead.

With lodging settled and a good weather forecast, we pointed the truck south into North Carolina from Virginia Beach.

Expectations were high.

And maybe that was the problem.

At the north end at the Kill Devil Hill and Kittyhawk area, we encountered the first of our two main OBX experiences.

Rampant consumerism.

Not in the Pigeon Forge, Tennessee style of busy theme parks and highrise hotels, but still. T-shirt shops. Hammock stores. Restaurants. Kite stores.

The retail districts back up to ocean-front residential areas, which are a virtually solid fence of tall houses that block out the ocean view.

We drove on, anxious to get out of the commercial areas.

And went straight into OBX experience number two.

Long, monotonous stretches of road.

Looking at the map of the Outer Banks, we expected to have constant views of water.

The reality?

For much of the drive, sand dunes obscured views of the ocean on one side and scrubby trees obscured the sound on the other.

Our Outer Banks visit wasn't entirely a disappointment.

We got our first glimpse of dolphins in the wild. We had our first sampling of fresh seafood. We walked beaches. We rode on ferries. We watched people fishing in the surf.

And we learned an important lesson.

Maybe it's because we didn't rent a beach house. Maybe it's because we were there in the off-season. Maybe it's because we came from West Michigan - which has some of the nicest beaches in the country.

But we learned.

We enjoyed traveling more when we had no expectations of the area we were in. No up-front research. No stories from other people's favorite family vacations.

Better to appreciate an area for what it is, than resent it for not being what it was supposed to be.

The Outer Banks of North Carolina are a series of barrier islands separating the mainland from the Atlantic Ocean. Learn more at outerbanks.com.

Photos:

1. Shells on the beach in the Outer Banks of North Carolina.
2. Miranda looks for treasures on the Atlantic Ocean shoreline.
3. Our first experience with fresh seafood.
4. The view while driving through the Outer Banks is a bit less scenic than we expected.
5. The Cape Hatteras Lighthouse had to be moved 2,500 feet inland in 1999 to keep it out of the ocean.

14 Beaufort, SC

"Recalculating."

That's what Mr. Ferguson (our GPS) would say when I didn't follow his route.

I'm convinced that the Garmin programmers added nuance to that word. I always heard it along with just a hint of disapproval.

Like Mr. Ferguson really wanted to say "You couldn't just turn when I told you to? Fine. (Heavy breath through the nose, eye roll.) Recalculating."

We were headed to a state park on the coast of South Carolina. Between us and our campsite for the night was the town of Beaufort.

It was dark.

We were running late.

And I had turned too early.

Recalculating.

Mr. Ferguson sulked off to create a new route.

But we weren't paying attention to the GPS.

We were looking at road closed bar-riers. And backed-up traffic. And crowds of people milling about.

Parents pushing kids in strollers. Couples holding hands. Groups of friends. All in stocking hats, winter coats, and scarves.

We'd been on the road all day. It took our tired brains a few minutes to realize what was going on.

It was mid-December. Those were holiday decorations.

This was Beaufort's Christmas Parade.

Mr. Ferguson's screen flashed. His new route showed a left turn at the next intersection.

Onto the parade route.

I got out to see if we had any options for turning around.

Cars lined both sides of the street. Late parade-goers trickled in behind us. There was an alleyway on one side of the street, but it was narrow and its entry was surrounded by parked cars. I didn't see the space I needed.

We were stuck. In the middle of the street.

I got back in the truck, set the parking brake, and shut off the engine.

Humans are funny creatures. We talk a lot about plans. Career plans. Marriage plans. Family plans. Travel plans.

All based on the arrogant belief that we can both account for and control all

DRIVEN TO WONDER

the variables necessary to determine the outcome of a complex sequence of events.

The great pugilistic philosopher Mike Tyson put it this way; "Everyone has a plan until they get punched in the face."

We can't always be in total control of every plan. What we can control is our reaction when the plan fails.

Recalculating.

MsBoyink volunteered to stay with the truck and RV in case some city official was unhappy with our mid-street parking spot.

The kids and I got out and walked to the closed-off street. We mingled with the holiday crowd. We toured an open art gallery. We watched the parade until Santa passed, then walked back to the truck.

A policeman slid the barriers aside and we followed Mr. Ferguson's directions out of town and to the state park.

It was now after-hours. The gate was locked. We hadn't called ahead - because we had planned to be there earlier.

Just as we resigned ourselves to spending the night on the road in front of the gates, headlights appeared behind us.

Another camper, returning late. He had the gate code. We convinced him to let us in as well. We found a campsite in the dark, plugged in, put the jacks down, and fell into bed.

Not the day we had planned.

But a day we remember more than many.

Because we recalculated.

Beaufort, SC has been used as a location for many well-known films including Forrest Gump, The Big Chill, and The Great Santini. Learn more about Beaufort at beaufortsc.org.

Photos:

1. Miranda walks on the Atlantic Ocean beach in Hunting Island State Park outside of Beaufort, SC.
2. Salt water marshland.
3. This initially sounded painful, but turns out to be an erosion preventative measure.
4. Miranda shows the large knobbed whelk shell she found while beachcombing.

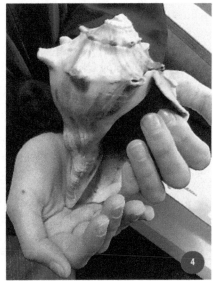

15 Dillon, SC

9/11 changed my life.

No, I didn't lose a relative in the horrible building collapses. And no, I didn't have any close friends who were first-responders to the scene.

I watched it all happen from the safety of my corporate job in West Michigan. A large TV on a distant wall had the news playing, and like prairie dogs we all stood up in our cubicle offices to watch.

I remember watching the second plane flying into the tower. I remember seeing people leaping from the burning towers. And I remember seeing the towers collapse.

I remember feeling numb.

And not knowing what to do.

The numbness melded into mourning. And eventually, the mourning ebbed away as life picked up again.

But it wasn't the same life.

People were scared. Scared people don't move the same way. Decisions that could be delayed were. Projects that could be canceled were.

The Dow-Jones dropped *700* points. An existing recession got deeper.

The company I worked for began to slow down. A round of layoffs took some coworkers. I felt bad for them, but was relieved to still have my job.

Six weeks later came another round of layoffs. I said goodbye to more coworkers, now starting to resent the additional workload their absence would mean.

Another six or eight weeks passed.

Then one morning my boss appeared at my desk, whitefaced. He asked me to accompany him to the conference room. Sitting inside were two men I didn't recognize. My boss stammered out an apology and left.

The two men laid out my termination package. Then a security guard escorted me back to my desk, waited while I packed up, then walked me to the door.

I don't remember the drive home. Only walking into the house and MsBoyink saying "What are you doing home so early?"

We were a single-income family.

MsBoyink was at home full-time with our two young children.

9/11 was a successful act of terrorism. Lives were lost. Great physical damage was caused. Millions of people - like me - were indirectly impacted.

But, like after a forest fire, new growth returned. And what grew wasn't what burned.

I looked for a new job. I got offers for projects instead. I started a business to take on those projects. Those projects led to others.

My income became location-independent.

Which, a few years later, gave us the ability to travel by RV full-time.

So on that day, when we rolled into a South Carolina rest area, and saw a semi trailer carrying steel salvaged from the World Trade Towers, it gave me pause.

9/11 had indeed changed our lives. For the better.

I'm not always comfortable with that thought. So many people lost their lives that day.

So we dedicate our travels - and these retellings of them - to the Americans that made the ultimate sacrifice on *9/11*.

And hope that they would join us in

being thankful that, in one small way, the terrorists didn't win.

Learn more about the 9/11 terrorist attacks at 911memorial.org.

Photos:
1. MsBoyink and the kids talk about what a piece of the World Trade Center means.
2. A semi truck carrying pieces of the World Trade Center is escorted by police on its way to Florida where the wreckage will become a memorial sculpture.

16 Atlanta, GA

We were glad to be back on the road. We had gone home for Christmas.

We'd left Savannah, Georgia, dropped our RV off at friends near Albany, Georgia, and headed for Michigan.

In Kentucky, we'd been knocked off the road by a distracted driver. A shop bandaged our truck back together enough to limp home.

A three-day visit had turned into two weeks while we waited for the body shop to finish the repairs.

And now we were driving south on a tight schedule to get back to Atlanta. We had a training business and had scheduled a class there.

Some students were local, but we also had people flying in from other states and other countries.

Then we started passing bucket trucks.

A brigade of them.

We'd only been on the road a couple of months, but the sight was unusual. I got curious. While taking a break at a rest area I grabbed my phone and started nosing around.

Checking the weather provided the answer.

Atlanta was expecting a heavy ice storm.

Those trucks were carrying a portent of powerline workers.

Comparing the storm's pace to ours, if we pulled a long driving day we could get to Atlanta before it did. I got us back on the highway while MsBoyink called ahead and added a night to our hotel stay.

We arrived late, unloaded, and tucked the truck down in the parking garage.

And waited.

How often have you heard predictions for bad weather that don't come true?

This one came true.

Freezing rain became snow became more freezing rain became two inches of ice.

Atlanta was paralyzed.

People were stranded. Restaurants were closed. Streets were nearly empty.

Between our accident and extended holiday in Michigan, we didn't have much for food. The ice storm had changed our plans to eat out.

My son and I went to the grocery store next to the hotel.

And found a new dilemma.

The shelves had large empty places.

On the one hand, we needed food. I felt the responsibility of feeding my family weigh heavy on my shoulders. Survival mode was kicking in.

On the other hand, I didn't want to get caught up in the hysteria. We considered ourselves Christian, with faith in God's provision for our lives.

But we realized just how easy that is to do when the store shelves are full.

I bought just enough food to last until our hotel stay was over.

And hoped I'd never be in that situation again.

The weather forecast changed. A thaw was coming.

Until then, we made do. We visited a local church. We found an open store and bought some games. We finally found an open restaurant.

A couple of our students had also made it in before the storm. The hotel let us do our training in their conference room at no cost.

The thaw came. People chiseled out. The hotel got the ramp out of the parking garage cleared. We repeated our class for the rest of the students.

After ten days with four of us in one hotel room, we were able to fetch our RV and continue traveling.

I know.

The coronavirus isn't just a spring ice storm. Hurricanes do more damage. And fires are so destructive.

It's going to get worse before it gets better.

But we are strong.

And our God is in control.

We'll get through this.
Together.

If you get directions to an address on "Peachtree" in Atlanta, double check your GPS. The city has 71 streets with "Peachtree" in the name. Learn other fun facts about Atlanta at atlanta.net.

Photos:
1. The brigade of bucket trucks carrying a portent of powerline workers.
2. Miranda, Harrison, and MsBoyink attempt to navigate an ice-covered Atlanta sidewalk.
3. An iced-in minivan in a downtown parking lot.
4. Harrison holds a chunk of ice.
5. Miranda holds a chunk of ice.

17 Comer, GA

"Many a trip continues long after movement in time and space have ceased."

- John Steinbeck, *Travels With Charley*

Steinbeck traveled with his dog, Charley.

We traveled with kids. Which, with deference to Mr. Steinbeck, is way, way harder.

For some, trips do indeed continue long after movement in time and space cease. But we found that, for others, trips don't start until after movement in time and space begin.

We started traveling when my daughter was 12.

She didn't want to go.

In retrospect, maybe cramming puberty into a 30-foot RV wasn't our best idea.

During our early travels she wouldn't even talk while riding in the truck.

Describing her as "the black hole of anger in the back seat" probably didn't help.

This went on for weeks.

I began to wonder if she would ever join us.

The truck accident knocked her off her axis. Then came the unexpected extended stay in Michigan. And the unexpected extended stay in the frozen Atlanta hotel.

Finally leaving the hotel, Miranda said "I just want to go home."

Same song, but with a different tone.

I stopped and asked her "Back in Michigan or in the RV?"

"I don't care. I just want to be home."

Her trip had finally begun.

We picked up the RV from where we had stored it with friends.

We parked in an otherwise-empty Georgia state park.

And tried not to hum *Dueling Banjos*.

Miranda accompanied us on family walks. We threw rocks through ice-covered water raceways and watched air bubbles form and try to escape.

We jumped from rock to rock in the stream below the falls. We watched the water create swirling eddies on its way downstream.

We watched water spill over a dam next to a covered bridge.

Miranda was engaged in a way she hadn't been.

She didn't know it yet, but the best parts of the trip were still in front of her.

She had yet to fall in love with ocean beaches. Or the Arizona Desert. Then a Texas horse ranch.

She had not yet met Gus, the alpaca guard dog in Texas. Or Leroy, the apparently-stranded baby seal in Washington.

She had not yet met Joel, Emily, Kristin, or any of the other dozens of fellow RVing kids we'd meet during our travels.

And now?

She's an adult. Married. Living a "settled down" life in Western Missouri.

It's hard to know if Steinbeck's quote applies.

But I do hope that now, as it was in Comer, Georgia, that the best parts of her trip are still in front of her.

Watson Mill Bridge State Park is two hours east of Atlanta, GA. Learn more at gastateparks.org/WatsonMillBridge.

Photos:

1. The covered bridge at Watson Mill Bridge in Comer, GA.
2. Miranda studies the currents of South Fork River.
3. Miranda perches on a rock below the dam.
4. Harrison and Miranda explore ruins of a mill.

18 Mobile, AL

He sat at a card table stacked with copies of a book. In his dress uniform, with decorations cascading down the front. He had the bearing of a visiting diplomat.

We were in the gift shop at the USS Alabama Battleship Memorial Park in Mobile, Alabama. It was just my son Harrison and I - the girls weren't impressed with our plan to tour the *680*-foot-long WWII battleship that serves as the main attraction in the park.

But a soldier with a story? That battleship wasn't going anywhere soon. We walked over and made introductions.

His name was Colonel Glenn Frazier. And his story?

It started out like a Hollywood adventure movie. Jilted lovers. A Harley Davidson ridden into a bar. Chased out with shotguns. Joining the Army to escape.

All at *16* years old. In *1941*.

Frazier was deployed to the Philippines, serving under General Douglas MacArthur.

From there Frazier's story turned gruesome.

The U.S. ended up surrendering the Bataan Peninsula to the Japanese. Frazier was one of the approximately *75,000* men forced to make the "Bataan Death March" to Japanese prison camps.

Their captors treated them brutally, starving and beating them. Many captives were mercilessly bayoneted along the side of the road.

Frazier survived the march. And further torture in the prison camps. He made it home. When we met, he was the

last known survivor of the Bataan Death March.

A movie would end the story there. Happily ever after and all that.

Real life goes on.

Frazier had nightmares. He developed a drinking problem. And a fierce hatred for his captors.

Just seeing a Japanese car on the road would put him into a rage.

The hatred went on for years, sabotaging his health. And his relationships.

There are many topics Colonel Frazier could school an audience on. Sacrifice. Endurance. Survival. Heroism.

But the subject I remember most from our gift shop conversation?

Forgiveness.

Frazier met a Japanese nurse training to be a pastor. She washed his feet. She prayed for him. She reconnected Frazier to the God that he gave his life to at 13.

"God made a way for me to forgive the Japanese," he said. "And the nightmares finally stopped. I could finally sleep. My health got much better."

We never did tour that battleship. We used our money to buy a book from Colonel Frazier instead.

World War II veteran and former prisoner of war, Colonel Glenn Frazier, died September 15, 2018, in Daphne, AL, at the age of 94. More about his life and his book Hell's Guest *can be found at colonelfrazier.com.*

Photos:

1. The USS Alabama docked in Mobile, AL.
2. Harrison poses with Colonel Glenn Frazier in the gift shop of the USS Alabama Memorial Park.
3. Flags fly at the Veterans Memorial.

19 Stennis Space Center, MS

Gainesville, Mississippi vanished on January 10th, 1962. Ninety one residences, two churches, two cemeteries, two stores, a nightclub, and a school.

Gone.

Logtown, Mississippi disappeared September 30, 1963.

Somewhere between those dates the nearby communities of Santa Rosa, Napoleon, and Westonia also fell off the map.

Not overnight. And not without a fight.

In the early 1960s, America was on a mission.

We wanted to conquer space. We wanted to put a man on the moon.

Before the Russians did.

To do that, we had to build rockets. New rocket designs had to be tested.

And those rockets?

Loud.

Not freight-train loud. Not 747 loud. Not even headbanging heavy-metal rock-band loud.

Loudness is measured in decibels (db). A 1972 Deep Purple concert set a record by hitting 117db. Loud enough to knock three fans unconscious.

At the launch pad, a rocket engine hits 180db.

But decibel math is tricky. Decibels don't increase at a linear rate, they increase logarithmically.

Which means a rocket engine isn't just half-again as loud as a Deep Purple concert.

It's 64 times louder.

NASA needed a place to run dangerously loud tests - dangerous to humans, and dangerous to buildings.

Sound travels. NASA needed a big place. Two hundred square miles big. Ideally forested to help absorb the sound.

It also needed water access. Rocket engines are too big to transport on highways. They needed to be carried by barge.

NASA found what they were looking for in Southern Mississippi and Louisiana. Official documentation described the area as mostly "a boggy swamp and a desolate forest." Cutting through the trees was the Pearl River, which connected to the Mississippi River and provided the necessary barge access.

Identifying the rocket testing site was the easy part.

Now NASA had to acquire it.

Inside the proposed site, 2,750 people owned large timber businesses, farms, homesteads, and empty building lots in residential subdivisions.

As you might imagine, not everyone was happy about being forced to sell. Conflicts flared up. Committees were formed. Senators were appealed to. Relocation costs were negotiated.

Meanwhile, the clock was ticking. Deadlines set by the Apollo program hastened the inevitable.

Faced with eventual forced eviction, deals were struck. People started moving.

Many took their houses with them. Reports described "a line of big trucks hauling houses, awkwardly jerking and swaying on trailers, slowly rolling down old Highway 43."

One of those homes swaying down the highway belonged to Cora Blue Davis.

Government officers had tried to negotiate with her. But Cora would not leave her home. Not for money. Not for some government man in a suit. And not to help put a man on the moon.

Irresistible force meets immovable object.

But this wasn't physics class. Someone understood human pride. Maybe a whisper was made into the ears of those government men.

And that's why, on that day in 1962, Cora Blue Davis sat in her rocking chair, on the front porch of her house as movers towed it down old Highway 43.

By December of 1962, flag-raising ceremonies had been held and officials had moved in.

The first static test firing of the Saturn rockets destined for use in the Apollo program took place at Stennis Space Center on April 23, 1966.

And on July 20, 1969, Neil Armstrong was the first man to step out onto the moon.

Back on earth, Cora Blue Davis and hundreds of other people watched Armstrong from new homes, or old homes on new properties.

They realized that, like it or not, they had contributed to Armstrong's "giant leap for mankind."

They had helped put a man on the moon.

Tours of the John C. Stennis Space Center can be booked via the nearby Infinity Science Center: visitinfinity.com.

Photos:

1. A rocket testing stand at the John C. Stennis Space Center in Southern Mississippi.
2. Cora Blue Davis on the porch of her house. (Hancock County Historical Society Photo.)
3. A rocket engine on display.

20 Toyahvale, TX

We were fresh on the road. A few months in. Still finding a groove to the whole full-time travel thing.

The road had been bumpy at times.

We had endured through accidents, ice storms, wrong turns, detours, and delays.

Each bump a lesson.

We learned to expect weather anomalies. We learned when to trust our eyes more than our GPS. We learned patience.

We had made it from Michigan to New York to Virgina to Southern Texas.

And school was not yet out.

Our truck had the unfortunate combination of a thirsty big-block engine and a small fuel tank. While towing it would eat through a tank of gas in just over *200* miles.

In most places it wasn't a problem.

Then we got into the wide open spaces of West Texas.

With our sights set on Balmorhea State Park, we were on I-*10* heading through Fort Stockton.

The exit appeared on the horizon.

MsBoyink asked if I was planning to fill up.

I looked down at the gauge.

Less than a half tank.

The exit got closer.

Newton's First Law of Motion states that "objects in motion tend to stay in motion."

It held true on travel days. Once all hooked up, everyone seat-belted in, no one needing a potty break, and no one dying of hunger, I hated to stop unless I had to.

I looked at the "distance left" number on the GPS. I knew what our average fuel mileage was.

The exit loomed. Now or never.

I calculated we had enough gas.

I drove past the exit.

MsBoyink may or may not have bit her lip.

Many cities have additional exits and fuel options once past the main exits.

Not Fort Stockton.

That exit was it.

We were committed.

I-*10* stretched out in front of us as far as we could see, dipping through a low valley then heading uphill towards a ridge of short peaks in the distance.

We settled in for another hour of driving.

All while watching the needle on the gas gauge slipping lower and lower.

No gas stations in sight.

Wondering if I'd made the big mistake.

Our route took us off I-*10* down a county highway to the State Park.

We pulled into the parking lot.

Not quite on Empty. But close.

MsBoyink checked us in while I walked around the truck. I was hearing a loud humming sound from under the bed that I had not heard before.

The fuel pump.

Singing away.

Evidently I had never run it this low on gas.

We found our campsite.

Got situated.

And explored the park.

The main attraction is a spring-fed swimming pool. The water is crystal clear. Which means you can see what you are sharing the waters with.

Fish. Turtles. Ducks.

The kids and I wanted to swim. The water was cool, so we had to decide on a gradual or all-at-once entry.

The boy and I chose the latter. We jumped into the deep end and swam back to the side.

My daughter decided to wade in slowly. A school of small fish swarmed around her, nipping here and there to see if she was food or not.

She decided she wasn't and got back out of the pool.

As we swam, the gas situation was on my mind.

Back home for dinner, the gas situation was on my mind.

Trying to sleep that night, the gas situation was on my mind.

I got up early the next morning. Either I'd find gas or get stranded in the effort. I left everyone else back at camp. No sense all of us waiting for a tow truck somewhere.

On the way out of the park I asked a ranger if he knew of any nearby gas stations. He waved vaguely down the road. I pointed the truck that way.

Fuel pump singing.

Gas gauge now touching "E".

A few miles down the road came salvation.

A tiny country party store.

With a single gas pump.

And a per-gallon price of nearly *50%* more than the going rate in town.

I didn't care.

They could have charged me $10 per gallon and I would have gladly paid, left a tip, and sent a Christmas card.

I filled up.

And felt relief wash over me as I headed back to camp.

We hitched up and headed down the road with Carlsbad Canyons dialed into the GPS.

And I never let that gas gauge fall below halfway again.

Learn more about Balmorhea State Park at tpwd.texas.gov/state-parks/balmorhea.

Photos:

1. The Davis Mountains at sunset, viewed from Balmorhea State Park in Toyahvale, TX.
2. We had the spring-fed swimming pool all to ourselves.
3. Visitors share the pool with ducks, fish, and turtles.

21 Carlsbad, NM

You'd think the story came from the pages of *Boy's Life* magazine.

Or from the pen of Jack London.

Ten-year-old Jimmy hates school. Wants to be a cowboy.

He is from Texas, after all.

His family is already in the cattle business, so it wasn't a big stretch.

But he doesn't stay in Texas.

Jimmy's dad brings him to the southeastern corner of New Mexico Territory.

Other cowboys in the area knew about the big hole in the ground.

But one day, Jimmy, now 16 and going by Jim, saw something they hadn't.

Bats.

Thousands of them.

Swirling and curling like so much smoke.

Coming out of that hole.

Jim later wrote "any hole in the ground which could house such a gigantic army of bats must be a whale of a big cave."

He returned with tools and a lantern. Made a ladder from rope and sticks.

And all alone, Jim lowered himself into that hole.

In the dim beam of his kerosene lantern, an underground wonderland opened up. Gigantic stalagmites. Hundreds of stalactites. A rainbow of color. Pools of water.

And bat poop. Thousands and thousands of pounds of it.

For the next 20 years, Jim explored the caverns, building trails and naming the different rooms and features. He worked as a bat guano mining foreman and ran a bed-and-breakfast to pay the bills.

He also guided visitors to the caverns, lowering them down in the bat guano bucket. Each time, he'd hope this was finally the visitor that would realize the beauty and significance of what he'd found, and want to help promote it.

That visitor never came.

So Jim turned to the government instead. A visit from a mineral examiner from the local Land Office started the process that led to President Calvin Coolidge declaring Carlsbad Caverns as a National Monument in 1923.

And Jim?

The government let him be a guide.

And sell his story about finding the caverns for 75¢ in the cavern lunchroom.

But he wanted more. He wanted to be officially recognized for what he'd already been doing for decades.

He wanted to be named Chief Explorer of Carlsbad Caverns.

The Park Superintendent lobbied for him. The Governor of New Mexico lobbied for him. Jim submitted a petition that included their signatures along with other important people from the area.

No dice.

You know how it goes with bureaucracy. That title didn't exist in the park system. If they created it, would other people want it? Would other parks require that same position? And Jim

didn't have any sort of college degree. Shouldn't a chief position require that?

It took a New Mexico Senator to pass a bill just to allow Jim and his wife to continue to sell their books at the park.

They also let Jim continue to guide others through the parts of the caverns he knew so well.

After 30 years spent below the dry scrubby plains of New Mexico, Jim "Mr. Carlsbad Caverns" White died in 1946.

He'd discovered the largest cave chamber in America, then went on to map out 19 miles of cave connecting to it. He promoted the caves by introducing thousands to their wonders. He'd helped establish one of the nation's most popular and unique National Parks.

Not bad for a kid who just wanted to be a cowboy.

Learn more about Carlsbad Caverns at nps.gov/cave. Jim White's book can be found by searching for "Jim White's Own Story" on Amazon.com.

Photos:

1. All photos from inside the Carlsbad Caverns National Park in Carlsbad, NM.

22 Deming, NM

I had a rockhound on board. I had to keep checking her storage areas, lest she eat up all the weight capacity in the RV by squirreling away what amounted to a gravel driveway.

We were staying at Rockhound State Park just outside of Deming, New Mexico. Most state parks tell you to "take only pictures, leave only footprints."

Not Rockhound State Park.

There, you can cart off 15 pounds of rocks per person. At no extra charge. The entire park area is open to exploration and sampling.

We got the RV situated in a site, then drove to another place rockhounds go.

The sign out front read Basin Range Volcanics Geolapidary Museum and Rockshop.

Fancy name for a modest, flat-roofed building connected to arrays of solar panels and water tanks.

The sign said open. There was a pickup truck parked in the gravel drive.

We parked and stepped inside.

To darkness.

Just for a second.

Then the battery-operated lights came on, revealing worktables, bins, and shelves.

Rocks everywhere.

And not just any old kind of rocks. Geodes.

Many uncut.

And many cut, the polished inner surfaces displaying a rainbow of colors, varying textures, and shapes.

The rocks were memorable.

But for me?

It was the men.

Paul and Christopher.

Paul wasn't the social one. Or maybe he wasn't feeling well that day. He stayed tucked into a corner, focused on a task.

Christopher greeted us and showed us around.

He could have been an extra in a cowboy movie. He was tall and gaunt, with long gray hair pulled back in a pony tail. His bearded face showed the signs of someone with a long history of being outdoors in the New Mexico sun. Talking about geodes dropped some years from his countenance, but he used a walker while showing us his outdoor specimens.

While Christopher talked with

MsBoyink and the kids, I wandered around the museum with my camera. I photographed some geodes and looked at various papers and posters visible on the wall.

Two things became clear.

First, these men weren't just enthusiasts. They were professionals.

Paul discovered his first geode at age 11. At 15 years old he left home to become a full-time agate miner. He became known as the "Geode Kid" and went on to author a number of books about the formation of thundereggs and his experience collecting them.

Christopher joined Paul in the 1970s, and together they owned rock shops, mines, and the museum. What we were touring was very much the life's work of two highly focused and intelligent individuals.

Second, these men held beliefs that directly contradicted our own. Religious beliefs. Political beliefs.

But we didn't travel to meet other people just like us.

We wanted to break out of the bubble as a family and explore a more diverse world than our hometown offered.

We had mixed success. RVing is a bubble of its own.

But that day in Deming, we met people who were very unlike us. We interacted with respect. We learned a bit of each other's story. We didn't seek to change, just understand.

My rockhound bought a small, cut geode from Christopher. It remains one of her few souvenirs from our travels.

What I treasure is the lesson of the geode. Gray and unremarkable on the outside, the real beauty only becomes visible when you get a glimpse of the inside.

May we all have the patience, and diligence, to see people for more than what's on the outside.

Paul "The Geode Kid" Colburn passed away in 2013. Christopher Blackwell continues to run the Basin Range Volcanics Geolapidary Museum and Rockshop in Deming, NM. Learn more at www.zianet. com/geodekid.

Photos:
1. Sunset over Deming, NM.
2. Christopher Blackwell shows us more of his uncut geodes.
3. MsBoyink views geode samples with Christopher Blackwell at the Basin Range Volcanics Geolapidary Museum and Rockshop.
4. A cut geode reveals its inner beauty.

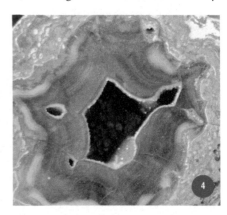

23 City of Rocks, NM

As a kid, it was dunes. We lived in Michigan. We had a dune buggy. Every few weeks during the summer, we'd hitch it up behind our motorhome and head north.

I'd watch out the front window, anxious to see the golden sand expand to fill the horizon.

Up a hill. Around a corner. A parting in the trees. The dunes would come into view, across the blue waters of an inland lake.

In New Mexico, it was rocks.

The drive to the City of Rocks seems flat. The horizon - a rippled ridgeline of mesas - stays in sight almost the entire time.

And yet, the land rolls. Enough to hide surprises.

A turn off the main highway. Up a small crest. Around a corner.

And the rocks come into view.

Their color isn't the unlikely thing. It's their size - some of them dwarfing the RVs camped next to them.

And it's their shapes.

The main field of rocks is a square-mile of columns, pinnacles and stacked boulders suitable for scrambling, hide-and-seek, and "Daddy take my picture" poses.

The City of Rocks State Park may just be the best natural laser tag arena in the country (bring your own gear).

Outside the main field are other outcroppings with their own shapes. One

even resembles a giant rabbit nibbling at some greenery.

Scientists will explain the City of Rocks with talk of volcanic eruptions, erosion, and lots of time.

That may well be.

I prefer to imagine a bemused Creator tucking little unexpected delights into His work for us to stumble across.

City of Rocks State Park is about halfway between Silver City and Deming, NM. The park features a visitor center and 51 campsites. The park offers hiking, mountain biking, and pretty sunsets. Learn more at www.emnrd.nm.gov/spd/find-a-park/city-of-rocks-state-park.

Photos

1. Rock formations at the City of Rocks park in New Mexico dwarf the RV parked next to them.
2. The kids walk into the rocks.
3. This rock formation looks like a foraging bunny.
4. Sunset over the rock formations.

24 Silver City, NM

In the movie *The Secret Life of Walter Mitty* Sean Penn plays photographer Sean O'Connell, who is suffering a remote location, deep cold and extreme altitude to get a photo of a rare snow leopard.

Finally, one of the big cats wanders out between some rocks and Penn's character frames it up in his telephoto lens.

Then just watches.

And watches.

All that prep time.

All that waiting.

And O'Connell isn't taking the shot.

Walter Mitty - played by Ben Stiller - asks "When are you going to take it?"

O'Connell says "Sometimes I don't. If I like a moment for me, personally, I don't like to have the distraction of the camera. I just want to stay in it."

Mitty says: "Stay in it?"

And O'Connell responds "Yeah. Right there. Right here."

In our camera-saturated social media world, it's often-shared advice.

Come out from behind the camera. Quit trying to capture that perfect photo. Be in the moment. And stay in the moment.

To which I have to say....

Hogwash.

Well, partially anyway.

There certainly have been times where, by the time I got the camera out, turned on, set correctly, and framed the shot, the moment was past. In trying to capture it I missed it.

Most of those moments involved our kids when they were younger. It seemed like the minute the camera was out they stopped doing anything cute.

But there have also been many times where a particular moment or experience would be lost to our faulty and incomplete memories, were it not for the pictures I took.

The photos trigger our memories and allow that moment to stay part of us in a way that it wouldn't otherwise.

I don't claim to have a photographic memory. But I took around 15,000 photos during our eight years on the road.

Show me any one of those pictures and I can usually tell you the city and state it came from.

And also recall some details about our visit to that spot. Something that happened to us. Or someone that we met. Or something I had to fix.

Silver City, New Mexico was largely a forgettable stop on our travels. We didn't do much there. We had hoped to visit the nearby Gila Cliff Dwellings National Monument, but we worried about getting there and back without being able to fuel up our gas-guzzling truck.

I did some client work. MsBoyink did laundry. The kids and I went bowling on free passes the RV park provided.

And then we got the hitch-itch.

We wanted to head west and get into Arizona.

Silver City would have faded from our memories by now.

Except I had taken a walk.

A photo walk.

Just ambling about looking for interesting shots.

Which Silver City provided in spades.

Its heritage as a Spanish frontier town meant interesting architecture. A vibrant arts scene meant plenty of color and culture.

Windows. Stairs. Street art. Fenced in vintage trucks. Art deco theaters. Colorful storefronts.

All captured in photos.

Documenting a moment from our travels.

A moment not forgotten.

Silver City, NM features prominently in the history of Henry McCarty, aka Billy the Kid. Henry and his mother Catherine lived in Silver City for a few years. Catherine is buried in a Silver City graveyard. Learn more at historynet.com/billy-the-kid.

Photos:

1. Colorful downtown storefronts in Silver City, NM.
2. A derelict coffee shop.
3. A VW bus parked by the Gila movie theater.
4. In case you forget what you are looking at the sidewalk reminds you.
5. A vintage truck waits for a new owner to spring it from prison.
6. Stairs as artwork.

25 Green Valley, AZ

I'm old enough to remember. Fifth grade. *1976*.

The previous December, just in time for America's bicentennial celebration, President Gerald Ford signed the Metric Conversion Act into law.

The Metric Conversion Act declared the metric system as "the preferred system of weights and measures for United States trade and commerce."

In West Michigan, where I went to school, the teachers took it seriously. They made sure we learned how to measure size, distance, weight, volume, and area using the metric system.

Because that was our future.

Years later though, we're still working in inches, miles, pounds, ounces, and acres.

What happened?

The law hasn't changed. The metric system is still, officially, the preferred system for the United States.

The problem? Ford's law didn't have any teeth.

Conversion was "completely voluntary."

Change is hard. Change costs money. Change takes time.

So most places simply chose not to convert.

Most, but not all.

Consider I-*19*.

It's a *63*-mile-long "Interstate" existing entirely inside the borders of Arizona. It connects Tucson to Nogales near the Mexican border.

And in *1980*, the State of Arizona joined my teachers in taking Ford's law seriously. The state paid to have all of the I-*19* distance signs renewed, using only metric measurements (speed limits remained posted in miles per hour).

Decades later the metric signs remain.

I had to squint at the small numbers on our speedometer to figure out my speed, then do the math to calculate the time until our next exit.

After years in the intense sun, the signs are showing their age. Arizona wants to replace all *2,000* of them.

With distances measured in miles.

But when the issue comes up the locals vote it down.

Changing the unit of measure for distances means changing the exit numbers.

Businesses that have spent years advertising their location as "off exit *55*" would have to start over.

Ultimately? The metric signs have become part of the I-*19* and South Arizona culture.

Change is hard. Change costs money. Change takes time. Maybe some things will never change.

I-19 has mile markers installed, but they face away from traffic and are for use by state road crews only.

Photo:

1. Highway sign on I-*19* in Arizona.

26 Picacho Peak, AZ

"A must-do hiking destination!"

"Some of the best scrambles in all of Arizona."

"Tall rock cliffs, steep drop-offs, and a high mountain saddle."

"A brief but almost-vertical cable-lined ascent to the top of a mountain ridge."

"Our boys loved it!"

I've said it before. We weren't great hikers. Yes, we were inherently more active while living on the road.

But we still spent more time doing work and school on screens and keyboards than we spent hiking, biking, or kayaking.

At least during our stay at Picacho Peak, Arizona, there was an attempt.

Well, by the boy and I anyway. The girls had zero interest.

Two motivating factors had my son and I finding our hiking shoes and filling water bottles.

One was camping next to a peak that looked potentially scalable. Maybe it's a male thing - but we couldn't help but look up at the top of Picacho Peak and not want to stand on top of it as conquerors, surveying the domain around us.

The second was learning the hike was relatively short.

Just four miles round trip.

Maybe there was a third motivating factor. Friends told us the final stretch of the ascent was strenuous enough to require post and cables to assist (and protect) hikers.

We weren't faint of heart. We didn't suffer from vertigo. We were healthy men.

We could do this.

Right?

After gearing up, we drove to the trail head and got started.

The trail may be short in length.

But it has nearly *1,800* feet in elevation gain.

Which felt almost straight up.

We wore gloves. We held onto rocks to steady ourselves against the loose shale under our feet.

We followed the switchbacks up the side of the peak.

Slowly. With lots of breaks. Drinking water and getting our breath back.

Taking in the view as we got higher and higher over it.

But definitely feeling the impact of the climb. We were getting worn out.

Do you know the word penultimate?

It means "next to last" or "second from last."

There was a penultimate destination on this hike.

The "saddle."

The saddle was the midsection between two peaks. The trail flattened out. We had nearly 360-degree views. We found rocks to sit on, drank more water, and enjoyed the views.

There was room, at that penultimate peak, for an elephant. We ignored it for a while, tracking tiny semis on I-10 off in the distance and looking at the white-dot RVs in the campground.

But eventually, the moment came. We had to talk about the elephant.

We had covered most of the distance on the trail. But the last stretch was more difficult.

It was getting warm. I had client work waiting.

I looked at my son.

"What do you think?"

He thought a minute.

"Not sure. I'm pretty tired. What about you?"

There are moments in life.

Hard moments.

Moments where you have to set aside false bravado and evaluate yourself with brutal honesty, because the ramifications could be bad.

This was one of those moments.

It wasn't getting to the final peak that concerned me. I felt like I had stamina enough to do that.

It was getting back down. My concern was becoming so flat-out exhausted that I couldn't keep my balance.

I was the primary wage-earner, the driver, and the fixer of problems. How would that work with a sprained hand, a broken arm, a twisted knee, or bum ankle?

I shook my head.

We took a few more pictures, headed back down the trail, and got home without incident.

It was the right choice.

Probably.

I still wonder, though.

Whenever I scroll through the photos from that hike, I feel like they are incomplete. Evidence of giving up too easily. A missed life lesson to impart to my son.

It doesn't help that the first question friends asked when we told them where we were was "did you climb up to the peak?"

No.

We didn't.

But.

The peak is still there.

Which is good.

Because I have unfinished business with it.

Located midway between Tucson and Phoenix, Picacho Peak has long been used as a landmark by travelers. Learn more about Picacho Peak State Park at azstateparks.com/picacho.

Photos:

1. View from not-quite-the-top at Picacho Peak, AZ.
2. Trail sign.
3. Harrison steadies himself on a rock as he makes his way back down the trail.
4. Looking back up at the saddle as we hike down.

27 Scottsdale, AZ

Sometimes we had a lake view. Sometimes we parked next to a river and fell asleep to its gurgling sounds. Other times we looked out our windows at majestic mountain vistas.

Scottsdale was not one of these times.

Arizona is tough enough to RV through if you are young. So many northern "snowbirds" travel there for the warm winters that most RV parks limit themselves to the 55-and-over crowd.

Dogs and cats welcome. Kids not so much.

We had scheduled a training class in Scottsdale. We needed to find lodging close to the class venue.

We had learned to look for fairgrounds when RV parks and campgrounds were scarce. Fairgrounds will often offer sites for RVs between scheduled events.

The Scottsdale fairgrounds?

WestWorld.

You may recognize it as the place where the Barrett-Jackson auto auction takes place.

They had openings for RVs. The $25 per night rate was attractive. We booked the nights we needed.

Only after paying for the campsite did we think to check their event calendar.

There were two things going on.

The first was an equine event. Bonus deal. We had an animal fanatic on board that would love to watch.

The other?

Arizona Biker Week.

Whooboy.

In a spot where we hoped to sleep?

We called the WestWorld office back. They assured us that the RV spots were at the opposite end of where the bikes would be. A mile away.

With no other real alternatives for lodging, we kept the booking.

Getting to our site was an unlikely intersection of mobile cultures. Lovers of the four-legged. Lovers of the two-wheeled. And us, lovers of our living room, kitchen, and bedroom all mounted on wheels.

Our spot was in a parking lot under dozens of high-tension electric lines.

Coming and going each day, we'd find our way into the stream of dually diesels pulling horse trailers, small swarms of motorcycles, and other RVs towing small cars.

And in between our work responsibilities we met some of our temporary neighbors.

There was Jack, retired from own-

ing a *300*-employee contracting firm in New Mexico. He and his wife of *60* years now lived in a beautiful diesel pusher motorhome.

Jack brought us a bag of freshly picked oranges. Then he gave us his card, offering a spot in his driveway if we ever got to his home town of Albuquerque. I told him I'd love to go there if only to make a left turn (if you get that joke I can tell you how old you are).

We met a local biker at the show, who said he wore a vest lined with pockets. Each pocket held a freezer pack. They kept him cool in the Arizona heat.

I asked him how the different subgroups of motorcycle owners got along. He said at Bike Week everyone from Harley riders to pocket-rocket riders did well together, because for that week "they were all just bikers."

We came across a gorgeous chopper getting prepped for a photo spread in a national magazine. It was painted lime green with orange flames. The entire engine was chromed.

The owner talked to me about having the bike custom built, and how it had been painted by his one-armed uncle.

I asked him how it rode. He gave me a strange look.

"I don't ride it," he said. "I've never even started it. If I did the exhaust pipes would get discolored."

I asked if he couldn't just have a second exhaust to use for photos.

"I don't want to spend another *$1,200*," he said.

Once the photographer was done, his friend rolled up in a lifted pickup towing a matching covered trailer. They pushed the low-riding bike up a long aluminum ramp and secured it inside the trailer.

They had to leave the show early as they had a *16*-hour drive back home to Colorado.

Different interests.

Different priorities.

Different lifestyles.

We appreciated the contrast.

Because what we mostly found in Scottsdale proper was uniformity and conformity.

Scottsdale must have strict building and zoning laws. Every strip mall, outlet store and office building looked alike. Business signage - where you could see it - was all in red.

Gas stations were hard to find. Pumps were hidden behind low walls, and price signage was all small and at ground level.

I'm sure the goal was to create a "consistent upscale experience."

But the result?

Without obvious waymarkers, every street looked the same. It was hard to navigate and hard to spot destinations.

We felt lost. We felt out of our element. This was not a city for us.

With our training class over, we broke camp and went back to our "RV friends in low places."

Scottsdale, AZ is known for its 51 golf courses, spa resorts, and Parada Del Sol Rodeo. Learn more at experiencescottsdale.com.

Photos:
1. The sun sets behind some equestrian competitors at WestWorld in Scottsdale, AZ.
2. A row of motorcycles at Arizona Biker Week.

28 Mesa, AZ

Birds do it.

-Cole Porter, 1928

You know the song. Covered by many singers, but the best known versions are from Ella Fitzgerald and Louis Armstrong.

In addition to the birds and bees, the song mentions sponges, oysters, clams, jellyfish, electric eels, goldfish, and monkeys that either "fall in love" or enjoy other activities that you might imagine.

No mention of rattlesnakes.

But rattlesnakes do, in fact, do it.

And when they do, at least at Usery Mountain Regional Park in Mesa, Arizona, they are not only left alone by the park staff, but given a roped-off campsite to enjoy.

But not much in the way of privacy.

Word spread through the campground. Rangers came by. Camp hosts came by. Other campers came by.

We watched.

We talked.

We took photos.

Some people saw it as a great opportunity to learn more about a native desert creature.

Others saw it as a great opportunity to kill two snakes with one bullet.

We were in the former camp. We loved the desert and wanted to spend more time in it.

We were scared of rattlesnakes, but wanted to fight that fear with knowledge.

We attended a presentation by a local rattlesnake expert. He taught us about the 19 different species of rattlesnakes in the Arizona desert.

And he taught us how to avoid getting bitten by one while hiking.

The first rule was to not step quietly. Snakes can pick up your vibrations and will actively try to avoid you.

The second rule was to watch where you were stepping.

And if you did step on one?

This rattlesnake expert had created a fake leg with a boot on the end of it. Every

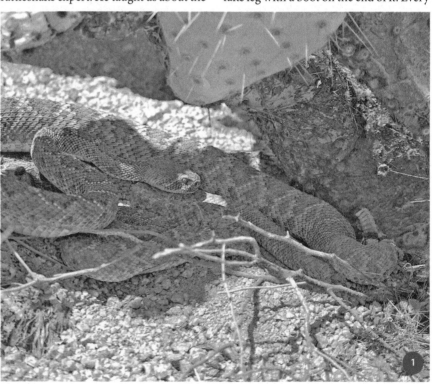

time he came across a rattlesnake in the wild, he'd step on it using the fake leg.

Only one snake out of *100s* tested ever struck back.

He figured that one was just having a bad day.

And if you do get bit?

Don't try to suck the venom out like in the movies. The venom will have been absorbed by the time you try.

Also no tourniquets, ice, alcohol, or electricity.

And don't try to catch or kill the snake for identification.

Just lightly wrap the wound with gauze and get yourself to a medical facility as soon as you can.

But don't let the chance of a snake bite keep you from enjoying the Sonoran Desert.

Deaths from rattlesnake bites are rare in Arizona - in the single digits each year.

According to the expert we talked with, most rattlesnake injuries were among men aged *25* and under, and the incident followed the phrase "hold my beer."

As for us? Arizona became one of our favorite states. We spent months there at different times in our travels.

We hiked and mountain biked different trails.

And never saw another rattlesnake in the wild.

A female rattlesnake reproduces every two to three years. She carries eggs but gives birth to eight to ten live young, who get no attention from their mother. Learn more at desertusa.com/reptiles/rattlesnakes.html.

Photos:

1. Rattlesnakes mating in the cactus in Mesa, AZ.
2. Park staff close off the campsite where the snakes are mating.
3. Rattlesnake season coincided with the desert bloom.
4. A saguaro cactus sprouts a bloom.

29 Mesa, AZ

What does the sheep say? Turns out, when they are part of a large herd on the move through a southern Arizona campground, not much.

Mostly what you hear is the scratching of hooves on the pavement.

And the whistle of the shepherd.

This was a long-standing yearly tradition. Moving the sheep from a winter pasture in the south to a summer pasture in the north.

One shepherd with a stick, a small rucksack, and a good pair of boots.

And a dog.

The shepherd's whistle wasn't for the sheep. Sheep, in a large group, behave exactly as you might expect.

The whistle was for the dog.

I couldn't tell the difference between the whistles the shepherd made.

But the dog knew.

One moment heading around the far side of the herd to group them up tighter. Then nipping at the heels of the slow-movers in the rear. Then back on the near side, close to the shepherd again.

The shepherd and the dog worked together to move the herd uphill, taking up the entire campground road.

The few spectators taking pictures didn't slow them down. A few yards from the main road, the two turned the herd into the gravelly scrub and cactus land running next to the road.

And it was over.

Not just for this year.

Over for good.

This was the last year the herd would be moved on foot.

For reasons that probably made sense to some suits somewhere - cost, safety, local ordinances, regulations, who knows - next year the sheep would make the trip as passengers. They'd be herded up into trailers, hitched behind semi trucks, and hauled down busy I-*10* like so many Amazon Prime packages.

And as that shepherd followed his herd into the Arizona sunset, I was a bit sad.

We were seeing an old-world, non-technological, labor-based way of life come to an end.

I wondered if the sheep would arrive at the summer pasture in better or worse condition for not having the journey.

I wondered if the shepherd and his dog would find other work.

And I wondered. Those suits who made the final decision to truck the sheep instead? Did they stop to think about the people who would miss hearing the clatter of hooves, the whistle of the shepherd, and the yip of the sheep dog?

Photos:

1. Arriving campers find themselves in a sheep-jam.
2. The shepherd guides his flock.

30 Lake Montezuma, AZ

You know the question. Come across any body of water and someone will ask it.

You've asked it yourself.

Especially if it you have to walk or drive through it.

How deep is it?

The deeper, the more interesting. We love the idea of a "bottomless" lake, with lost cities, mermaids, or monsters.

I hate to break it to you.

Bottomless waters only exist in the works of science fiction writers like Jules Verne.

There are, however, deep lakes.

Crater Lake in Oregon is *1,943* feet deep.

Lake Baikal in Siberia is the deepest in the world at *5,315* feet.

But lakes don't have to be bottomless to be mysterious.

Take the Montezuma Well National Monument in Arizona.

It's no Crater Lake. It's not going to bowl you over with serene grandeur and inspire you to wax philosophical about the color blue.

Not to say that it's not interesting. Every day, even during droughts, the well generates *1,500,000* gallons of water.

The Well contains five species (a snail, a scorpion, an amphipod, an algae, and a leech) not found anywhere else. The water has a high concentration of carbon dioxide gas which keeps fish from living in it.

Cliff dwellings perch along the rim. Different indigenous tribes have used the Well for irrigation over the years. The Yavapai people claim the spot as the birthplace of their race.

The first ever underwater archaeological survey took place at the Montezuma Well in *1968*.

Which brings us back to that question.

How deep is it?

The first person to measure the depth was Captain Day of Fort Verd in *1873*.

His answer wasn't the answer he was hoping for.

Day had hyped up the idea that the Well was bottomless. So when his long rope found bottom at 65 feet, an embarrassed Day tossed the rest of his rope in the water to get it all wet. He then pronounced to the onlookers that he'd been correct. It was bottomless.

Subsequent divers proved Day wrong. Montezuma Well did indeed have a bottom at about 55-65 feet.

Or so they thought.

It wasn't a normal lake bottom.

Reports described the bottom as "creepy," "boiling like a thin mush cooking," "boiling oatmeal," or a "white lava flow."

That the last 20 feet down to the bottom was "filled with thousands of free-swimming leeches" probably didn't help the creepiness factor.

Then in 1962, one diver made an odd suggestion.

What if the bottom wasn't?

It took 44 years.

In 2006, divers from the National Park Service Submerged Resources Center in Santa Fe, New Mexico finally came to check things out.

And found that what other divers had been assuming was the bottom of the Montezuma Well was not the actual bottom.

It's a false bottom.

A false bottom made up of a five to ten foot thick layer of "fluidized sand." It's denser than the water above it, so won't float to the surface. From underneath, the layer of fluidized sand is held in place by pressurized groundwater entering the bottom of the well.

Divers found another 40-82 feet of depth past the false bottom.

A pond within a pond.

It's a unique phenomenon. The researchers said none of them or any of their colleagues who had dove all over the world had seen or heard of anything like it.

They say still waters run deep.

From the surface, the waters of the Montezuma Well look placid.

But even Jules Verne would be interested in what goes on there.

Down in the not-quite-bottomless depths.

See video of the bottom of Montezuma Well at nps.gov/featurecontent/moca/ Montezuma%20Well%20Dive.MP4.

Photos:
1. Harrison looks over the Montezuma Well in Arizona.
2. Harrison and Michael on the walking path around the well.

31 Winslow, AZ

A blank stare. An uncomfortable pause in the conversation. A dawning realization that the ten years between our ages represented a wider gap in our pop culture knowledge than I imagined.

I had just told a friend that "We had to stop in Winslow, Arizona to go stand on the corner."

I had a little grin on my face, waiting for his reaction.

It didn't come.

"You know...the song?" I added.

He shook his head.

I hummed a few bars.

No good.

I suddenly felt very old.

This friend was no spring chicken. One of the reasons we bonded was our age. We had joked about creating an "old curmudgeons group" in our profession of web development.

He was married with three kids and a mortgage. He owned a successful business with multiple employees.

All of which, evidently, didn't make him old enough to have ever heard the very first song from the very first album by The Eagles.

Take It Easy.

Written by Jackson Browne and Glenn Frey.

First released in *1972*. (when I was five years old, by the way).

One of "*500* Songs That Shaped Rock," according to the Rock and Roll Hall of Fame.

Covered by Bruce Springsteen, Travis Tritt, Buck Owens, Jimmy Buffett. And countless tribute bands, jazz bands, string bands, karaoke singers and acoustic soloists.

Still in rotation on classic rock radio stations across the country.

The history behind how the song came to be is a bit unclear.

As many histories are.

Jackson Browne may or may not have broken down in Winslow. Or was it Flagstaff? And that girl, my Lord. Was she in a Toyota? Or was it really a Ford?

No matter, really.

The Eagles recorded the song. It became a hit.

And in 1999, the town of Winslow, Arizona opened the Standin' on the Corner Park.

The guitar-holding man statue is said to be Jackson Browne.

A flatbed Ford is parked nearby.

A trompe l'oeil mural on the building forming one edge of the park visually references other lyrics from the song.

In 2016, Glenn Frey passed away, and Winslow added a statue of him to the park as well.

One hundred thousand people per year now stop in Winslow.

Just to stand on the corner.

And for Winslow, the railroad town where the trains stopped stopping, and the Route 66 town bypassed by the interstate?

That's a fine sight to see.

Learn more about Winslow, AZ at winslowarizona.org.

Photos:

1. Harrison, Michael, and Miranda join Jackson Browne in the Standin' On The Corner Park.
2. Crissa Boyink poses as the girl, my Lord, in a flatbed Ford.
3. Other parts of Winslow, AZ still show the effects of I-40 bypassing town.

32 Grand Canyon, AZ

We had gotten up at 3 a.m. Dressed. Made coffee. Ate something. Made more coffee. And drove the hour-plus from our campsite to the Grand Canyon.

All in the dark.

We used flashlights to find our way to the overlook on the south rim of the canyon.

Along with a couple hundred other people.

Hushed voices spoke in strange accents and foreign tongues. If we had taken a survey, I'm sure it would have found slight differences in our beliefs.

And yet, we were one. Here for a single reason.

The eastern sky lightened. Black turned to blue. Long shadows fell on the ground.

The outline of a cross appeared against an angry sky.

Easter morning.

A slow-reveal first view of the Grand Canyon.

The incredible depth. The vast width.

The colors. The endless outcroppings of rock. So incomprehensible your brain tells you it's really just the biggest tourist trap roadside ball of twine con game ever.

And the cross. Standing as a mute counterpoint.

It caused our own dawning realization.

As vast, as big, as unfathomable as the Grand Canyon is, it's a mere teaspoon compared to God's love for us.

With everything going on right now, it's easy to feel like we're standing on the edge of an abyss, with a large Grand Canyon of our own stretching out before us.

A canyon of fear. Of uncertainty. Of doubt.

A popular saying says "we'll cross that bridge when we get to it."

I think that has it the wrong way around.

When it's time to get to the other side of that canyon?

We'll bridge that cross.

Find Easter service availability and details at grandcanyoncommunitychurch. org/easter-sunrise-service-2.

Photos:

1. Easter Morning at Mather Point Overlook at the Grand Canyon.
2. The cross basks in the first sunlight of the day.

33 Petrified Forest, AZ

The National Park System in America is a vast and wonderful resource.

Without destinations like the Grand Canyon, Yosemite, Yellowstone, the Great Smoky Mountains, or any of the other 419 National Parks, Preserves, Monuments, Memorials, Rivers, and Scenic Trails, people embarking on the "Great American Roadtrip" would have few places to visit.

We learned to watch for brown signs while traveling. A brown sign meant there was a location nearby that was special for its natural beauty or historic significance.

We followed brown signs to Crater Lake. To Gettysburg. To the Grand Canyon.

And many, many more places.

Once we arrived at a particular place, however, both the tone and content of the signage often changed.

We saw signs that said:

"Stay on designated paths."

"Please don't touch any of the displays."

"Even by breathing, you are changing this environment."

"Take only photographs, leave only footprints. Actually, if you could, like, not even leave footprints that would be great."

Well. Ok.

I may or may not be embellishing.

Less than you might think, however.

Overall, if the signs at many National Parks were written honestly they'd say:

"In the interest of preserving this national treasure for future generations, we'd prefer you didn't visit. But since you came anyway, please make amends for the damage you're sure to cause in the form of a donation."

The Petrified Forest National Park was a particularly egregious example of a National Park with a passive-aggressive attitude towards its visitors.

First were the rangers at the check-in booth. After accepting our entrance fee, they gave us a short lecture on not removing any petrified wood from the park.

We didn't think it was an unreasonable request.

No one is going to pay $10 per car to look at where some petrified wood used to be.

Driving further in, however, we encountered the same message in sign form.

"Collecting Petrified Wood Prohibited."

Yes, already.

We get it.

We parked at the visitor center and went in.

National Park Visitor Centers often have films about the park. The film will talk about the history of the park, illustrate its beauty with sweeping videography, and guide you to various points of interest within the park.

And, in the case of the film at the Petrified Forest National Park, go over the top in convincing you to not steal petrified wood.

Most of the film was a dramatization

of a young white male getting chased down by TWO ranger vehicles, pulled over, yanked out of his vehicle, spread-eagled, and frisked.

And found to be carrying a chunk of petrified wood large enough to explain why his pants were falling down.

The movie (and other NPS communications) claimed that petrified wood disappears from the park at the rate of 12-14 tons per year.

Which begged the question.

How do you weigh something that isn't there anymore?

The movie wasn't done yet.

Knowing that humans don't always respond to logic and reason, the film delved into mysticism.

I'm not kidding.

By removing petrified wood from the park, you are placing a curse on your life that won't go away until you return the wood.

The movie didn't say that directly of course. But it featured interviews with and quotes from people who believed it.

The visitor center lobby had a display of letters from the accursed souls who had stolen petrified wood and returned it in an effort to stop "bad things" from happening to them.

The returned rocks can't realistically be put back to whence they came, so the NPS dumps them in a "conscience pile" next to a private service road.

Where no visitor will ever see them.

Your tax dollars at work.

We ended our visit to the Petrified

Forest National Park Visitor Center by visiting the gift shop.

You might guess what we bought.

A small chunk of petrified wood.

Guaranteed curse-free, of course.

Located on Interstate 40 between Flagstaff, AZ and Albuquerque, NM, the Petrified Forest National Park has a website at nps.gov/pefo.

Photos:

1. Petrified wood at the Petrified Forest National Park in Arizona shows a rainbow of colors and textures.
2. Somehow this "millions of years old" petrified tree trunk was in need of a cement support.
3. Dark objects are sections of petrified tree trunks scattered on the desert floor.

34 Sandia Park, NM

"You are bound to the wheel and your eyes to the car ahead and to the rear-view mirror for the car behind and the side mirror for the car or truck about to pass, and at the same time you must read all the signs for fear you may miss some instructions or orders.

No roadside stands selling squash juice, no antique stores, no farm products or factory outlets.

When we get these thruways across the whole country, as we will and must, it will be possible to drive from New York to California without seeing a single thing."

-John Steinbeck
Travels With Charley

Steinbeck published those words in 1962. He could already foresee how interstates would create a "Generica."

That same year, Ross Ward began building the type of roadside attraction Steinbeck was mourning the loss of.

Not that Ward had any intentions of trying to attract traffic from nearby I-40 heading east from Albuquerque to his home in the foothills of the Sandia Mountains.

He was just creating a place for his artwork.

Enjoying a hobby.

Settling down after 30 years spent traveling with the circus, painting backdrops, attractions, and setting up traveling displays of his work.

By 1983, enough people wanted to see Ward's "hobby" that he opened it as a museum.

Like the City Museum in St. Louis, Tinkertown is hard to describe in a few words.

It features hand-carved circus dioramas. Gypsy wagons. Murals. Skeleton sculptures. Snake Charmers. Miniature saloons set in Wild-West scenes. Animated jug bands that play for a quarter. Animatronic fortune tellers living in glass booths that spit out wisdom on paper slips.

Paintings. Etchings. Drawings. Antique memorabilia. Clothes from the world's tallest man. Arcade games. Farm equipment. Old tools. Old toys. Found art.

All housed in what Ward considered an in-progress work of art in itself - a sprawling, rambling, 22-room structure with 51,000 glass bottles encased in 20 tons of rock and cement.

Tinkertown reviews use words

like "eccentric," "odd," "a half-forgotten story," and "cute, playful and a bit creepy."

I'll add one more: melancholy.

Few places give such a sense of what it's like to be inside someone else's brain. Wandering the tight isles and low ceilings of Tinkertown, you get a vivid sense of what Ross Ward was fascinated with, his delight in creativity and whimsy, and his nostalgia for circus days gone by.

Who he was, really.

Then, having just "met" him, you learn that Ward passed away in 2002.

After being diagnosed with Alzheimer's in 1998.

Ward's daughter Tanya came home to help care for him during that time.

She wrote about how the disease began to affect him. She said he grew "less tethered to this world" and got "frustrated with his tools as he forgot how they worked."

Alzheimer's didn't stop Ward completely, however. In an 2013 interview with the *LA Times*, Tanya said Ward was "sometimes angry and frustrated, but he continued to draw and paint even after he was moved to an Alzheimer's care unit."

Also caring for Ward during those final years was his wife, Carla.

Tanya said "his love for her seemed to keep one little light on in his brain even after most everything else had gone dark."

Carla Ward still runs the Tinkertown Museum, opening it each season in memory of her late husband.

Who, as it turns out, took a playful, posthumous poke at us.

And at you.

Painted on the end of a glass bottle in a Tinkertown wall are the words:

We did all this while you were watching TV!

So, what are you doing tonight?

Tinkertown is located 30 minutes from downtown Albuquerque, NM.

Check venue availability at tinkertown. com. Leaving Tinkertown by Tanya Ward Goodman is available on Amazon.com.

Photos:
1. The Tinkertown sign.
2. One of the circus dioramas created by Ross Ward.
3. Bottles encased in cement form a wall at Tinkertown.
4. Artwork created by Ross Ward.
5. Ward's challenge to the world.

35 Moab, UT

What if we break down? What if the weather turns nasty? What if we run out of money?

What if CPS knocks on our door?

What if we can't stand living with each other in a 30-foot RV?

What if.

The "what if" questions came fast and furious when we were trying to decide if we wanted to travel full-time as a family.

Questions from friends. Questions from relatives. Questions from the dark recesses in our own psyches.

What if questions can be pragmatic. Logical. Reasonable.

What if questions can help you plan and be prepared for different situations.

But often, what if questions are something else in disguise.

Fear.

Fear is skinny. It can slip in through a crack in the door.

Fear has slipped into a lot of our doors these days. We're afraid of disease. Afraid of demonstrations and riots. Of the police. Of terrorists acts.

We're afraid of each other.

COVID-19 has us calculating risks each time we need to venture out into public. Am I six feet away from that person? Is their mask on properly? Did I just hear her cough?

Looking back through our travel photos, Moab caught my eye. Yes, the scenery is stunning. Yes, Moab is Mecca for people who love to hike, bike, and go off-roading.

But it was more than that.

It was the people.

We didn't make arrangements to meet anyone in Moab. We didn't know anyone who lived there.

I just knew we were in the area and I wanted to go off-roading. We found a campground to park the RV in, and I went out and rented an SUV.

I asked the rental agent for trail recommendations based on my experience and comfort level.

The next day we packed up and headed out early.

And the what-ifs started.

What if we get stuck? What if the SUV breaks down? What if I total a rental?

We never did this alone. We always went off-roading with other people. Having other people and rigs around was always a comfort in case something went awry.

But the rental was paid for. The cooler was packed. The camera was at hand. I figured if the trail looked too intense, we'd turn tail and go find something easier.

We were only alone until we arrived at the trailhead. There was already a number of vehicles queuing up to begin the trail. It was obvious that some of them were there as a group or club.

We found a spot in line between two of the groups.

What happens on most club runs is the group moves along until an obstacle comes along. The group leader is usually a more experienced driver who can get through the obstacle on his or her own. They then park and walk back to the obstacle to "spot" the lesser-experienced drivers through the tough spot.

Using a combination of hand signals they communicate to the driver which way to point their tires, which line to take through the obstacle, when to use a bit more throttle, etc.

These spotters didn't quit when the last of their club went through. They saw us coming, saw that we were alone on the trail, and kept right up with the finger pointing and arm waving.

Like anywhere else in life, having an experienced guide helping a novice through a tricky place makes all the difference in the world. People are safer. Vehicle damage is minimized.

And fear is diminished.

We stayed with the group the rest of the day. Took breaks with them. Ate lunch with them. They took pictures of us. We took pictures of them.

Years later, I have no clue who they were. I remember they were a club out of Colorado, but that's about it.

But looking at the photos, I remember their actions. I remember how welcoming they were. I remember they helped us enjoy the day more by being less stressed.

They give me hope. Hope that no matter what flavor of crisis we find ourselves in, no matter what fears are gripping us, no matter what obstacle is before us, there are people who have gotten through it.

And one of them will be willing to turn around and spot others through that obstacle as well.

We just can't be afraid to let them guide us.

National Parks, off-roading, mountain biking, whitewater rafting and more are available in Moab, UT. Learn more at discovermoab.com.

Photos:

1. A spotter helps Michael negotiate an off-camber downhill turn in Moab, UT.
2. The Moab scenery is spectacular.
3. This club from Colorado welcomed us in and let us ride with them.
4. Another spotter helps me do a controlled slide down a steep trail section.
5. Taking a break from the trail.

36 Antelope Island, UT

They should call it "Maybe Antelope Island." Because maybe it's an island. Or maybe it's a peninsula.

It all depends on the current water levels in the Great Salt Lake. Too little water and the connecting land becomes visible.

We visited Antelope Island State Park while staying in Salt Lake City, Utah. True to its name, it was an island at the time.

The antelope part was also true. In addition to bison, chukar partridge and other wildlife, we spotted a few pronghorn antelope roving the grasslands.

Good thing.

Otherwise?

We'd remember Antelope Island as "Bug Island."

Some people experience dense infestations of biting no-see-ums on Antelope Island.

For us, it was "midge flies."

We happened to visit the island smack in the middle of the big yearly hatch.

We first spotted them on the seven-mile causeway leading into the park.

I thought the shoulders were on fire.

Every bush or clump of grass had a cloud of thin black smoke swirling above it.

Then the splatters on our windshield told us the truth.

That wasn't smoke. Each twisting, drifting black mass was a swarm of flies.

By the time we got into the park, the entire front end of our truck was coated with dead midge flies.

According to the park service, midge flies don't bite.

So it must have been something else that attacked us when we got out of the truck.

After a quick walk down to verify that the Great Salt Lake was, in fact, salty, we retreated back to the truck for a slightly less aerobic driving tour of the rest of the island.

With its rolling grassy plains, sweeping vistas, green and brown foothills, and distant snow-covered peaks reflecting in the waters of the lake, there was no doubt. Antelope Island is beautiful.

Years later, what I remember most are those black clouds of bugs.

They've become a visual metaphor for me.

I imagine them swirling above people's heads. Little black clouds of fears. Of past hurts. Of physical sickness. Of addictions. Of failed relationships.

The clouds remind me that each person is more than they appear.

Something up in that cloud of nastiness may be influencing the words they are saying, or the actions they are taking.

And I'm no different. I have a cloud of my own.

But there is a Son who can shine through that cloud. I pray that His light cuts through your cloud.

And mine.

Antelope Island State Park is about an hour's drive out of downtown Salt Lake City, UT. Current bug conditions are reported at stateparks.utah.gov/parks/ antelope-island/current-conditions.

Photos:

1. Antelope Island State Park, on the Great Salt Lake in Utah, boasts one of the nation's largest bison herds.
2. Driving to the island, the black shadows over the water are large swarms of midge flies.
3. Miranda ensures that Salt Lake is actually salty.
4. Our license plate covered in dead flies after visiting the park.

37 Salt Lake City, UT

If you have read *Something Wicked This Way Comes* or *Fahrenheit 451*, you know of author Ray Bradbury.

If you know of Ray Bradbury, you've enjoyed the benefits of a public library. After graduating high school, Bradbury didn't go to college. He went to the library.

Over the course of ten years, he spent two or three days a week there. He'd say he "graduated from the library" at age 28.

I didn't spend that much time in our local library back in Holland, Michigan.

But one of my first memories of "freedom" as a nine or ten-year-old was being given permission to ride my bike the three miles to the library on a Saturday morning.

I'd load up as many books as I could carry, cart them home, stack them next to my bed, and spend the entire day engrossed in the *The Hardy Boys, Encyclopedia Brown*, and *The Boxcar Children*.

My library use didn't stop as an adult. As a homeschooling family, we remained heavy users of that same library - by this time rebuilt, enlarged, and modernized.

Our biggest problem was the lending limit.

They would only let us check out *100* items per card.

We prevailed, however. We used multiple cards. The kids had their own as soon as they could scratch their name on it.

Our library use continued while traveling.

Other traveling families planned visits around state capitals, sports arenas, and national parks.

We visited libraries.

For entire days, sometimes.

I'd use the wifi to catch up on work. The kids would find books or take part in planned activities. MsBoyink would research where we were or where we were headed.

We'd often tailgate in the parking lot - cooking soup or making sandwiches on the back of the truck.

Then heading back in for another couple of hours.

The libraries we visited were as varied as the towns that contained them.

The Las Vegas, New Mexico library was modest. It was one of the *1,689* libraries built between *1883* and *1929* using grants from the Carnegie Foundation.

The Hoover Public Library in Hoover, Alabama, was bigger. It reimagines the role of a library in the life of a city by offering live theater, art collections, music concerts, children's entertainment, technology demonstrations, gaming competitions, and sci-fi festivals.

But the most impressive and memorable library we visited was the Salt Lake City Library.

Five stories tall.

225,000 square feet.

$78 million to build.

Glass walls and roof.

Rooftop garden.

Amphitheater.

Coffee shop.

Hidden stairways.

300-seat auditorium.

Fireplaces.

Waterfalls.

Beehives.

And *500,000* books.

You might think the Salt Lake City Library houses the large genealogical research facility that the town is known for.

That's actually a separate facility known as the Family History Library. It has *2.4* million microfilmed genealogical records.

Our time in Salt Lake City was more scheduled than in most places. People to visit. People visiting us. RV repairs to coordinate. Ball games. Rodeos. Antelope Island.

We didn't get a full-on day to enjoy the library.

But we did explore it, visited the rooftop garden, found the beehives, settled in to read for a little while.

And wondered.

If Ray Bradbury had been born in Salt Lake City, how long would it have taken him to graduate from this library?

Learn more about the Salt Lake City Library at slcpl.org.

Photos:

1. Looking up in the Urban Room at the Salt Lake City Public Library.
2. MsBoyink and the kids walk through the Urban Room at the Salt Lake City Public Library.

38 Yosemite, CA

The memories are sweet. Bridalveil Fall. El Capitan. Half Dome. Years later, I can still recall the beauty and majesty of the Yosemite Valley.

As usual, the photos don't do it justice. My skeptical brain likes to look at them and whisper "it's all a painted backdrop strung across the roof of a strip mall."

The rivers were full the day we were there. Every view we had of water was accompanied by the sound of it roaring over rocks.

We wore light clothes against the mild temperatures and hats against the brilliant sun (those of us unconcerned with the appearance of our hair, anyway).

Memories.

Sweet ones.

But incomplete.

I went back to the notes I kept at the time and reread our full experience at Yosemite.

We started at a campground who could have rented out their "level campsites" as sledding hills when it snowed.

Getting situated required every leveling block and spare piece of lumber I had on board.

Then we noticed we had no cell service on either our AT&T or Verizon phones.

MsBoyink headed up to the office to get the code to the campground wifi.

"We don't have wifi."

I worked online to fund our travels.

I needed internet access. With no cell and no wifi we couldn't stay.

The following morning we backed the trailer back down the Evel Knievel ramp we'd created to get level and headed out to setup at another campground that promised cell service.

And fell in right behind county trucks laying down a fresh application of chipseal.

You know what chipseal is, right? A layer of hot tar followed by a layer of small, loose gravel. Chipseal relies on traffic to compact it to a hard road surface.

Which is all great.

Unless you are the first of that traffic.

My truck's front tires picked up the gravel and sprayed it down the sides and undercarriage. The rear truck tires sprayed gravel against the front of the RV.

It sounded like wind-driven hail against a window.

To a guy who is kinda picky about his cars, it was like nails on a chalkboard.

I crept down that road at ten miles an hour.

Making fast friends with the traffic behind me.

We got to the next campground and marveled at how full it was.

With families.

Oops. We did it again.

Made plans completely forgetting "normal people."

People with houses and kids in school and two weeks of vacation all used during the summer.

We were in a popular National Park during the busiest time of the year.

We parents rolled our eyes.

But our kids?

They were thrilled.

A busy park meant playmates. Frisbees, soccer balls, and baseballs were quickly unearthed from the bowels of the RV.

The kids we couldn't usually convince to go outside suddenly didn't want to come back even when it was bedtime.

After a couple days of working an hour from the Yosemite entrance I finally cleared most of a day to drive into the park.

I was excited.

MsBoyink was excited.

The kids?

Not so much.

For them, a pick-up ballgame with other kids was more interesting.

They offered to let MsBoyink and I go while they stayed behind.

I said the things most dads would probably say in that moment.

Sentences that started with "we didn't come all this way..."

Or "you can play baseball anywhere, but..."

They protested.

I prevailed.

But my popularity ranking suffered.

Once inside the park we did what one does in Yosemite. We stopped at the scenic overlooks. We hiked up to the base of the falls. We found a restful spot by the Merced River to eat lunch.

I'd like to report that the experience of actually being in Yosemite chased the bad attitudes out of the truck.

And for the most part, that was true.

But we learned (again) the downside to the company the kids were so happy to have.

Traffic.

Bumper-to-bumper.

Waiting for someone to pull out of a parking spot so we could pull in.

Once we decided to head home it took another hour and a half to see the park gates.

For MsBoyink and I, the memories of Yosemite are sweeter than the real thing.

The beauty persists. The rest fades.

I hope it's the same for our kids.

Yosemite National Park is the fifth most popular National Park, drawing up to five million visitors each year. Learn more about the park at nps.gov/yose.

Photos:

1. Our lunch spot by the Merced River with El Capitan looming.
2. The classic Yosemite Valley overlook.
3. Hiking to the base of Bridalveil Fall.
4. Bumper-to-bumper park traffic.
5. Waterfalls and graffiti.

39 San Francisco, CA

We weren't big city people. Holland, Michigan - our hometown - isn't as small as our current residence of Ava, Missouri.

But Holland is no sprawling metropolis either.

If it wasn't a weekday at 5 p.m., the other side of town was only twenty minutes away.

There was public transportation, but it was limited. Useful for some, but having a car was preferable.

Traveling full-time didn't change our feelings about big cities. Visiting them usually meant staying in hotels. Costs aside, we preferred staying in our RV. It truly became our home with our beds, our chairs, and our kitchen.

And we wanted to see natural beauty. God's handiwork, not man's.

So we skirted around big cities like Chicago, Nashville, Miami, Dallas and Los Angeles.

But you can't set out to "see America" and bypass all the big cities. Some of them are far too ingrained into the fabric and identity of America.

San Francisco is one of those places. Skip "The City" and you haven't truly seen the country.

One of the ways we funded our travels was by hosting software training classes.

Scheduling a class in San Francisco made sense on two fronts. We could both make some money from the training class and write off the costs as a business expense.

Which helped, because we paid more per night to "camp" just south of San Francisco than anywhere else in the country. I put quotes around the word camp because it was less a campground than it was a tightly-packed, paved parking lot for RVs.

But the campground had three things going for it:

- It was right on the coast. We had a view of the Pacific Ocean and could hear the sound of the surf from our RV.
- It was about a mile from a BART

station, so getting public transit to downtown San Francisco was relatively quick and easy.

- It attracted many international travelers, which made for several interesting conversations around the campground hot tub.

Once our class was done, we stayed on a few more days to explore the city.

We walked down Lombard Street (the "crookedest street in the world"), ate seafood and sourdough bread on Fisherman's Wharf, had crepês at the Cable Car Cafe, chocolate at Ghirardelli, and (maybe the most surprising) found tasty BBQ at a place called The Pub just under the Ghirardelli store.

And then, evidently being too stuffed to walk anywhere, we did what you absolutely have to do when in San Francisco.

We rode the cable cars.

There are two main cable car lines in San Francisco - the California and the Powell.

They are mostly independent of each other.

Each line has its own cables the cars grab onto.

The Powell line runs north and south. The California line runs east and west.

There is one spot where they cross - at the likely-named intersection of Powell and California streets.

I'm not sure how all this got negotiated, but at that intersection, the Powell cars have to drop their cable and coast. Once past the California cable, they can latch onto their own cable and be under power again.

And just to make sure this all happens without incident?

There's a little green booth.

With an employee sitting inside of it.

Watching for collisions.

At the ready.

All day.

During our visit, the California line was down for repair.

But the collision-avoidance guy?

Still on duty.

Must be a union job.

Learn more about the San Francisco cable cars, Alcatraz Island, the Golden Gate bridge and more at sftravel.com.

Photos:

1. A cable car heads uphill in San Francisco.
2. A view from the cable car, looking towards the Bay.
3. The collision-avoidance hut at the intersection of the competing cable car lines.

40 Chico, CA

What you gonna do in Chico? Years later, that question still comes to mind.

People understand Los Angeles. No one questions Yosemite. They get San Francisco.

But Chico?

Chico, California is a railroad town. A lumber town. An Army town.

And a college town.

In *1987* a certain "men's magazine" ranked Chico State University as the *#1* party school in the nation.

None of which are reasons for anyone driving around the United States to stop in Chico.

Sure, Chico has attractions. A yo-yo museum. An air museum. An art museum.

Still, Chico doesn't rank highly as a tourist town.

In *2017* one website actually ranked Chico as the 7th "Most Miserable City in America." Some online reviews mention high welfare rates, lack of jobs, a high rate of homelessness, pervasive drug culture, and high crime rates.

But we didn't know any of that.

We just wanted to visit some friends who lived there.

And we needed downtime after a stressful business-related visit to San Francisco and a hectic "oops we forgot it was a holiday" visit to Yosemite.

We needed a week in a quiet place with no agenda.

And no expectations.

So, what did we do in Chico?

- Had dinner with the friends we came to town to see.
- Enjoyed a clean, shady RV park with a nice pool.
- Had our first taste of In-N-Out burgers.
- Toured the Sierra Nevada Brewing Company, a prime mover in both the craft beer and sustainability industries.
- Visited Bidwell Park, a *3,670*-acre municipal park with mountain biking trails and swimming holes. The afternoon we were there a live band was playing blues.

All good stuff.

But it's not what we remember Chico for.

Let me back up.

In our romantic envisioning before leaving on this trip we saw ourselves driving down smooth back roads with the

dappled sun shining through the canopy of trees. We'd be singing along to the Beach Boys (in perfect four part harmony of course) but pause the CD to stop for fresh fruit and vegetables at small road-side stands. Pushing our folded dollars through the small square hole cut into the top of a used coffee can, we'd pull away and wave happily to the farmer on his tractor out in the field, satisfied that we'd both be supporting the small local business and eating healthy in the process.

The reality? We were in places out of season. Or going through town on the wrong day.

Our food shopping turned into trips to Walmart, pushing a cart, dodging other tired people doing the same, forgetting which town we were in because looking out from inside of the store it all looks the same.

But in Chico?

We struck gold.

It's not just that we were in the right place at the right time.

The Farmers' Market in Chico was nothing short of remarkable. It went on for several blocks and it was packed with tents, vendors and people. And they did it twice a week.

We bought local honey, cherries, blackberries, strawberries, apricots, peaches, green beans, yellow beans, onions, peppers, oranges, and zucchini. We sampled beef jerky, fruit curds, and our first maple-bacon donut.

There were also turnips, kale, flowers, pies, bread, nuts (Chico is in almond country), mini-cacti, jewelry, leather goods, coffee, eggs, kombucha, and a ton of other locally-sourced products that I either missed or have forgotten.

Local musicians, yo-yo performers, and other entertainers kept the mood light and the people moving.

A water park at one end of the market provided a place for overheated families to get some relief.

All in all?

The Chico Farmers' Market was more than just a place to go get some fresh veggies. It was a place to be entertained, bump into neighbors, and feel like an active part of a community.

Not at all what we expected.

But expectations are a funny thing. It's hard to visit well-known places without some expectations for what you will experience.

But the higher your expectations, the greater the odds are that the place won't live up to them.

We didn't expect much from Chico.

And maybe that's why the town charmed us as much as it did.

So much we visited a second time two years later.

Even though our friends had moved.

Chico is known both as the "City of Roses" and the "City of Trees." Learn more at visitcalifornia.com/uk/attraction/chico.

Photos:

1. All photos taken at the Chico Farmers' Market.

41 Crescent City, CA

In the *1920*s, whiskey bootleggers needed to outrun the law. They modified their cars to run faster. It led to races for bragging rights. The racing became as popular as the whiskey, and now stock cars race *1,500* times per year at *100* tracks in *48* states.

In *1937*, a man and his wife were tossing a *5¢* circular cake pan back and forth on the beach. Someone offered them *25¢* for it. A business was born. Wham-O bought the idea, improved it, and our world now has disc golf, disc dogs, freestyle competitions, and international associations.

In *1975*, a California kid sold his VW bus. His friend sold a scientific calculator. They pooled the money to start a company named after a fruit. These days, their company has more money than Mexico, the Netherlands, or Switzerland. You may have one of their products in your pocket right now.

Humble beginnings.

We love stories where humble beginnings lead to majestic endings.

Rags to riches. Zero to hero.

Your favorite superhero probably started as an orphan. Or as a small, weak, bullied child suffering from a debilitating disease.

For Americans, maybe we love these stories because we see ourselves in them. Pilgrims tired of being oppressed by a rich, entitled king risk it all in a wild, unsettled land. And become a world superpower.

Or maybe we love these stories because they parallel the Gospel. An innocent Savior, born in a lowly manger to working-class parents, cares for the weak and powerless, takes on the powerful established religion, and ends up offering his life for all of us.

"Tall oaks from little acorns grow."

Whoever wrote that never encountered a Redwood tree.

You could fit *100* redwood seeds inside an average oak tree acorn.

And tall?

The tallest oak tree is around *100* feet tall. Redwoods can easily triple that. And then some.

Rags to riches is never a direct path. Heros don't immediately spring from zeros.

There are trials involved. Villains to vanquish. Planets to save.

Early redwood preservationists thought the best way to save them was to keep fire away from them. An easy, risk-free life would be best, right?

But redwoods need fire.

Fires clear out smaller trees and underbrush that can crowd the soil and nutrients that the redwood needs to thrive. The redwood's thick, non-flammable bark helps the tree tolerate the fire.

Maybe we like stories with humble beginnings for another reason.

If heroes can come from zeros, if there are riches to be made from our rags, if the oldest and largest living thing on our continent needs a little fire now and then to thrive?

Maybe there's hope for us yet.

Learn more about the Redwoods at Jedediah Smith State Park at parks.ca.gov /?page_id=413.

Photos:

1. Trying to see the top of a redwood tree at Jedediah Smith State Park in Crescent City, CA.
2. Redwood trees dwarf our RV.
3. Three of us can't even come close to hugging this redwood.

42 Cape Flattery, WA

I had two goals for our trip to Cape Flattery. The first was wanting to visit all of the four corners of the country. Cape Flattery was the obvious choice for the northwest corner.

The second was salmon.

Smoked salmon.

Fresh smoked salmon.

There aren't many foods I'd blow the entire grocery budget on, but fresh smoked salmon is one of them. The Makah Indians run fishing boats out of Neah Bay and then sell smoked salmon from places in town.

At least, they do when not closed for COVID-19 concerns.

We easily met my two goals during our pre-Coronavirus visit to Cape Flattery.

But the most interesting visitors to the Cape Flattery area had only one goal for their visit.

Rescue.

The first Japanese people to ever set foot in the State of Washington never intended to.

In October of 1832, a crew of 14 Japanese sailors left on a "business as usual, around the corner and up the coastline of Japan trip" to Tokyo.

A typhoon took out their rudder. The crew cut down the mast to stabilize the ship.

And they drifted.

For 14 months.

And 5,000 miles.

Existing on rice, fish, and rainwater.

Their families gave them all up for dead.

Eleven men did die.

Sailors Otokichi, Kyukichi, and Iwakichi were the only survivors of the group.

They washed up on the Washington shore, just south of Cape Flattery.

Only to be captured by the Makah Indians and bound up as slaves.

Neither group was aware that the other existed.

Japan was closed to foreigners. Natives couldn't leave and were prohibited from returning if they did.

Indian tribes like the Makah had limited exposure to European fur traders. They had never seen an Asian person.

News of the castaways reached Fort Vancouver, located across the Columbia River from current-day Portland, Oregon.

John McLoughlin was the boss man

DRIVEN TO WONDER

there, employed by the Hudson Bay Trading Company, headquartered at that time in London.

McLoughlin brought the castaways to Fort Vancouver, initially thinking they were Chinese. After determining they were Japanese he decided to send them home, hoping to use them as a lever to open up trade between Britain and Japan.

But McLoughlin first wanted to impress them with Britain, so they could pass the word in Japan. He sent the three castaways to London.

Without really asking London first.

The London folks didn't know what to do with the three sailors. After quarantining them on their ship for a week, the three were allowed a one-day tour of the city.

The sailors were then put back on a ship - headed for China.

Because, you know, it's close to Japan.

The three sailors spent two years there waiting for a chance to go home. While they waited, they learned English and helped translate the Bible into Japanese.

Finally, an American Chinese silk dealer named Charles W. King decided to see about returning them to Japan in 1837. King loaded the three on a ship and sailed for Japan.

But Japan wasn't having them.

After twice encountering cannon fire from the Japanese, King gave up and brought the castaways back to China.

After surviving 14 months at sea, getting rescued out of bondage, being inundated with new languages, cultures, and religion, and then co-opted as tools to increase corporate profits, and with the shores of home within sight, the men couldn't go home.

Two of the castaways fade into history at this point.

Otokichi - the youngest of the three castaways - became a translator, working for the British in China. He became a British citizen, married a British woman, and changed his name to John Matthew Ottoson.

Through his work, Ottoson was able to visit Japan in 1854. Japan - finally - offered repatriation.

Ottoson refused.

After a second marriage and fathering several children, Ottoson died in Singapore in 1867 at the age of 49.

In 1983 the story of the Japanese castaways was made into a movie entitled Kairei, *a Japanese film with English dialog and Japanese captions. It's unclear whether* Kairei *was ever released in the United States. Were it not for one notable American actor starring in the role of John McLoughlin, the film would hardly be remembered at all. That actor? One white-wig-wearing Johnny Cash.*

Kairei *is available on YouTube.com.*

Photos:
1. A fleet of fishing boats in Neah Bay, WA.
2. Looking out at the Pacific Ocean from the trail at Cape Flattery, WA.
3. A fishing boat floats in front of Tatoosh Island.

43 Hoh Rainforest, WA

Save the rainforests!

If you saw someone walking through an airport wearing a shirt that said that, you'd probably expect to see them getting on a flight to Madagascar. Or Borneo. Or New Guinea.

You know, where the rainforests are. Someplace warm. Lush. Wet. Green.

Imagine our surprise coming across signs for a rainforest in the United States.

And no, we weren't in Hawaii.

The Hoh Rainforest, one of a few rainforests in the 48 contiguous states, is in the Olympic National Park, about 100 miles (as the crow flies) from Seattle.

The Hoh is lush. There are spruce trees, hemlock trees, fir trees, maple trees, and cottonwood trees. The forest floor is covered in different varieties of ferns.

The Hoh is wet. It gets an average of 140 inches of precipitation per year.

And the Hoh is green. There are apparently no rolling stones in the park, because everything is covered in moss.

But here's where the Hoh is different from the rainforests in places like Borneo or New Guinea.

The Hoh is temperate, not tropical.

Scientifically, the definitions get fussy. Suffice to say temperate rainforests are cooler, have fewer tree species, more trees with needles than leaves, and older trees than tropical rainforests.

The other temperate rainforests in the lower 48 states include areas of the Redwood National Park in California, Mount Rainier National Park and North Cascades National Park in Washington, and portions of the Great Smoky Mountain National Park in North Carolina/ Tennessee.

The Hoh has its own campground, but without reservations made well in advance, we weren't able to get into it.

Instead, we parked the RV at the ocean-front Kalaloch campground and daytripped into the Hoh. The drive took about an hour.

On the way, we spotted a Roosevelt Elk bull feeding along the edge of a pond. The Olympic National park is home to approximately 5,000 of these "Rosies." They are the largest species of elk, with

bulls weighing up to *1,100* pounds. President Theodore Roosevelt created the Olympic National Park mostly as an elk reserve for them.

And yes, you can hunt the elk.

Once into the rainforest itself, we found a couple of options for exploring.

For those who aren't hardcore hikers - like us - there are two nature trails that total about two miles.

Between the moss-covered trees, fern-rich forest floor, and view of the Hoh River, there's plenty to point a camera at.

For the more experienced, there is a *17*-mile-long trail that brings you to the shoulder of Mount Olympus.

No matter which way you go, the Hoh is well worth a visit.

Even if just to be able to say you drove to a rainforest on your vacation.

Plan your visit to the Hoh Rainforest at nps.gov/olym/planyourvisit/visiting-the-hoh.htm.

Photos:

1. Sword ferns abound in the Hoh Rainforest.
2. Walking under moss-laden trees.
3. Anything stationary - like these tree trunks - ends up swaddled in thick moss.
4. The Olympic National Park is home to approximately *5,000* Roosevelt Elk.

HOH RAINFOREST, WA

44 Port Angeles, WA

The tide pools were fascinating. The sunsets had more drama than the local movie theater.

Cruise ships, commercial vessels, and surfaced submarines could often be spotted in the Strait of Juan de Fuca.

The forests were lush and the mountainsides vibrant.

Nature even played its trump card of cuteness - a baby seal.

But we couldn't wait to leave.

"Spend a summer relaxing on the beach!" That's what we had signed up for.

It turned out to be a lie.

Mostly.

The beach part was true.

There was one half-mile of sandy Washington shoreline on the Strait of Juan de Fuca. It was privately-owned and attached to an RV park that we had taken "work-camping" jobs at.

Most RV parks have hosts or work-campers, who trade hours worked for a campsite.

Our funds had taken a hit from an unexpected RV roof repair. I had a large client project that would get us back in shape financially.

By stopping down for the summer, we'd save gas money. We'd work for the campground part of the week to pay for our campsite, and I'd have time for client work the rest of the week.

The campground also offered to employ the kids. They could earn spending money while getting a summer job experience.

And we could day-trip around the Olympic Peninsula, visiting rain forests, waterfalls, and oceanfronts.

It all sounded good.

In theory.

So we committed to an eight-week camphosting gig.

But it was all one big giant fail.

First, the beach wasn't enjoyable. Biting sand fleas, piles of washed-up kelp, cement-hard sand and salt water made us miss the soft, clean freshwater beaches of Lake Michigan.

Second, there was no summer. Days were damp, drippy and overcast. Three times in eight weeks the sun burned through enough to warm things up over 70 degrees.

Third, there was little relaxing.

2

Another host couple didn't show up, so the park increased our work hours.

Finally, the duties weren't as advertised. While talking to us before we got there, they described one of my jobs as "walking the beach each morning and cleaning up trash."

Turns out, what they meant by "trash" was any person or dog who didn't pay their $6 day-use fee.

And their "morning" was a six-hour shift.

They wanted me on the beach from sun up to noon, alone, confronting any beach-goers not wearing the campground wristband, and demanding payment.

Their beach had no obvious signs or fences helping visitors understand when they were on private property.

It seemed like the campground owners wanted people to trespass, so they would be justified in confronting them for the day-use fee.

I wouldn't do it. There were enough other issues - micromanagement, shoddy repairs, sewer overflows, etc. - that I didn't care if they wanted to fire us for not being their beach hitmen.

We didn't get fired. But it made for an awkward, uncomfortable working arrangement.

We endured the summer. I finished the client project. Our finances looked better.

Then, eight weeks to the day after arriving, we hitched up and left.

One of the owners was outside sweeping as we pulled out.

She didn't wave goodbye.
And that was OK with us.

Port Angeles, WA is located on the Strait of Juan de Fuca. Learn more at visitportangeles.com.

Photos:
1. A ship travels through the Strait of Juan de Fuca at sunset.
2. This baby seal showed up on the campground beach. Miranda named it Leroy.
3. Starfish, anemones and mussels found while tidepooling nearby.
4. Seagulls keep us company while tidepooling.

45 Port Angeles, WA

"Why is she looking in our windows?"

We were having lunch in the picnic area for Madison Falls - one of a number of scenic waterfalls in the Port Angeles, Washington area.

Our truck was parked a short distance away, and a woman was standing alongside it, looking intently at the rear passenger window.

She was mid-thirties. Reddish hair. An average build. Someone you'd see at the grocery store or coming out of a hair stylist.

Our truck came from Florida with dark tinted windows. It was almost impossible to see anything inside it on a sunny day.

As she kept staring at the truck, it quickly became apparent she wasn't interested in what was inside of it.

She was using the window as a mirror.

Out of her bag came a festive red dress with black and gold trim. She pulled that over her street clothes.

Then came earrings, arm bands and leg shakers.

Then she retrieved a large headdress. It had blue, brown and white feathers radiating out from a pink and gold headband.

She used our large side mirror to set it in place on her head.

Our unremarkable parking lot woman had just transformed herself into an American Indian princess.

In another parking spot, a man about her same age had just finished a similar transformation. He was in brilliant blue, silver, and purple clothing, with headdress, armbands and leg shakers.

Three others in similar-but-different dress joined in as the pair started down the path to the waterfall.

We followed them, curious to see what they were up to.

Once we got to the falls, they climbed down to stand in front of the waterfall. One of them had a camera, which they

DRIVEN TO WONDER

passed around while the others posed in various ways.

We managed to have a short conversation with one of their members.

English wasn't their first language, but - so far as we understood - they were an Indian spiritual dance tribe. They were from and performed in the Olympic Peninsula region.

Sadly, they weren't here to dance. They had only stopped to get some updated publicity photos.

I often think about that parking lot woman, and how she transformed herself into something unexpected.

It helps me remember, as I move about and meet people at work, in stores, in restaurants, etc.

There's always more to a person than meets the eye.

That stressed cashier might be raising her grandchild. That soft-spoken mechanic might have just donated half of his salary to a Guatemalan orphanage. That elderly man pushing along his walker might have saved his buddy's life in the war.

I know people who have an ability to always see the best in others. I used to think they were born that way, but I've come to believe that it's a skill that can be developed.

Seems worth a try to find out.

Madison Falls are located approximately 11 miles southwest of downtown Port Angeles, WA. Information about Madison Falls and the other waterfalls in the Olympic Peninsula can be found at olympicpeninsula.org/drive-the-loop/waterfalls.

Photos:

1. American Indian dancers pose by Madison Falls in Port Angeles, WA.
2. By this time a crowd of onlookers had gathered, taking photos.
3. A solo dancer sounds a call through the forest.

46 Wallace, ID

Huckleberry ice cream. That was the bait I used to get a family bike ride going while in Wallace, Idaho.

I probably didn't have to mention the huckleberry part. The kids were up for anything that ended with ice cream.

Rails-to-trails paths were MsBoyink's preferred way to ride. Flat, straight, and no cars to worry about - our best family bike rides were on Michigan's large rails-to-trails network.

I've mentioned that we weren't hardcore bikers.

But that day?

We killed it. The kids took off ahead of us. MsBoyink and I followed, pedaling and talking. But making good time at a quicker pace than usual.

We did the five-mile ride and arrived at the ice cream shop. Most rides I'd get off the bike feeling my age. This ride had me thinking maybe I was finally starting to get into shape.

I thought about suggesting we have our treat and then continue on a longer ride.

But I didn't push my luck.

Our ice cream came. Our verdict? Huckleberry ice cream tasted a lot like blueberry ice cream. Good, but not something we'd necessarily drive across the state for.

We got back on the bikes.

After riding the first half-mile back towards the RV I wondered if they had drugged the ice cream. Or maybe I was allergic to huckleberries.

My legs were heavy. The bike was

heavy. The wind had turned against us. My brakes were locking up.

None of that was true, of course.

But it felt that way.

Try as we might, we just couldn't get a decent pace going. By the end of the slog home I was feeling every minute of my age. Sweaty. Tired. Gulping water.

You probably already know what had happened.

Full-time RVing is good for several things. Meeting new people. Seeing new places. Trying new foods.

And exposing new things you are ignorant of.

We had only ridden rails-to-trails paths in Michigan. While Michigan isn't as flat as say, Kansas, it isn't mountainous like Idaho.

The Michigan trails probably were flat. But this Idaho trail? It had a slight grade. Not enough to see. Not - like some other bike paths in Idaho - steep enough that you could coast the entire time.

Just enough to make us feel like superheros going one way and superzeros going the other.

Looking back on that day, I see a lesson.

Well, yes, if riding bikes in the mountains, it's a good idea to check the elevation profile of the route in advance.

But more than that.

The tilt of the land acted as an invisible agent on our ride. And it didn't take much to be a noticeable help in one direction and an even more noticeable hindrance going the other way.

I think the same idea applies to relationships. Every interaction I have with someone has the potential to tilt their world.

If I'm going to be a world-tilter, I have choices. I can choose the direction and the degree of my efforts.

I'm not going to be radically destructive. That's the stuff of criminals and psychopaths.

But it doesn't take much to tilt someone's day a degree towards ruin.

A honked horn. A sarcastic comment on social media. A stolen parking spot.

I can also choose to tilt peoples' worlds in their favor. When it comes to "helping people" I always feel like I need to do something impressive. Go on a mission trip. Write an inspirational book. Build an orphanage. Drill a fresh water well.

Those are noble callings, but they aren't universal. And there might be more pride than philanthropy in them.

Maybe I can just be a one-degree positive tilter, nudging people along with a smile, a kind word, or a generous tip.

Working as an invisible agent on peoples' lives, helping them feel like superheros but not knowing why.

Sounds better than a bowl of ice cream to me.

Learn more about the rails-to-trails biking available around Wallace at railstotrails.org.

Photos:
1. MsBoyink and the kids bike towards ice cream in Wallace, ID.
2. A dish of huckleberry ice cream.

47 Yellowstone, WY

We didn't see Yellowstone. Not really. Oh, we visited. We spent the better part of two days in the park.

We waited for Old Faithful. We braked for buffalo.

We walked through sulphur-smelling steam coming from colorful cauldrons bubbling with caustic water. We joined roadside crowds to watch elk in the distance. I filled up a memory card taking photos and video.

We bought souvenirs and checked the park off our list.

All said and done, we had what was probably an average tourist's Yellowstone experience.

Which means we barely saw anything.

Yellowstone is the second-largest national park in the lower 48 states (only Death Valley is bigger). There's 3,500 square miles of it - more than the states of Rhode Island and Delaware combined. Yellowstone is three times larger than Yosemite National Park.

While living on the road full-time

in an RV gave us great freedom, it also came with constraints.

We weren't on a vacation - I needed internet service to keep our online businesses afloat. We had to be careful with our budget. To satisfy those two constraints we had to sleep one hour and two states away from the entrance to Yellowstone.

We weren't hardcore outdoors people. We had a saying: "Your tolerance for inconvenience defines the level of your adventure."

As a family we could tolerate living in an RV, but all four of us weren't excited

about long hikes, sleeping in tents, cooking over campfires, and worrying about bears.

Schedule was another constraint. In-park camping and backcountry hiking options in national parks like Yellowstone and Yosemite are very popular. They need to be reserved months or a year in advance. We learned that reservations brought stress. Without having to be somewhere on a certain date and time, we could change plans and directions to suit the weather, availability of friends, or work opportunities.

It all sounds logical to explain. Yet,

I can't think about our time at Yellowstone without some angst over what we didn't see.

What wildlife did we miss out on? What photos of great mountain vistas could I have taken? Who might we have met out there in the backcountry?

Our time on the road was a huge blessing, an experience few families will have. I have to be thankful for whatever part of Yellowstone we got to see.

And who knows? There's always the chance for another visit in the future. And maybe our constraints will be different then.

Yellowstone National Park is open year-round. Plan your visit at nps.gov/yell.

Photos:

1. Some natural colors from Yellowstone thermal pools.
2. The pools at Yellowstone National Park are colorful but dangerous.
3. A buffalo crosses a river at Yellowstone National Park.
4. Miranda opines on the sulfur smell of the thermal pools.
5. Old Faithful viewed from the distance.
6. A sunset as we exited the park.

48 Rapid City, SD

What is art? What artwork is good? What artwork isn't? Who gets to say whether a particular piece of art is "good?"

What would happen if an art gallery wasn't juried? What if any artist could participate?

Questions like this get answered in different ways.

Some answers are more formalized. In Grand Rapids, Michigan, the yearly "ArtPrize" event opens the city up to all types of artists, and the public uses a smartphone app to vote on who wins the $450,000 in prizes.

Other answers are messier.

At the Cadillac Ranch in Amarillo, Texas, anyone can stroll up to one of the ten half-buried Cadillac cars and become an artist.

For a moment, anyway.

No matter how much time you spend planning and creating your artwork, it's all fair game the moment you step away. The next "artist" may even ask to borrow your can of spray paint in order to desecrate your just-completed work (don't ask how I know).

In Rapid City, South Dakota, the "Art Alley" is another place where answers to those questions are pondered.

Running between busy downtown streets, Art Alley is just that - a true alley with the backside of buildings, dumpsters, power poles, and resident parking.

And every surface is covered with paint.

During our visit, Art Alley was an unregulated art anarchy.

There was graffiti. There was art. There were murals.

But it operated like the Cadillac Ranch. Paint what you like, anywhere you like, but understand the temporary nature of your work.

The local police essentially threw up their hands about patrolling the alley, saying it was difficult to determine who was an artist and who was "vandalizing property."

Since then?

Graffiti started to edge out the murals.

"Concerned citizens" groups formed. Building owners wanted more control over the type of art that appeared in the alley. Tourism dollars were at stake.

The city council voted in a system. Artists needed to file for permits, present their plans for artwork, present proper ID, sign a liability form, and agree to an "Art Alley Policies" form.

All managed by the local arts council.

The city was confident they were going to make the Art Alley "more beautiful than it was."

Three years later?

Local artists commented that the once-vibrant space was now "really stale." Rapid City had to develop a plan to "revitalize" the space.

Questions over nature and ownership of art continued to get asked.

And answered.

In 2019, a properly permitted, planned, approved, and signed-off breast cancer awareness mural had some unapproved graffiti added.

And in a space that used to be described with words like organic, fickle, and bohemian, some new words are getting used.

Words like suspects, vandalism, damage, suspicious activity, and mischief.

As humans, we'll probably never stop asking what art is.

But at least in Rapid City, the city police now have an answer.

Art is done by people with permits.

Learn more about the Art Alley of Rapid City online at artalleyrc.com.

Photos:

1. A graffitied wall in Rapid City's Art Alley.
2. It's hard to tell where one artist stopped and another started.
3. There was a tacit agreement that cars were exempt from becoming artwork.

49 Mitchell, SD

The arena was buzzing. People in the stands. Competitors on the floor.

Coaches. Teammates. Scorekeepers. Referees.

Shouts. Whistles. Grunts of effort. Cheering.

Matches coming down to differences of a tenth of an inch.

Results sending competitors collapsing into the arms of family and coaches, emotional after finishing the final effort of not just this match, but their entire career.

Their competitive pedal-tractor-pulling career.

Not kidding.

We were at the Corn Palace in Mitchell, South Dakota.

The Corn Palace.

The Palace of Corn.

Or just possibly, the nation's largest shrine to corn.

Built in order to prove to the world that South Dakota actually has the weather and land to grow things like corn.

Each year the building reinvents itself with fresh interior and exterior murals.

All made with ears of corn.

The process starts in late May by removing last year's murals. The new ones are usually completed by October.

For us, the Corn Palace was one of a string of attractions close to I-90 starting with Mt. Rushmore, Custer State Park, Wall Drug, and other various touristy photo opportunities including giant prairie dogs, giant cement president heads, dinosaurs, and jackalopes.

And while the exterior of the Corn Palace was mildly interesting for us, the event going on inside was more memorable.

The National Pedal Pull Championships.

Seventeen different states ranging from Kentucky to Oregon have sanctioned pedal tractor pulling teams.

Contestants are organized by age and gender, from four years old to 13.

Apparently, past teams have found ways to game the results. According to the rules posted on the National Pedal Pullers Association website, contestants are now prohibited from wearing "weight

jackets" or carrying extra weights in their pockets.

And no "standing on the pedals." Lifting off the seat ends the pull right there.

To compete at the Corn Palace, they have to have won a first, second, or third place at the state level.

Behind the state-level events are local-level events. In between all levels of competition are boards, committees, vouchers, host rotations, rules and regulations.

Companies that own the tractors and "sled" the competitors pull.

And parents hitching cement blocks to toy pedal tractors for their kids to practice with at home.

Recently, some pedal tractor pulling events are starting to let adults compete.

The biggest debate?

Whether they should take a cue from the motorized tractor-pulling events and have classes for both "normally fueled" and "alcohol-powered."

A live video feed of the corn palace can be viewed online at cornpalace.com/157/ Corn-Cam.

Photos:
1. The exterior of the Corn Palace in Mitchell, SD.
2. Watching the National Pedal Pull Championships.
3. Prepping a pedal-tractor-pulling contestant during the national event.

50 Holland, MI

This wasn't supposed to become a new way of life.

This whole travel thing.

It started off as a lark.

Sitting on the couch with MsBoyink, we realized we were homeschoolers who owned an online business with clients who mostly weren't local.

We could do this anywhere.

I joked that we could buy an RV and take life on the road. Rather than read about places like Gettysburg we could just go there.

The joke started to run. The running joke got serious. We mentioned the idea at a networking event and got a challenge in response.

Why don't you?

I had one big question.

Could we keep our house? Or would we have to sell it to afford to travel?

I looked at our finances and researched the cost of RVing. The numbers said we could keep it.

Which was good. Because we didn't dare go all in.

We had a *12* and *13* year old, so we were looking at compressing puberty into a 30-foot box.

Would the RV survive?

Would the parents survive?

We decided we'd travel for a year. We'd keep the house and find a friend to live in it. We'd store our stuff in the basement. The house would be our safety net.

In case that puberty thing wasn't so funny after all.

We bought a used truck and fifth-wheel and hit the road.

Six months later we hadn't even made it halfway around the country.

Most days I forgot we owned a house.

I didn't like it when the memories came back. The house was a big anchor of worry several states away.

We were enjoying travel and the adventure of visiting new places.

We'd been able to handle that puberty thing. So far anyway.

The country was just too big. A year wasn't going to be enough to see what we wanted to see.

Sitting in a little private RV park in Cortez, Colorado, we held a family meeting. We decided to stay out for the planned year, then go back to Michigan and sell the house.

And go all in.

We continued on to the Pacific coast and then north up to Oregon and Washington.

We spent a few weeks working for a campground in Washington, then pointed the nose of the truck back towards Michigan.

Via Yellowstone, Mount Rushmore, the Badlands, Wall Drug and more.

We arrived back home in West Michigan after having been gone just over a year.

We moved back into our house as winter set in.

Faced with a question.

All the stuff stored, untouched, in the house for a year. What do we do with it?

Just sell it, right? Put it up on Craigslist or Facebook and get some money back out of it.

Some bigger items sold easily. Then I tried selling the smaller stuff. The stereo speakers. The table saw. The hose reel.

Between "will you take half that," "do you have more photos," "can you meet me across town," "is this still available," and "oh sorry I wasn't able to make it," the process quickly became too much hassle for the money.

We decided to give it all away.

We scheduled a "house cooling" party and invited friends over for a meal and conversation. But they had to take a fabulous parting gift with them when they left.

We were able to bless a young gal just getting started on her own after extensive surgery that kept her living with her parents. We gave furniture to newlyweds. A bed went to a young family with growing kids. My tools went to a local rescue mission that had an auto mechanics training program. Homeschooling materials disappeared into a dozen minivans.

The gratitude we felt from giving stuff away was worth more than money. As the pile of our possessions got smaller the weight on our shoulders got lighter.

And the house? Sold to the first realtor who came through.

Eventually the day came. Time to go. We threaded our way through painters, carpenters, and electricians prepping the house for the new owner.

We put a few last things in the RV, hitched up, and drove away from the only house we'd ever owned.

We were houseless.

But we weren't homeless.

Save for a few boxes stashed at my parents' cottage, everything we owned was with us in the truck and RV.

It probably didn't look like much going down the road.

But.

We'd never felt so rich.

Photos:

1. A basement full of stuff to get rid of.
2. Piles of stuff to sort in the garage.
3. Miranda sorts through her belongings.
4. We left our house behind as a crew of contractors came in to get it ready for the new owner.

51 Spencer, TN

There is a theory, in the psychology world, that we have two selves.

The experiencing self and the remembering self.

The experiencing self lives in the moment. The experiencing self is the one answering questions like does this hurt, is it hot outside, or are you tired?

The remembering self answers different questions.

Questions like, how was it on the whole? What did you learn there? How would you describe it to someone else?

The remembering self is described as a tyrant.

Because it's the self that keeps score, that decides what we learn from living, and uses those memories to make decisions in the present.

But the remembering self?

It's not always right.

Or consistent across people who shared the same experience.

One of the most interesting aspects of our travels is talking about them with our kids, now that some time has passed.

My memories of a specific location are often radically different than theirs.

I remember things they have no concept of.

They talk about meeting people that I would swear we never met.

Sometimes I can prove them wrong with the photos that I took.

Other times I start to wonder if it's my own memory that is starting to slip.

We each remember a different aspect of our visit to Fall Creek Falls State Park in Tennessee.

For my baseball-loving son, it was the place where a random campground conversation led to buying a wooden baseball bat from a pig-farming pharmacist who made them on the side.

For my daughter, it was the place where we let her experience some independence. After carefully reviewing the park map and setting a time to be home, she left on a short solo bike ride to look at horses the park kept in stables.

She wasn't back when she was supposed to be.

As the clock ticked.

Our worry increased.

The clock ticked.

We wanted to give her the space to figure things out for herself.

The clock ticked.

We didn't want to be helicopter parents.

The clock ticked.

It was a very hot day.

The clock ticked.

MsBoyink finally caved. She got in the truck and started off in the direction Miranda had gone.

A few minutes later, Miranda pedaled into the campsite.

From the opposite direction.

A wrong turn on a park loop had lengthened her ride to ten miles, by herself, on a hilly 40 mph road with no shoulders or shade.

But she had stopped for help, figured out her error, gotten directions and water, and made it back.

For MsBoyink, our visit to Fall Creek Falls was a sentimental one, recreating a camping trip she had taken with her family while in college.

And for me?

Fall Creek Falls was the place where I decided just looking at a waterfall wasn't enough.

I wanted to stand under it. I waded across the water, climbed up on wet rocks, and let the falling water beat through all my clothes, drenching me to the bone.

The heat aside, the worry over Miranda aside, the baseball bat aside, that's what my tyrant remembers.

At 256 feet tall, the Fall Creek Falls waterfall is one of the highest in the Eastern United States. Learn more about the park at tnstateparks.com/parks/fall-creek-falls.

Photos:

1. View of the Cumberland Plateau from Fall Creek Falls State Park in Spencer, TN.
2. Michael encourages an uncertain Miranda into wading across the water to join him under the waterfall.
3. Harrison with a wooden baseball bat purchased from a pig-farming pharmacist who made them on the side.

52 Brownsville, MN

Maybe the term came from the *2007* movie with Jack Nicholson and Morgan Freeman. Maybe it's older than that.

A "bucket list."

That list of stuff to do before you die.

I've never had a formal bucket list. But once on the road we wanted to try new things.

On my list were:

- Go to a rodeo
- Go to a roller derby match
- Drive a race car
- Learn to surf
- DJ a blues radio show

And?

Live on a houseboat.

After our first year on the road, we sold our house. We paid off the mortgage and had some extra money.

Not enough to buy a houseboat.

But enough to rent one.

I found rentals on Lake Powell, Arizona. Then on Lake Cumberland, Kentucky. And then, the Mississippi River.

Live on a boat, on the Mississippi River? Like Huck Finn? Tom Sawyer? Mark Twain?

Game over.

There's a lot to remember from our time on the river. Piloting a 55-foot long box-kite boat on a windy day. Negotiating with oncoming river tows. Locking. The pelicans, herons, bald eagles, and fish. Seeing a classic Mississippi Riverboat chugging up-river.

But mainly?

We remember wing-dams.

Wikipedia says: "A wing dam is a man-made barrier that extends partway into a river. "

The Mississippi River has thousands of wing-dams. They keep the water deep enough for commercial boats.

And houseboats, as it turns out.

While I had visions of being able to

DRIVEN TO WONDER

explore every nook and cranny of the river, our boat's draft required us to stay in the shipping channel.

Until we stopped. Then we could beach the boat and secure it with multiple anchors.

But we had to find space between wing-dams.

Hidden wing-dams, that is. Wing-dams don't protrude from the water. They lurk, invisible, under the surface.

We had a book that estimated their locations, but to be sure we didn't hit one we had to go back.

Back to Mark Twain.

A name, yes. But a pseudonym. Chosen from Samuel Clemens' time as a Mississippi riverboat pilot.

A riverboat needed two fathoms of water to float. A crew member would drop a weighted, marked rope into the river to check the depth. They would call out "mark twain!" when the waters reached the second mark.

We used a marked pole rather than a rope, but the idea was the same.

I faced the boat towards shore. My son knelt on the bow, pole in hand. I nudged the throttle. He stabbed the pole

into the water. If he called out "wing-dam!" I'd quick-reverse the boat. If he called out "clear!" I'd goose the throttle and beach us.

We were always relieved when we were finally beached and anchored.

Wing-dam.

We've never rented a houseboat again. But that phrase - wing-dam! - has stayed with us.

When we are in a situation where hidden obstacles threaten delays or damage we'll think "wing-dams!"

And start testing the waters with prayer, seeing if God wants us to wait, back up, or charge ahead.

Houseboating is more popular on the scenic upper Mississippi River. There are multiple rental outlets in Iowa, Wisconsin, and Minnesota. Prices vary by boat configuration, size and length of rental.

Photos:

1. Beached overnight on Crater Island near Brownsville, MN.
2. The Boyink kids playing on shore in the cove.
3. Michael piloting the houseboat up the Mississippi River.
4. A surprise sighting of a classic Mississippi River steamer.
5. Miranda shows why the river is called "The Big Muddy."
6. MsBoyink and Harrison set one of three required anchors.
7. A family shot after our first successful beaching of the boat.

53 White Sands, NM

"It might have been the American tendency in travel. One goes, not so much to see but to tell afterward."

-John Steinbeck
Travels With Charley

Simple words. Written in the early 1960s. In them, Steinbeck efficiently skewers a entire modern-day "travel writing" industry, from travel bloggers, to YouTube vloggers, to #vanlife Instagram influencers.

And yes, also this very book.

I'll confess. Part of the reason I wrote these stories and compiled them into this book is simply to "tell afterward."

But there's more to it than that.

The rear view mirror can be clearer than the windshield.

The real value, the real lesson, or the real takeaway from an experience doesn't always show up right away.

Like White Sands National Park.

At the time, we were just checking another "National" something off our list (during our visit White Sands was only a National Monument. Since then it apparently aced the final exam and graduated to full-on National Park status).

It happened to be my birthday. I decided I wanted to eat cake while barefoot on a gypsum dune somewhere in the 145,762 acres of the park.

We went to the visitor center first to pick up a map. We found a trailhead parking area and drove to it. We took the requisite birthday photos.

Then we had to book it before a rainstorm swept through the valley. We drove back and parked next to the visitor center for a half an hour while the worst of the rain poured down.

And then went back to the campground where we'd left the RV.

Done and done.

Now, years later, I see our day in a different light.

It's a narrative.

Almost a Psalm.

Our time in the park began in "life as usual" mode. Celebrating yet another birthday in a string of them longer than I care to count. Visiting yet another new place in a string of new places.

Then comes the unexpected drama.

A nasty looking storm. A curtain of black rainclouds moving in our direction. Rain coming down sideways. Tornadoes

do occur at White Sands. People have died in this park.

David might say "my deadly enemies compassed me about."

We scrambled first for cover inside the truck, then for safer parking by the visitor center. We hoped there was a shelter inside if it came to that.

And, like David, we prayed for deliverance.

As the storm passed over the lighting became dramatic.

Spooky, even.

It was like we had parked on the dividing line between day and night. Out the passenger side of the truck it was pitch dark. The driver's side of the truck was lit up in a brilliant sunset.

And birthed out of that division?

A rainbow.

Literally a symbol of God's faithfulness. A promise that things would be OK.

And just in case we maybe had a few remaining doubts about our safety?

God doubled down.

A second rainbow appeared next to the first.

We're off the road now.

But that doesn't mean that the storms stop coming.

But we've been here before.

We'll take the action we need to take.

We'll find shelter.

We wait on God.

And we'll see His promise.

Just like at White Sands.

White Sands National Park is located about an hour northeast of Las Cruces, NM. Learn more at nps.gov/whsa.

Photos:

1. View from the trail at White Sands National Park, NM.
2. The Boyink kids trying to outrun the rain back to the truck.
3. A rainbow arches over our truck at the park visitor center.
4. Vegetation at White Sands.
5. A second rainbow appears over the first.

54 Mesa, AZ

"Can I be a cactus expert?"

There are rare moments, as a parent, when you actually hear the sound of a paradigm being shifted, of a self-identity expanding, or of a potential future being tried on like a new pair of jeans.

We were in Mesa, Arizona, working as camphosts in a county-owned campground.

MsBoyink and I staffed the park entrance booth, checking in campers, selling day-passes, and giving directions to the hiking, mountain biking, and equine trails.

In return, we got a covered RV parking spot with full hookups, access to laundry, and use of a car wash station.

As homeschoolers, the kids were old enough to be mostly self-directed. MsBoyink worked with them to develop a curriculum and a weekly plan. The kids would take it from there.

And once their studies were done, this park held an additional attraction for them.

The Turners.

Another family. With kids about their age.

Like us, the Turners had moved out of a house and into an RV in order to explore the country as a family.

We'd met them during a previous stay at the park and become fast friends. We stayed in touch and when a camphosting spot became available, the Turners hooked us up.

They had also created a model for engaging with the park as a family. The Turner kids helped other camphosts at the gift shop or assisted the maintenance crews.

Our kids followed suit. Harrison swept floors after nature center talks, raked campsites between campers, and helped direct traffic during archery tournaments.

And Miranda?

She fell in love.

Let me back up.

Miranda was our introvert, normally just as happy to sleep in late, then stay dressed in PJ's inside the RV all day reading, writing, or emailing her friends.

When we made her go outside, she would usually let her more outgoing older brother lead the way into games with other kids.

DRIVEN TO WONDER

But here?

She'd get up on her own, shower, wolf down breakfast, pack a snack and water bottle, and sail out the door before we adults were even due in the entrance station.

She'd ride her bike over a mile to the other end of the park where she'd join one of the park's ranger-led hikes.

While hiking, the ranger would teach the group about the desert. What was edible? What came out at night? What would flower in the spring? What should you do if you come across a rattlesnake?

Miranda soaked it all up, falling in love with the Sonoran Desert. She made friends with the ranger and the other camphosts who staffed the nature walks. She bought her own desert plant and animal identification guide from the park bookstore.

Then one of the camphosts - a former teacher - challenged Miranda. "The next time we do this talk, why don't you cover the barrel cactus?"

She accepted. She studied up. First she presented about the barrel cactus. The next week they added the creosote bush. Then the hanging chain cholla.

Week by week, bush by cactus by bird species, Miranda learned to present an entire "Sonoran Desert 101" talk to park visitors.

When people learned we were homeschoolers, they would often express concern over social skills. How on earth could kids who didn't spend all day in a school building possibly learn to socialize with other people?

I present Exhibit A.

A self-taught, self-motivated 14-year-old girl fearlessly presenting her science knowledge to a group of complete strangers.

There was no need for Miranda to ask if she could be a cactus expert.

She already was.

See Miranda's presentation at vimeo. com/travelersfilms.

Photos:
1. The Sonoran Desert.
2. Miranda leads a Christmastime desert walk in Mesa, AZ.
3. Harrison rakes a campsite to prepare it for the next camper.
4. Miranda teaches a group about the Saguaro cactus.
5. Moonrise over Pass Mountain.
6. Miranda talks about the jumping cholla bush.

55 Mesa, AZ

Ted was thirsty. Which was a problem. Because Ted lived in the desert.

Ted and his wife, Alice, had purchased a plot of land in Mesa in *1936*.

If real estate success is location, location, location, then Ted and Alice had chosen wisely.

Their plot of land had access to Highways *60*, *80*, and *89*. The "Apache Trail" went right past their door, leading to the Superstition Mountains and Saguaro Lake.

Ted and Alice moved a house onto the property, then built a gas station and small store to serve the people enjoying the new American pastime of automotive roadtrips.

Ted wasn't the only thirsty one. Business was booming. All those people and cars needed water.

Not one to be deterred by a challenge, Ted simply hauled water in barrels from downtown Mesa.

After three years he decided to sink a well. He hired a drilling crew and they went to work.

And were successful.

They found water.

Full of minerals.

And hot.

The thermometer said *113* degrees.

They'd struck a hot spring.

But it was undrinkable.

Ted and Alice made lemonade from lemons.

They piped the hot mineral water into a bath house and added changing rooms and overnight cottages.

Buckhorn Mineral Baths was born.

Ted and Alice added a cafe, nine-hole golf course, trading post, Greyhound station, and a museum full of the mounts from Ted's taxidermy hobby.

Their business grew. Up to *100* people were enjoying the baths each day.

One of those people was Horace Stoneham.

Horace happened to own the New York Giants baseball team.

Horace liked the Buckhorn Baths so much he made it the team's official base of winter operations.

The big names started showing up.

Baseball names like Willie Mays.

Ty Cobb. Joe DiMaggio. Political names like Margaret Truman and JFK. Entertainer names like Elvis and Burt Reynolds.

Other teams followed the Giants into Arizona for the winter.

The so-called "Cactus League" was eventually formed.

Buckhorn Baths was at the center of it all. Ted and Alice hosted barbecues for the teams and players that would attract 4,000 people - which is how many people lived in Mesa at the time.

Ted, Alice, and a staff of 25 ran Buckhorn Baths into the 1960s and 1970s.

Then, like all good things, it slowly came to an end.

Ted died in 1984. Highway 60 got rerouted in the 1990s. Large hotel chains had come to town. Alice finally closed Buckhorn Baths in 1999. She was 93 years old.

And the Buckhorn Baths, now on the National Register of Historic Places, have been in limbo ever since.

The property sat for sale for years. The City of Mesa tried to buy it but couldn't reach an agreement. In 2017, a private company purchased the property and buildings. The taxidermy collection was donated to Arizona State University, but no other work has taken place at the property.

In 2020, the City of Mesa hired a new historic preservation coordinator, who mentioned the Buckhorn Baths as her top "must-do" item.

Meanwhile, the classic Buckhorn Baths sign sits in Mesa, reminding passers-by of a time when a thirsty man drilled into the desert and struck gold.

Buckhorn Baths is at 166 N Recker Road in Mesa, AZ. While the facility is closed and parts are fenced off, the classic sign is visible from the road.

Photos:
1. The classic Buckhorn Baths sign.
2. The entrance to the men's side of the hot mineral baths.
3. Sign for the Wildlife Museum at the Buckhorn Baths complex.
4. Under the front porch roof at the hotel.

56 Canyon Lake, AZ

Derek was a fast driver. We were in his black, diesel-powered Chevy pickup truck, attacking the twisty Arizona back roads like we were second place in a rally race.

My son was in the back seat. There were kayaks on the roof and coolers on the floor. The three of us were heading to Canyon Lake for a day on the water.

I looked over at Derek and said "You could be an axe murderer, for all we know."

He laughed.

I'm pretty sure he laughed.

We had only met the previous day. MsBoyink and I were working the entrance booth at a campground in Mesa, Arizona. Derek checked in on the way to his campsite. I saw the boats on his roof

and reminded him that we were currently in the middle of a desert.

He said Canyon Lake was a few miles away and he was planning a day kayaking there. I said it sounded like fun and waved him on.

He backed up.

"Want to go?"

His wife had stayed home so he had an extra kayak.

I looked at MsBoyink. She shrugged. "Always say yes," she smiled.

We had already talked about this. One reason we started traveling was to

get out of our routines. We wanted to be open to new experiences. And new people. We decided that unless an offer was illegal, immoral, or unsafe, we would say yes to it.

Karaoke on the beach with off-duty Coast Guardsmen? Yep. Sunday dinner with reality TV show stars? Absolutely. Swimming with manatees in Florida? Yes, yes, yes.

Kayaking on a remote lake with an absolute stranger?

Yes.

We left early the next morning and I got to know Derek on the hour-long drive to the lake.

He owned a delivery company in Wisconsin. He had a son about the same age as mine. His parents lived in the Phoenix area. Derek kept his kayaking gear stored in their garage and was able to visit a few times a year. He had spent a lot of time on Canyon Lake.

We rented a third boat for my son. We explored up river mouths. We saw bald eagles and Peregrine falcons. We beached the boats and rock-hopped up riverbeds to see snow-melt waterfalls. The conversation flowed easily.

It was one of the most memorable days of our time on the road.

And I know Derek at least smiled at my axe murderer joke.

Canyon Lake is approximately 50 miles east of Phoenix and is in the Tonto National Forest. The lake offers boating, fishing, kayaking and swimming. Learn more at fs.usda.gov/recarea/tonto/recarea/?recid=35545

Photos:

1. Derek and Harrison explore a small cove off the main lake.
2. Derek and Harrison on the main waters of Canyon Lake.
3. Michael kayaks with the one-lane Canyon Lake Bridge visible in the distance.

CANYON LAKE, AZ

57 Mesa, AZ

We were invisible. Car after car would drive by. And the driver would ignore us.

Sometimes they would hand us money.

But without looking at us.

We were in Mesa, Arizona.

Working in what was affectionately called the "monkey house."

The monkey house was the entrance booth to a county park complex that included an archery range, nature center, campground, and trails for hiking, biking, and horseback riding.

To most people driving into the park, we were invisible.

Just a quasi-secure, money-taking utility. Cheaper to provide than an automated solution.

In exchange for approximately 25 hours-per-week working in the monkey house, the county provided our campsite and laundry facilities.

And invisibility.

People would pull up to the window and hold out money or day pass while staring straight ahead. Or having a conversation with others in the car. Or with someone on the phone.

So we made up a game.

Just to try and get them to see us.

Not just notice we were there. We wanted to interact with them as fellow human beings.

We'd comment on their cars. Or their clothes. If they were eating or drinking something we'd ask if they brought enough to share. If they had bikes I'd see if they wanted trail recommendations. If we recognized them as campers we'd tell them "welcome home."

It all became our monkey house shtick.

And it worked.

Mostly.

Many visitors were repeats, and with them one-off jokes became running gags. We actually did get offered food.

One RVing couple stopped by our campsite just to say goodbye before they hitched up and left for their next park.

To them, we had become visible.

But it didn't work with everyone.

There was one young gal who came to the park almost daily to walk or run the trails. She was always on the phone with her car stereo blaring. She would keep looking straight ahead and talk while holding out her pass for us to swipe. She would just keep her hand out for us to put the card back in.

She never saw us.

Invisible people.

Invisible people are everywhere. Grocery store cashiers. Bank tellers. Waiters. Hotel maids. Janitors. Delivery drivers.

It's so easy to take others for granted. They're just there to do their job. Provide us a service. Make our lives easier.

That year in Mesa, we celebrated Christmas with other invisible people. Maintenance workers. Archery range coordinators. Nature center staff. Group hike leaders. Restroom cleaners. Camp hosts.

My challenge to you?

Claim a superpower for yourself.

See the invisibles.

Look them in the eye.

Remember they are God's child.

As are you.

Wish them a good day. Thank them for their work. Make a positive comment about something they said. Or did.

And mean it.

Usery Mountain Regional park is one of 14 parks and recreation areas maintained by Maricopa County. Learn more at maricopacountyparks.net/park-locator/ usery-mountain-regional-park.

Photos:

1. Sunset over Mesa, AZ.
2. MsBoyink peeks out the window of the monkey house.
3. An end of season party with other "invisible people" - rangers, campground staff, and volunteers.
4. Christmas mimosas with other invisibles.
5. Sunset from the monkey house.

58 Pasadena, CA

"Oh, by the way."

I was self-employed for 16 years. I did OK, but my legacy won't include any college business schools bearing my name.

I did learn a few things.

One of them being that hearing "Oh, by the way" late in negotiations isn't usually a good thing.

We had a training business and were talking with a new client.

We had locked down dates. Agreed on a price. And were happy to hear the venue - a small Christian college in Pasadena, California - actually had a few RV sites on campus. Long hotel stays weren't one of our favorite aspects of business travel.

But then I heard it.

"Oh, by the way, there will be a powwow of Christian American Indians going on while you are here. Hope that's ok?"

Oh?

I didn't really know how to respond.

We didn't know anything about powwows. We were intrigued by the intersection of Indian culture and Christian faith.

And?

We needed the money.

So we went.

We arrived as the powwow was getting started. Cars lined the streets. People crowded the vendor booths. Drums were already sounding.

We threaded the truck and RV into a full parking lot and through a little-used side gate. The spot wasn't much - just a gravel pad with hookups - but we were happy to have our home with us.

Once setup, curiosity took over. What actually happens at a powwow? We walked over. At the middle of the event was a large grass circle for the different dances.

We watched the Grand Entrance - when all the costumed dancers line up and make their way into the circle for the ceremonial beginning to the powwow.

After that there were ceremonial solo dances and social group dances. All were accompanied by a drum circle of six to eight men.

Newbies like us, however, couldn't just jump into the group dances. You had to be invited in.

My son and I got into a conversation with a man who had the title of "Arena Director." William described his role as the Indian version of Head of Security.

He pulled us into the ring.

Our feet found common ground as we learned a simple two-step.

And our hearts found common ground as we shared our story.

We were nomads, at that time living without a permanent place to call home. We had packed up family, house

and home. We often traveled to where the work was. Where the sustenance was.

For many Americans, that's nonsense. The American Dream is found safely inside the white pickets of a fence, not inside the white stripes of a highway.

As an American Indian though, William got it. His ancestors were nomadic. They often packed up family, house and home and moved to where the sustenance was.

We wrapped up our conversation. William wished us well. And he let us know that, now that we had been invited into the circle and learned the dance, we were welcome in the other group dances.

Indians and White people. Not always a history to be proud of there.

But on that little chunk of grass in sunny Southern California, we had connected. We found shared experiences. We respected each other.

So we danced.

Best known for hosting the Rose Bowl, Pasadena was originally settled by the Hahamog-na tribe of Native Americans. Learn more at pasadenahistory.org.

Photos:

1. Beaded purses for sale.
2. The Boyink kids join an American Indian dance circle.
3. (This page) Other handmade items for sale at the powwow.

59 Desert Center, CA

The answer is Desert Center, California.

And the question?

Where is the birthplace of prepaid, managed healthcare?

Desert Center is aptly named. It's in the desert. And it's located in nearly the center of an otherwise unpopulated 100-mile stretch of I-10 between Indio, California and Blythe, California.

Driving through it, you'd hardly expect any kind of healthcare, much less healthcare history.

In the 1930s, however, things were different. There were nearly 5,000 men in town digging the Colorado River Aqueduct. And when they got sick, they had to travel 50 miles to Indio to see a doctor.

Learning this, Dr. Sidney Garfield borrowed money from his dad and put up a small clinic near the construction site.

But the trouble?

The men would receive care, promise to pay on the next payday, but when that time came - feeling healthy - they'd head to the bar instead.

Garfield was going broke. He announced he was closing the clinic.

Enter Henry J. Kaiser.

Yes, that Henry J. Kaiser.

Kaiser shipyards. Kaiser Motors (if you are a street rodder and know what a "Henry J" is, now you know where the name came from). Kaiser Aluminum. Kaiser Jeeps. Kaiser Broadcasting.

The non-paying men were Kaiser's employees.

Kaiser didn't want Garfield to close the clinic.

Instead, Kaiser proposed that he would take a nickel a day out of the men's paycheck to prepay for future medical care. Another nickel would cover injuries during non-work hours. Yet another nickel would cover wives and children.

It worked.

Garfield soon had a steady income stream. His clinic stayed open.

And Kaiser Permanente, now the largest managed health care system in the world with 12 million members, 39 hospitals, 700 offices, and 300,000 employees was born.

We knew none of this on our day in Desert Center.

We just needed gas.

We had stopped for fuel up the road at the Chiriaco Summit fuel station on the first leg of a week-long Arizona-California-Arizona trip. Knowing the lack of gas

options in this stretch of I-10, I planned for another stop on the way back.

It was a Saturday afternoon. The station was packed.

And there was an unhappy vibe in the air.

Usually when people are pumping gas they keep to themselves, watch the pump, or look at their phone.

These people were heads up, looking around.

The guy at the pump in front of me asked if I knew why his pump wasn't working.

I noticed my pump wasn't working either.

I went in to ask an employee and he came outside to check things out.

Then the station PA system came to life.

"We are out of gas."

A discernible ripple of fear went through the crowd. This wasn't a suburban fuel station with two other options across the street or up the block.

The next station to the east was 60 miles away.

The next station to the west was 30 miles away.

The guy in front of me said "I'm on empty. I need to be in Phoenix tomorrow. What am I supposed to do?"

I didn't have an answer.

Our truck had the unfortunate combination of a small gas tank and single-digit miles per gallon when towing.

I had learned to refuel early.

I still had a third of a tank.

The unrest in the crowd continued to spread and grow. Voices began to get an edge to them. I have never been in a crowd that turned to riot, but I was afraid this one might.

Unlike most other customers, we had options. We had our house on our back. I could go park in the corner of the lot for the night and get gas when the fuel supply truck showed up.

But honestly?

I was scared.

I didn't want to be sitting in a vehicle that had *any* fuel next to a crowd of people who were desperate for it.

So we pulled back out onto I-*10*.

Backtracking west.

Because *30* miles was closer than *60* miles.

That station had lines at the pumps. Maybe word had gotten out.

We filled up, and once again headed east. I don't remember being able to see who was left at the gas station while driving past it again on I-*10*.

And that's probably a good thing.

Desert Center is mostly a ghost town these days, yet has a functioning post office serving the population of around 200 people.

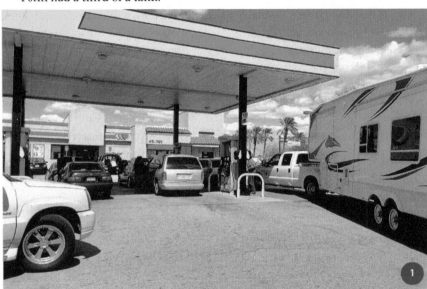

Photos:
1. We normally wouldn't have tried to get into such a busy gas station while towing.
2. Looking happy to be gassing up after backtracking *30* miles.

60 Phoenix, AZ

Mmmph. That's the sound I heard from the other side of the RV.

I looked over at MsBoyink.

She was staring at her laptop.

"What?"

"Just...something," she said.

I got worried.

"Something bad?"

"No," she said. "Just..."

"What then?"

"I wasn't going to show you this," she said.

"Show me what?"

She let out a heavy breath. She tipped her laptop towards me.

She was looking at GroupOn.com - a website that promotes limited-time deals by location.

On her screen was a deal for a stock-car "Driving Experience" being held at the nearby Phoenix International Raceway.

It wasn't that I was a die-hard stock car racing fan. I'd watched some races on TV but had never been to one in person.

Rather, back when we started traveling, I had the whole family pretend money, time, or access weren't obstacles and write down experiences they'd like to have or people they'd like to meet.

On my list?

Drive a race car.

Quarter-miler, circle-tracker, stock car - it didn't matter. I just wanted to drive a high-performance car used for some type of racing.

MsBoyink had seen my list.

She didn't like the thought of me in a race car.

But love isn't always expressed with cards or flowers. Sometimes it's expressed with race cars.

She handed me her laptop and I signed up for the deal.

The day came. Clear sky. Mild temps. The kind of day snowbirds move to Phoenix for.

The upsells started the minute we arrived. Insurance was an extra $60. Practice laps riding with a pro was another $80.

Training was next. Our instructor made it clear - this was a "driving experience," not a "racing experience." A race master would be talking to us the entire time, telling us when we could pass or when to move out of the way so we could be passed.

After training they size you up.

Not to see how fast you're going to be, but physically how big you are. For the firesuit and helmet.

DRIVEN TO WONDER

And the car.

Turns out, stock cars aren't generous on space. They had one car setup for "tall guys."

At six foot three inches, I'm often the tallest in a group of men.

Not this time.

I crammed myself through the window of a "standard sized" green and yellow #46 car that may or may not have been a leftover from the *Days of Thunder* movie with Tom Cruise.

I got strapped in. Installed the steering wheel. Put my helmet on. Got a feel for where the pedals and shifter were.

And waited.

And thought about how little I could actually move.

And waited.

And realized how warm it had gotten.

And waited.

And pondered claustrophobia in a way I hadn't before.

And waited.

I started to sweat. I wriggled a hand up to my helmet and took my sunglasses off for a bit of relief.

Finally the radio crackled to life. We all gave thumbs up to the race master. I put my sunglasses back on. Put the clutch in. Found first gear.

Start your engines! came over the headset.

And I did.

The flagman pointed to cars ahead of me. They launched. Then he pointed at me.

This was it. All of the buildup. The training. The trash-talking. The nervous jitters.

I feathered the gas and let my foot off the clutch.

And STALLED THE CAR.

I got it restarted. But it suddenly got about ten degrees hotter inside that car and I was glad no one could see my face.

From there the experience was a blur. The corners came up faster than seemed

possible. The car's reaction to jumping on the gas was impressive.

The answer to the your question? I don't know. There was no speedometer. I was too busy steering and shifting to be able to look at gauges anyway.

All too soon my three laps were over. I pulled into the pits without incident. Extracted myself from the cockpit.

And paid another $15 for the souvenir photo.

I'm usually too cheap to pay for those, but this time was different.

Because I had driven a race car.

Photos:

1. Driving NASCAR at the Phoenix International Raceway.
2. He's not gonna fit!
3. Just before stalling the car.
4. Post- race adrenaline high.

61 Sedona, AZ

It's a Missouri name. Made up in *1877* by Amanda Miller, an Amish mother from Gorin, Missouri. She thought it pretty enough for her newborn daughter.

Amanda's baby grew up. Ms. Miller became Mrs. Schnebly. She and her husband T.C. moved to the red rock wilds of Arizona. They built a house that became a hotel that became the first post office of a new town.

Washington, D.C. didn't like T.C.'s initial ideas for what to call the new town.

"Just name it after your wife," they said. So he did.

And Sedona, Arizona went on the map.

These days?

There's an RV model. A car model. A bike model. Cookware from Macys. Men's clothes from Kohls.

All named Sedona.

Marketers love it. It's a word with a lot to say.

It says sweeping views. Majestic red-rock buttes. Steep canyon walls. Pine forests. Hiking. Mountain biking. Being outdoors. Being active. Being healthy.

We wanted to love Sedona.

Friends did. Fellow full-time travelers as well. Sedona remained their favorite even after years on the road.

So we went.

Forgetting.

Being home-schoolers, self-employed, and living on the road we'd often forget.

We'd forget where we were. We'd forget which day of the week it was. And we'd forget to think about "normal people."

For normal people, the day we decided to drive into Sedona was smack in the middle of Spring Break.

Spring Break in Sedona means bumper-to-bumper traffic in town.

While we sat not going anywhere, we looked around at Sedona.

We saw Jeep tour companies. Helicopter tour landing pads. Bike rental shops. T-shirt shops. Souvenir shops.

We saw bohemian chic art galleries. We saw neo-hippie crystal shops. We saw offers for flotation therapy, abundance manifesting, and generational healing.

I'm pretty sure we saw a sign for organic, fair trade, grain-free, dairy-free, non-GMO, vegan coffee made by holistic, hyper-authentic, fully-woke, self-actualized, free-range nutritionists. Drinking it would balance the male and female energies in your microbiome and optimize your spiritual pilgrimage to one of Sedona's energy vortexes.

Not sure if that coffee still had caffeine, but we sure could have used some to help us stay awake waiting to get out of town.

There was beauty around Sedona, yes. The red rock was all that.

But, our timing aside, I couldn't get a photo of that beauty without also getting a power line, house, fence, or tower along with it.

A long-forgotten website said it best:

"Sedona is what happens when a place should have been a national park but isn't."

We have to wonder - what would Sedona Schnebly think of what became of her namesake?

Sedona is two hours north of Phoenix, AZ. Plan your visit at visitsedona.com. Avoid late April if you can.

Photos:

1. Cathedral Rock formation in Sedona, AZ.
2. Fences line a popular trail to keep hiker traffic out. Signage also mentioned armed guards.
3. A view of Oak Creek at Red Rock State Park in Sedona, AZ.
4. One of my few "human-free" Sedona vistas from Boyce Canyon.

62 Picacho Peak, AZ

Civil War soldiers and saguaro cactus. Two things you don't expect to see in the same photo frame.

Neither did we.

We had been to Gettysburg. From there, driving south until we found ocean, it seemed like every historical marker, National Monument, and National Park had to do with the Civil War.

It got to be too much for our home-schooled road-scholars.

"Can we learn some history that doesn't have anything to do with people dying?"

Fair point.

We pointed the nose of the truck west.

We refocused our learning on the Westward Expansion.

The Gold Rush. Lewis and Clark. The Wild West.

The Sonoran Desert.

We entered Arizona at the southeastern corner. The views confirmed what we learned from Roadrunner cartoons growing up - the desert consisted of vast expanses of bare graveled ground pop-ulated with scrubby trees and framed by silhouetted mountain ridges in the distance.

No anvils falling from the sky, however.

Then we saw our first saguaro. To a bunch of shade-tree-loving Michiganders the desert was already other-worldly. The saguaros just added exclamation points.

But we struggled to find a place to stay.

Arizona has RV parks. Scads and gobs of them.

But not for people under 55.

State parks don't age-discriminate, however. Tucson has the gorgeous and popular Catalina State Park.

Full up.

The next option heading an hour north was Picacho Peak State Park - less popular because it's more remote.

We found a site and setup camp amidst the saguaros - which seem to get

more populous as you move north from Tucson.

The park map mentioned an upcoming Civil War Reenactment.

Civil War? Here amidst the cacti?

Our students were not amused.

Turns out Picacho Peak hosted the westernmost battle of the Civil War.

And the smallest in terms of men involved - just two dozen men.

Percentage-wise, the numbers weren't great. Three dead. Three wounded. Three captured.

The battle represented a small, temporary victory for the Confederates.

And each year, more men show up to reenact it than originally fought in it.

We don't remember Picacho Peak for its Civil War history, however.

We remember it as the place we had our first date with a desert that we quickly fell in love with.

We'd go on to spend more time in Arizona than just about any other state during our travels.

Picacho Peak State Park offers a visitor center with exhibits, camping, and hiking around and up to the 1,500-foot top of Picacho Peak. Learn more at azstateparks.com/picacho.

Photos:

1. Sunset over the Sonoran Desert at Picacho Peak State Park.
2. Michael, Harrison, and Miranda wave from the top of a smaller peak visible from the campground.

63 Imperial Beach, CA

I wanted to visit the four corners of the country. You see the problem. The USA isn't exactly rectangular.

I researched to see where other people went. When I got to the point of having to use ridiculous phrases like "the south-southwesternmost point of the contiguous United States" to describe what I was after, I stopped researching.

Instead, I looked at a map and chose what felt right.

In the southwest, it was Border Field State Park south of San Diego, California.

The park's location is interesting. Its ownership is an onion of bureaucratic layers.

Border Field State Park:
- Is on the US and Mexico border.
- Contains a national monument.
- Is within the city limits of Imperial Beach, CA.
- Is within a national estuarine research preserve - managed by 14 governmental agencies including the EPA, US Navy, and US Border Patrol. I'm not sure there's another four

square miles in the USA where you could be ticketed by so many different officers.

Politics aside, what's the park like? Depressing.

We had to call ahead to see if it was even open. The area can flood, which closes all or part of the park down.

On our visit we had to park outside and walk. The main road was closed to vehicles.

The small, gravel parking lot was partially surrounded by a prison-like eight-foot chain link fence topped with rolls of barbed wire.

There was little in the way of ameni-

ties like bathrooms or interpretive trails. The gatehouse was abandoned.

US Border Patrol helicopters constantly flew overhead.

There were signs warning us about possible sewage in the water. Swimming was prohibited.

It wasn't a welcoming experience. But the hardest part?

Mexico.

It was a hot two-mile trek on an unpaved road cutting through barren sandy flats to get to the beach. No shade. No benches. No water fountains.

While we walked, we looked at Mexico.

On their side were hotels. Apartment buildings. Houses. A stadium. A lighthouse. Brightly colored roofs.

Arriving at the beach, we approached the border fence. Through it, we saw Mexican families enjoying the beach and playing in the surf.

We were alone on our side. Until a Border Patrol SUV came to check on us. The officer warned us to stay five yards away from the fence. He stuck around.

Feeling unwanted and under observation, we took a few photos and began walking back to our truck.

The news is full of talk about our borders. I don't know who to believe. Maybe we needed more fences. Maybe we didn't.

What I do know is on that day, we drove away from the border not feeling too proud to be Americans.

Border Field State Park is 40 minutes south of San Diego, California. Check the park status at trnerr.org before visiting.

Photos:
1. Walking towards the beach at Border Field State Park in Imperial Beach, CA.
2. Looking south, Mexican hotel and arena visible.
3. Border fence separating Mexico and the United States.

64 Encinitas, CA

We were from Michigan. Which is surrounded by water. On three sides anyway.

However, we weren't surfers. A few Michiganders surf, but not many.

When we decided to travel full-time, we put together a list of things we wanted to do. Ride horses. See the Grand Canyon. Swim with manatees.

And take surf lessons.

We could have surfed in Northern California, Oregon, or even Washington. We were in all of those areas our first year on the road.

But we were picky. It had to be in Southern California.

I blame the Beach Boys.

When our travels finally found us in the San Diego area, we booked lessons at a surf school in Del Mar (actually the first beach mentioned in "*Surfin' USA*").

That was the easy part.

The harder part was finding affordable camping options. California State Parks can be both expensive and rustic. Many sites have no electric or water hookups.

Once again, MsBoyink kept us on budget by looking for non-traditional places to stay. She booked us a reasonably-priced full-hookup spot at the nearby fairgrounds.

With RV parking sorted, we went down at the appointed time for our surfing lessons.

We started on the beach. We learned how to lay on the board, then tried "popping up" - doing a quick push-up maneuver in an attempt to get on your feet.

After a few rounds of landlubber practice our instructor took us out into the ocean.

There were four of us. And four different stories emerged that day.

Harrison was a natural, popping up successfully on his very first wave. He promptly declared himself "a Southern Californian at heart" and began talking about returning to the area when it came time to set off on his own.

It took me a few tries. Between launching on a wave and then stabilizing enough to pop-up, it's a lot to pack into a seconds-quick process.

But I wasn't quite an old dog learning a new trick. Years of snowboarding in Michigan provided some carryover skills that helped - once I was finally able to stand up on the surfboard.

153

Then there was Miranda. Surfing turned out to be a challenge for her. Wave after wave, launch after launch, she'd try to pop up on the board, only to lose balance and tumble into the foam.

She'd swim in, gather up her board, and paddle back out. Our instructor would patiently find a good wave, line her up, and push her off in front of it.

And again, she'd fall off while trying to stand up. I could see her strength flagging and my heart hurt for her. She was trying so hard. I knew she would be crushed if she failed while her brother succeeded.

Then finally, mercifully, everything went right. The instructor pushed her off. She transitioned from her belly to one knee. Then stood up on both feet. And stayed on.

She whooped in victory, arms over her head, thumbs pointed up. Her face resolved into a beaming smile and she put her arms out for balance. And stood up all the way in.

She was tenacious in the face of adversity and overcame it. Her success was all the sweeter for the work it took to earn.

And MsBoyink?

It was a day of conflicted feelings. Our surfing day happened to fall on her birthday. If you are "of a certain age" you understand how birthdays can uncomfortably force you to face the realities of growing older.

At the time, she didn't feel that she had the physical core strength required to pop-up on the surfboard. She thought the cost of the lesson might be better spent on a nice birthday meal out.

She grabbed the camera and took the photos you see here.

Seeing the fun the rest of us all had, she vowed that she would be in shape to surf by her upcoming 50th birthday.

But then life happened. Our travels went elsewhere. "Surfing by 50" became "surfing someday."

Then we got off the road. Thoughts of surfing in California disappeared into learning a new job, refurbishing a house, and integrating into a new community.

And that's OK. Every once in a while we need reminding that our plans are not always God's plans.

Then again, you never know.

Sixty isn't too old to take up surfing either.

The Eli Howard Surf School has been teaching people to surf since 1999. Learn more at elihoward.com.

Photos:

1. Miranda has her first successful pop-up while surfing in Southern California.
2. Michael, Harrison and Miranda follow their surf instructor into the waves.
3. Harrison rides one in.
4. Michael channels his inner snowboarder while on the water.
5. Miranda beams after riding in successfully.

65 Alcatraz, CA

Our visit to Alcatraz started on the mainland. We arrived at the docks and paid for tickets we had reserved in advance.

We entered a large staging area lined with photos of past prisoners and quotes from the Alcatraz rulebook.

The line to the ferry took us past a professional photographer. For $20, she would take a souvenir photo of our family's visit to the island.

She had a line of customers waiting. She would position them in a staged area and use her photographer magic to make sure everyone had open eyes and a smile on their face.

She'd take the photo and let customers know it would be printed and waiting when they returned.

What most caught my attention was the backdrop in that staged area.

It was a large photo of Alcatraz Island.

With the real thing waiting a short ferry ride across the San Francisco Bay, people were willingly paying $20 for a "souvenir photo" taken in front of an artificial Alcatraz.

I laughed about it then.

Now it makes me think.

How many times in life do I do the same thing?

In the queue of life. Ticket paid for by Christ. My final reward looms just a short ways off.

But I not only get sidetracked by distractions based on falsehoods, I pay for the privilege of doing so.

On the day of our visit to Alcatraz, we mumbled a quick "no thanks" to the photographer and continued down to the ferry. We were anxious to see the real thing.

May we live every day with that same intent.

Alcatraz Island served as a federal prison from 1934 to 1963. It's now a National Park visited by over a million visitors per year. Learn more at nps.gov/alca.

Photo:

1. Ferry boat view of the real Alcatraz Island in California.

DRIVEN TO WONDER

66 Crater Lake, OR

I could write about the horribly annoying swirling mass of recently-hatched mosquitoes.

Or I could write about the dozens of Willy-Wonka-esque squirrels, one of which mistook the enclosed underbelly of our RV for his hole-in-the-ground home.

But I didn't even remember those details until I reread the journal I kept at the time.

I only remember blue.

Paint manufacturers have creative names for their different shades of blue. Aztec Sky, Yucatan, Hacienda Blue, Peaceful River, Dynamic Blue, Hyper Blue, Jay Blue, Major Blue, Jamaican Dream, Cobalt Stone, Suddenly Sapphire, and Rave Regatta.

They are all blue.

But they aren't Crater Lake blue.

Scientists will tell you Crater Lake is so blue because the water is purer and deeper than any other lake in the country.

It's true.

We filled our water bottles from the lake and drank it down, just to say we did.

And at nearly *2,000* feet deep, you'd have to stack four of Missouri's Gateway Arches in Crater Lake before you'd see one break the surface.

Crater Lake is also unusual in that there are no rivers into or out of the lake. Snowmelt and rain fill it up, and evaporation takes it away.

All interesting, yes.

But what sticks with you is the blue.

We see blue nearly every day. If the sky is cloudy, there are blue jays, blue flowers, blue clothes, blue ink pens, and blue websites.

Blue is the world's universal favorite color - regardless of country, age, race, gender, or political affiliation.

Blue is so common, you might even take it for granted.

For us, Crater Lake was God's way of reminding us that He can transform the common into the uncommon, the familiar into the extraordinary, and the plain into the bejeweled.

And if He can do it with blue, He can do it with you.

Sitting at an elevation of 6,178 feet, Crater Lake National Park is usually only open from mid-May to mid-October due to snow. Check current conditions at nps.gov/crla.

Photos:

1. Crater Lake National Park in Oregon.
2. A small building tracks weather and lake conditions near the shoreline.
3. A scenic overlook on the Volcanic Legacy Scenic Byway.

67 Pasco, WA

I'm sorry, we're full," they said. Full? "Yea, for the holiday."

Ugh. We'd forgotten.

Again.

On long drives we'd often find a truck stop to overnight in. After a couple nights of that we'd book a proper campsite so we could fill what was empty and empty what was full.

But not in advance. We'd look at the clock and the map while driving. We'd choose a city an hour down the road, find the RV park, then pick up the phone.

Usually this worked.

Except for holiday weekends.

We spent one Memorial Day in a Walmart parking lot, cooking a frozen pizza and watching a movie on a laptop.

Because we'd forgotten.

On this weekend we had just said goodbye to friends in Oregon. We'd spent the day driving the beautiful Columbia River Gorge, headed east. After seven hours on the road, we were ready to stop down for a night or two.

Forgetting it was the third of July.

MsBoyink was on the phone with a campground in Pasco, Washington.

She looked over. "Full for the holiday."

Facepalm.

Back on the phone, she made a funny face.

"The hockey arena?"

Sure enough, Pasco has a hockey arena - part of a bigger event facility.

Which has an RV park attached.

And they had openings.

We booked a site, and drove the rest of the way there.

Entering the RV park, we noticed a baseball stadium next door.

It was Gesa Stadium, home of the Tri-city Dust Devils, a minor-league baseball team.

Who happened to be playing a home game that night. Our fanboy was ecstatic.

The next day there was a 5K fun run starting right behind our rig. Later that night was the big city fireworks show.

At the baseball stadium.

When in Rome, right?

We walked over to the baseball game that night. Supper was hot dogs in the stands.

The next morning I entered and (mostly) ran the 5K. That afternoon we

DRIVEN TO WONDER

grilled hamburgers and cut up watermelon on the tailgate of the truck.

At dusk, we put our camp chairs in the strip of grass behind our rig and watched the fireworks.

Once they were over, and the parking lot started backing up with homeward bound families, we folded up our chairs and walked a few feet "home."

We closed the curtains against the tailights of all the exiting traffic.

And went to bed.

The next day, with the parking lot empty around us, we hitched back up and got back on the road.

Headed east.

Planning may lead to more predictable results, but our most memorable experiences while traveling happened when we weren't sticking to a plan.

Pasco is one of the Tri-Cities area of Washington, along with Kennewick and Richland. The Tri-Cities are located at the confluence of the Yakima, Snake and Columbia Rivers. Learn more about Pasco at visittri-cities.com.

Photos:
1. Michael finishing a 5K run.
2. Attending a baseball game on an unplanned Fourth of July weekend.
3. Our baseball fan hopes to catch a fly ball at a minor-league game in Pasco, WA.

68 Pompeys Pillar, MT

Thirty five men. Gone two years, four months, and ten days.

Traveling *8,000* miles.

Spending the equivalent of *$870,000* in today's dollars.

Dealing with dysentery, VD, boils, ticks, hailstorms, grizzly bears, stolen horses, a stolen dog, tense standoffs with locals, and a near-miss by a Spanish delegation sent to capture and imprison them.

Still, the Lewis and Clark expedition of *1804 - 1806* was successful.

140 maps created of land that would become *11* states.

178 new plants identified.

122 animals categorized.

A number of mineral, rock, and fossil samples gathered.

Diplomatic relations established with two dozen indigenous nations.

The expedition also rose above social norms of the time being both gender and race inclusive. They employed a female Native American guide. Others were French Canadian, French Indian, and African American. At one point, the group took a vote and included everyone.

The expedition embodied "Manifest Destiny" and helped fuel the westward expansion of the United States.

Or at least that's what we all learned in school.

But, as usual, there's another side to the story.

The Lewis and Clark Expedition failed at one of its primary goals: finding the so-called "Northwest Passage" - a direct water route from the Missouri River to the Columbia River and out to the Pacific Ocean.

They weren't the first people to see the land they explored, white or otherwise. Most of their travels were on existing Indian trails, also used by trappers and traders.

Their cross-continent route went too far north to be useful by others. The maps they brought back were inaccurate.

Actual details about Sacagawea are scarce. But one thing is certain - she was not the primary guide.

For Native Americans, Lewis and Clark might as well have been spreading a plague.

Within *100* years after the expedition

passed through, every indigenous group they had encountered had lost their lands and had been placed on reservations. Forests were cleared and buffalo herds were decimated.

And all those plants, animals, and other specimens and artifacts sent back by Lewis and Clark?

Some never made it, sinking with the ship that carried them. What did survive was split up. President Jefferson got some. Some were exported to England. Some made it to museums. Other artifacts were stored in attics, sold, or stolen. Some burned in fires. Some were discarded as trash.

The main problem?

No one cared.

Journals from the expedition didn't get published on schedule. The War of *1812* came along. Then the Civil War. Other explorers found fame promoting more accessible routes west.

In a sense, Lewis and Clark only just became famous. A historic trail was established in *1978*. Stephen Ambrose wrote a book in *1996*. Ken Burns did a documentary in *1997*.

And Pompeys Pillar - a *200*-foot-tall rock formation alongside the Yellowstone River in Montana bearing William Clark's signature chiseled into the stone - became a National Monument in *2001*.

That signature is the only remaining physical evidence of the Lewis and Clark Expedition along the original route.

Was the Lewis and Clark Expedition a foundational building block for America?

Or is their story merely a convenient skeleton to hang some politically-correct modern myths on, and help us feel good about the means by which America became the country that it is?

I'll leave that one to you.

Pompeys Pillar National Monument is located 30 miles east of Billings, MT and is named after Sacagawea's son Jean Baptiste Charbonneua, whom Clark nicknamed "Pompy." Learn more at nps.gov/places/pompeys-pillar-mt.htm.

Photos:

1. Pompeys Pillar rises *200* feet above the Yellowstone River.
2. From the top of Pompeys Pillar the Yellowstone River is clearly visible.
3. This graffiti/signature of William Clark is the only remaining physical evidence along the route of the famous Lewis and Clark Expedition.

69 Holland, MI

People ask us where home is. It's a difficult question to answer.

MsBoyink and I have had long conversations about it.

We weren't from anywhere for eight years. Before we set off on these oddball travel adventures, we were from Holland, Michigan.

"You can't go home again."

Ever hear that?

It's the title of a 1940 Thomas Wolfe novel. It's the story of a novelist who portrays his home town poorly in a book. The people still living there are so unhappy with his words they sent him death threats.

He can't go home again.

We left Holland in 2010. In some ways, it's still home. We have friends there. We have a son there. It's a place to say we are from if we don't have time for the whole travel story.

And we've gone back. Multiple times.

In one sense, our travels made it clear how pretty Holland is.

Gorgeous beaches, Lake Michigan sunsets, a bustling farmers' market, miles of bike paths and a healthy job market all make Holland an attractive place to live.

But as we made our way about town, eating at restaurants where we used to eat, driving streets we used to drive, shopping at stores we used to shop at, I realized it wasn't just that I didn't want to buy a house and live there again.

No one knew us.

In public, I looked at the faces of people we encountered. I tried to subtract

years off their face and see if I recognized them.

I was successful twice. One a coworker from over twenty years ago. The other a casual acquaintance from church programs our kids were in.

In private get-togethers with friends and family, few were interested in our travels. We had simply been gone and now we were back. Conversations quickly turned to sports, weather, and celebrity dating news.

Holland, Michigan.

I was born there. Grew up there. Graduated high school there. Met MsBoyink there. Started businesses there. Bought my first house there. Had my kids there.

But it's not home. Not really.

And not because it changed.

We can't go home again.
Because we've changed.

Located just over two hours north of Chicago on the shores of Lake Michigan, Holland is home to 33,000 residents and celebrates its Dutch heritage with the annual Tulip Time Festival. Learn more at holland.org.

Photos:

1. Competitors from a weekly regatta return from Lake Michigan, passing in front of the "Big Red" lighthouse in Holland, MI.
2. Holland celebrates its Dutch heritage with an annual Tulip Time festival that draws a half-million people each May.
3. De Zwaan, an authentic Dutch windmill imported from the Netherlands in the 1960s, still operates as a grain mill.
4. Sunset over Lake Michigan.
5. Produce at the Holland Farmers' Market.
6. Holland's "Snow Melt" system pipes hot water under city streets and sidewalks to reduce wintertime plowing and shoveling.

70 Petersburg, KY

Simpler living. Closer family. Richer education. Uncommon adventures.

That was our family travel manifesto. Travel broadened our worldview. We met people we would not have met otherwise. We learned things we would not have otherwise. We lived simply and more closely than many families do.

And yes, there were adventures.

Some planned. Some not.

What that manifesto doesn't explicitly cover?

Faith.

Our travels happened in time and in space.

But we also went on a faith journey.

It took me years to process what happened. And I'm not sure the journey is over.

MsBoyink and I grew up in the church, met in a church, and got married in a church. We started a family and had our kids baptized in a church.

Then we left our church to hit the road.

And, over time, found that full-time travel doesn't fit well with the mainstream church.

We had a number of experiences, both negative and positive, that served as waypoints on our faith journey.

This particular one happened on the way to the Creation Museum in Petersburg, Kentucky.

We were on a smaller backcountry highway, intentionally staying off the interstate to enjoy glimpses of small town life.

We also liked being able to easily pull over when necessary - for potty breaks, fueling up, or eating meals.

It got to be lunchtime. We had cold pizza back in the RV. We just needed a parking lot big enough to pull into.

I spotted a church up ahead. It was a weekday and the lot was large and empty.

Perfect.

I swung in and parked. We went back and got in the RV to eat. Our RV had one large "slide-out" in the living area. It was tight for the four of us with that pulled in, so I pushed the button and gave us some room to eat.

Halfway through our cold pizza, we heard a knock on the door.

I opened it to a middle-aged man in a leather coat.

And he was not happy.

"What are you doing here? This isn't a campground. You can't stay here."

I explained we had just stopped to eat lunch.

"You have your slideouts all out like you are camping. I'm the pastor here and you don't have our permission to camp here."

I reiterated that we were just eating lunch and could be gone in five minutes.

He left in a huff, treating us to the loud exhaust on his motorcycle as he pulled out.

We put the rest of our cold pizza in the truck, pulled in the slide, and drove out of the church parking lot.

Only to notice the church name, painted in large letters on the side of the building.

The church name had three words.

The last word?

"Outreach."

Matthew 25:35 talks about welcoming strangers with food and drink.

Hebrews 13:2 recommends showing hospitality to strangers who might be angels in disguise.

Other verses in Leviticus, Romans, 1 Peter, Job, and Deuteronomy say basically the same thing.

Yet, as strangers we were literally kicked off the doorstep of a church with "outreach" in its name.

It'll make you think.

Now.

To be fair.

We told this story to some friends back home. Not trying to "name and shame" the pastor or the church, but rather just chuckling at the irony of it all.

One of our friends got a burr under his saddle. He approximated where we were and figured out which church it was.

And contacted the pastor.

And let him know what he thought of the "outreach" methods the pastor had demonstrated.

And to his credit, the pastor apologized. And invited us back.

We didn't make it back to that area until a number of years later. Long enough that it all just felt awkward. We didn't stop.

But we learned. Sometimes God gives us exactly what we say we want. We just need to be ready to receive it.

Photos:

1. Sunrise over the Ohio River.
2. Making a mobile neighborhood with another RVing family.
3. Sunset at the same campsite.

71 Washington, D.C.

We were in Washington, D.C. And I was a security risk. Detained by a guard. In a uniform. With a badge. And a gun.

Well, I'm pretty sure he had a gun.

He was telling me, based on his investigation, what I could do and not do.

My offense?

I was carrying.

Of course I was.

We had parked the RV outside of D.C. proper. Packed a couple of meals and water in a backpack. Taken the Metro down to walk the Mall, took in some of the memorials, and visited different museums.

And like any time we planned to be "away from home" for a long period of time, in a strange and possibly dangerous city, I was carrying.

Carrying my trusty Swiss Army knife.

You know, to be prepared for any thread that needed trimming, letters that needed opening, slivers that needed tweezing, or wine corks that needed popping.

I love my Swiss Army knife. It's a wide one with 32 different tools. I had my name engraved on the main blade.

I carried it everywhere.

But I had completely forgotten about the potential for tighter security in the buildings in D.C.

At first it wasn't an issue.

After getting to the Mall, we began visiting memorials and museums. Some let us enter freely with no metal detectors or bag inspections. Some locations searched our backpacks, but had no problem with my knife.

Then we got to The National Air and Space Museum.

The rest of my family had gone in already. They were on the other side of the metal detectors, looking back at me.

Along with the security guard.

And he was holding my knife out to me.

"Sir, you can't enter the museum with this knife."

I nodded and took the knife back from him.

I looked at him.

I looked at my family.

I didn't want to part with my knife.

Bringing it back to the RV meant at

least a two hour round trip of walking and metro-riding.

The only other option was not go in at all.

And miss the museum I was most interested in seeing.

"Sir."

I looked back at the guard.

"You can't enter the museum with the knife. But if you didn't have the knife there would be no problem."

Well, duh.

Wait, what?

I looked back at the guard. Was that a small angling of his chin towards the pavilion area in front of the museum?

I looked out the door.

Outside the front door of the museum were raised cement landscaping squares tall enough to allow people to sit on them. Inside the squares were a variety of shrubbery and ground cover.

I know he didn't wink.

Did he?

Suddenly I saw the only option that allowed me to both experience the museum and have a chance of keeping my knife.

I walked back outdoors.

And found a place to sit on the edge of a landscape square with my back to the bushes.

And casually, ever so casually, stretched out my legs.

I put my hands behind me.

For support, you know.

I dug a shallow hiding place for my knife.

Covered it with dirt and leaves.

And rested a few moments longer.

People watching.

Just acting natural.

Not feeling at all nervous that at any moment another armed guard with a gun and walkie talkie would come busting out to see what kind of incendiary device I might have just hidden behind me.

Or that somewhere, in a back room, there weren't three other guards gathered around a monitor, holding their sides in and howling at my white suburban boy attempt at subterfuge.

I wiped my hands on my pants.

And walked back into the museum.

I chose a different entry line with a different guard, of course. To save whatever face I may have left.

After a successful trip through the metal detectors, I rejoined my family.

"I had to bury my knife in the landscaping," I told them.

To all of the giggling and eye-rolling you might imagine.

"I just hope it's there when we go back out."

And you know what?

It was.

The National Air and Space Museum is the fifth most visited museum in the world. Learn more at airandspace.si.edu.

Photos:
1. The Washington Monument.
2. The Capitol building.
3. The National Archives.
4. The National Bank of Washington.
5. A *1940s* schoolbus at the American History Museum.

72 New Orleans, LA

We weren't supposed to like New Orleans.

MsBoyink and I were both raised in the conservative mainly-Dutch culture of West Michigan.

Churches on opposing street corners. Television antennas hidden in attics and television screens tucked inside cabinets with doors. So you could hide it when the pastor came calling.

And not much in the way of a social scene. Live music was mostly the church choir on Sunday morning. Our hometown was dry on Sunday. The town next door was dry all the time. Locals would tell visitors about the sidewalks that rolled up right after supper.

But then we found jazz.

I came to it via a musical journey that started with 80s hairbands, then went to rock-blues crossover artists like Stevie Ray Vaughn, then found blues-jazz artists like Bennie Goodman and the Dutch Swing College Band.

MsBoyink, a fair piano player herself when we first met, also became a fan.

Then we hit the road full time. What traveling jazz fans could avoid New Orleans?

The list of buts was long.

But...the obscene public displays during Mardi Gras.

But...the crime.

But...the homelessness.

But...Bourbon Street.

The buts kept us away. At least the first time. Mardi Gras was firing up and we thought all of Mardi Gras looked like the clips we'd seen on the news.

Not anxious to subject our kids to that, we drove past.

Our third year on the road found us in the area again. This time our list of buts was much shorter. We had talked to other traveling families who had explored New Orleans. We had learned about the diversity of Mardi Gras events - both in location and mood.

We found a nearby campground to park the RV in, and made our way into town.

For three days.

We ate beignets and drank chicory coffee at Cafe Du Monde. We stood in Congo Square. We went to a family-friendly Mardi Gras parade. We walked on Basin Street. We peeked into a cemetery. We ate a muffaletta. We toured the St. Louis cathedral. We got a free ukulele lesson on the sidewalk.

And we heard live jazz. On the street. In Preservation Hall. In the clubs lining Frenchmen Street.

The kids weren't impressed. They aren't jazz fans. They were bothered by the homeless population around the French Quarter. They thought the marchers in the Mardi Gras parades looked tired and defeated, and the attendees collecting throws like beads and candy were "greedy and first-world minded."

But MsBoyink and I?

We fell in love with New Orleans.

We returned several times during our travels - enough to refine a "$50 New Orleans date night" formula that included overnight lodging, drinks and live music. We know where to park and where to find the jazz music being played.

New Orleans is only a ten-hour drive from our new home in Ava, Missouri.

But any thoughts of another road trip to visit the Big Easy have been delayed first by COVID, and then Hurricane Ida.

We pray the city is able to recover.

Because we know what it means to miss New Orleans.

Public Radio station WWOZ is located in the French Quarter of New Orleans and specializes in promoting the local music scene. Listen online at wwoz.org.

Photos:

1. The St. Louis Cathedral in New Orleans.
2. Inside the Cathedral.
3. Tuba Skinny plays jazz at the D.B.A. Club on Frenchmen Street.
4. This streetside cafe looks like it should be in Paris.
5. A classic New Orleans balcony.
6. One of the many Mardi Gras parades.

73 San Antonio, TX

Memory lane has potholes. Sometimes I stumbled into them while researching to write this book.

Places we visited and loved got flooded out. Or burned out. Or closed.

Or it's people.

We met a lot of people while traveling.

The more people you meet, the more likely you're going to know people who were separated, divorced, or estranged.

Or passed away.

One pothole I stumbled into was learning that a favorite musician had died.

Somehow we missed the news.

I sat down to write about San Antonio.

San Antonio has been many things to us over the years.

Our favorite big city.

Home to our favorite restaurant.

The location of a memorable training class that led to long friendships and lucrative additional work.

The place where we got hired by the man who later became Donald Trump's campaign manager.

And the home of one of our favorite bands.

I first heard the Jim Cullum Jazz Band on WGVU, our local Public Radio station back in Michigan.

Live from the Riverwalk played on Saturdays when I was out in my garage, laying under a vehicle or working at my workbench.

Led by cornetist Jim Cullum, Jr., the radio show was about more than just playing jazz. It taught jazz history. Each show had a narrator that would talk about a historic jazz recording or musician. The narrator would end his spoken piece with a recording of the work he was talking about.

For a minute or so.

Then the magic would happen.

The scratchy recording of jazz would dissolve into the full sound of the live Jim Cullum Jazz Band, picking up right where the record had been playing.

Jim Cullum, Jr. was born into a jazz family. His father was a clarinetist and saxophonist who had toured with trombonist Jack Teagarden.

As Jr. aged, he and Sr. put together

a new band. In *1963*, they opened The Landing, a club on San Antonio's famous Riverwalk. Musicians like Benny Goodman, Earl Hines, and Louis Armstrong would join them onstage if they were touring in the area.

The club lacked what many other music venues couldn't dream of skipping.

Amplifiers and speakers for the musicians.

Cullum said he was a "purist" who wanted the audience to hear the music through the instruments rather than speakers. "I play the cornet, and when you hear that sound it's not the speaker vibrating, it's my lip."

MsBoyink and I managed to catch the Cullum Band playing at The Landing once before it closed down in *2009*. I remember the cheesecake. And I remember feeling saturated in sound when the four horn players playing that night all came in on a phrase.

On later visits to San Antonio, we caught a smaller version of the Cullum band at other local clubs and restaurants. Our favorite was so "intimate" we had to move our knees when the drummer showed up late.

Jim was a friendly man. We had a few conversations with him at that smaller club.

His openness and generosity was felt by other jazz musicians in San Antonio, who often found work as part of Cullum's stable. He helped young musicians by teaching jazz as part of Stanford University's Summer Jazz Workshop.

Cullum's Stanford connection is especially important now.

The Jim Cullum Band had a running repertory of *2,000* songs, all playable from memory.

A Stanford librarian became interested in the band, its songbook, and the history of jazz captured in the *450* episodes of *Live from the Riverwalk*. Stanford eventually archived all of the shows online at riverwalkjazz.stanford.edu.

You can search by song, guest, band member, or program.

Jim Cullum, 77, died of a heart attack on August 11, 2019. He had played gigs earlier that week.

Photos:

1. San Antonio-based traditional Jazz cornetist Jim Cullum (left) plays on stage at The Landing, his Riverwalk restaurant that closed in the early *2000*s.
2. The Riverwalk at night.
3. The Tower of the Americas is *12* minutes from the Riverwalk on foot.
4. The Hilton Palacio del Rio on the Riverwalk was built by stacking preassembled rooms that contained furnishings, lighting and artwork.

74 Crystal River, FL

"Where was your favorite place?"

That's the most common question we get asked after people learn about our travels.

And it's a surprisingly difficult question to answer. So many things could influence our experience in a place. Weather. Traffic. Health. Attitudes. Hype.

There were places friends raved about that we couldn't wait to leave (Sedona, Arizona). And there were backwater, unheard-of spots we lingered in because we kept finding more to do (Kinston, North Carolina).

But sometimes? We got exactly what we wished for. And more.

One of those places was Crystal River, Florida. We went there for one reason.

To swim with manatees.

We weren't morning creatures. But the manatees were, so I scheduled us for a 6 a.m. tour.

The day and time came. We got up early and made the drive in. We watched a training video. We donned wet suits.

We boarded a boat and went to a known manatee hangout. The captain threw out his anchor and shut the boat's motor off.

And then we encountered it. It rose up like a sea monster between our seats in the boat and the water.

Fear.

Not of the manatees. They are gentle grass-eating giants.

The fear was of drowning. One of our family had held it for a long time. It wasn't a "can't put my face in the shower spray" level of fear, but it was strong enough to have kept us from ever snorkeling.

We had discussed it before booking the tour. They wanted to overcome it. This was a good place to do it. We had an experienced instructor. We had the gear. We were in a protected, inland, fresh-water cove. We had the boat to retreat back to.

And manatees awaited.

One by one, we sat on the edge of the

DRIVEN TO WONDER

boat, put flippers on our feet, masks over our eyes, snorkels into our mouths, pool noodles under our arms, and slipped into the water.

Slowly, arched backs went prone. Raised heads relaxed into the water. Breathing became regular. We floated on our bellies and swam in circles, letting our eyes adjust to the underwater light.

I made eye contact with an adult manatee the size of a VW bus. It swam my way. I floated in place, reminding myself that it was an herbivore.

As it neared, it dipped and went underneath me. I stretched out my hand and brushed its rough, leather-like back as it swam past.

Turning, I saw one of our group having a special moment with a manatee calf. It wasn't until Miranda's grinning face popped out of the water that I realized it had been her.

All too soon it was over. We were heading back on the boat, shivering under beach towels and anxious for dry clothes.

But we did what we came to do.

We swam with manatees, yes.

But better than that?

We overcame fear.

There are multiple manatee tour companies in Crystal River, Florida. We were happy with our experience at River Ventures. Find them at riverventures.com.

Photos:
1. Miranda pets a manatee calf.
2. Miranda and an adult manatee.
3. Miranda snorkeling.
4. Harrison snorkeling.
5. Harrison photobombs a parental snorkeling photo.

75 Silver Springs, FL

Most people know about it as the place with the glass-bottomed boats.

You may have seen it as the backdrop for television shows or movies like *Sea Hunt* or *Creature From the Black Lagoon*.

We remember Silver Springs, Florida as the place with wild monkeys.

Wild monkeys.

In Florida.

Not natively, of course.

It all started in the 1930s. The glass bottom boats were already in action. Tourists were flocking to the area to see the incredible wildlife found below the surface of the crystal-clear waters.

And Hollywood was calling.

With ideas about filming a Tarzan movie in the area.

The guy running the boats? Colonel Tooey.

We don't know where he came from. Or where he went. Indeed, most of Tooey's life is lost to history.

Except for one notable decision. Maybe it was a mistake. Maybe it made Tooey a legend in Florida. Maybe it was both.

But Colonel Tooey is the guy who brought monkeys to Silver Springs.

Tarzan lives in the jungle. Jungles have monkeys. Monkeys would be a great addition to the glass bottom boat tours.

So Tooey went to work.

He made a home for the monkeys.

Tooey dredged an artificial island from the middle of the Silver River. The island would be a great spot for his guests to see the monkeys while on his glass-bottomed boat tours.

With the island done, Tooey purchased six Rhesus monkeys from a carnival in upstate New York.

He ferried the monkeys over to the island and released them.

It wasn't long before Tooey knew his mistake.

Because monkeys?

They can swim.

The monkeys quickly left the island and took up residence in the 500+ acres of dense Florida forest surrounding the river.

And started doing what monkeys do. Breeding.

By the 1980s, Florida had a "monkey situation."

Six monkeys became hundreds. And 25% of them carry the Herpes B virus, which can be communicated to humans.

Monkeys have now been found over 60 miles from Silver Springs. There have been reports of them ravaging orange groves and raiding deer feeding stations.

A YouTube video shows monkeys attacking a visiting family.

And with no natural predator, their population is ever-increasing.

Studies have been done.

One expert says the monkeys are a non-native, invasive species. Another says they've been in Florida long enough to be considered native.

Various plans for managing the monkey population have been published.

But people love the monkeys. And the government keeps shuffling its feet - citing public sentiment, funding, and the political climate.

So - for now anyway - Colonel Tooey's legacy as the monkey man of Florida is safe.

Silver Springs State Park is located approximately 1.5 hours northwest of Orlando, FL. Learn more at floridastateparks.org/silversprings.

Photos:
1. Kayaking in search of monkeys.
2. Finally! A wild Florida monkey.
3. Abandoned amusement park attractions along the banks of the Fort King Waterway.
4. The iconic glass bottom boats still operate at Silver Springs State Park.

Between *1998–2012*, The Florida Fish and Wildlife Conservation Commission tried to minimize the risk to humans by managing the troop population. They authorized the capture and sale of Silver Springs monkeys.

Eight hundred and thirty of them.

The public was outraged.

And the trapping stopped.

76 St. Augustine, FL

Charges of monopolization. Violation of anti-trust acts.

There was also trouble at home. Henry's wife Mary was sick with tuberculosis. Her doctor suggested a trip to the warmer climes of Florida.

Henry took a reduced role in the business and followed the doctors advice.

And found his next calling in life. Developing Florida.

Henry confirmed that his success in the oil business was no fluke. He built hotels. Bought existing railroads and added to them. Built mansions.

He was generous with his riches, donating land and money for churches, hospitals and schools.

But there are two reasons you've never heard of Henry.

First, he was modest. Henry didn't like things named after himself.

In Southern Florida he helped one

H enry was a rich man. Maybe the richest man you've never heard of.

Henry left home at age *14* to work in a store owned by an uncle. He started as a clerk, then became a manager, then left to start his own grain business. He then failed at a salt business and came back to the grain business.

He met a guy named John.

John was starting a new business, and needed capital. Henry borrowed money from a stepbrother and went into business with John.

The business?

Oil refining.

Henry proved to be a sharp businessman. He and John grew their oil business to the point of owning oil wells, refineries, pipelines, barrel plants, warehouses, and tank cars. They employed over *100,000* people. They sold *300* oil-based products including tar, chewing gum, and paint. They had corporate offices on Broadway in New York City.

Success, though, came at a cost. Protests. Vandalism. Bad press. Lawsuits.

city by financing new streets, water, sewer, and a newspaper. The residents wanted to name the city after Henry. He refused. They ended up calling it "Miami" instead.

Second, Henry's personal life was seemingly cursed.

Mary - his first wife - passed away shortly after that first Florida trip.

Henry had three children with Mary - two girls and a boy.

Jennie, his oldest daughter, died during childbirth at age 34. The baby died with her.

Carrie, his middle child, died at age 3.

Harry, his youngest, was in his 20s and managing one of Henry's hotels when Henry fired him. The two apparently never spoke again.

Henry did remarry. His second wife was Ida, one of Mary's nurses. Ida ended up suffering from dementia, was declared insane, and institutionalized.

While still married to Ida, Henry began a scandalous relationship with a young socialite named Mary Lily. He was 61, she was 23. At first it was platonic, but three years later the newspapers were starting to call out Henry publicly for having an affair.

Ida's mental health had only gotten worse. Henry wanted out. But incurable insanity wasn't legal grounds for a divorce in Florida.

So Henry did what only Henry could do.

He "influenced" the Florida legislature and got the law changed. With the law rewritten in his favor, he divorced Ida and married Mary Lily ten days later.

Four years later Florida repealed that law. Henry had been the only person divorced under it.

Eleven years later, Henry fell on some stairs and never recovered. He passed away at age 83.

With no children by either his second or third wives, and still estranged from his only son, the immense fortune of Henry Flagler, partner of John D. Rockefeller in the Standard Oil Company, and the so-called "King of Florida" all went to his third wife Mary Lily Kenan.

Making her the richest woman in the world.

Who you've probably never heard of either.

Learn more about the church that Henry Flagler built at at memorialpcusa. org.

Photos:

1. The Memorial Presbyterian Church in St. Augustine, FL.
2. Flagler donated the lot on which the Ancient City Baptist Church stands.
3. Flagler donated this building to the Grace United Methodist church in exchange for land.
4. Entrance to the Memorial Presbyterian Church.

77 Albany, GA

Speakers blared the countdown. Three! The riders tensed. Tires pushed against the gate. Two! Some parents held their breath. Others cheered. The ref holding the mic took a breath.

My gut ached. I wanted photos, but had a hard time watching.

Both my kids were in that lineup at the gate of a BMX track.

We were in Albany, Georgia in an almost-deserted county campground. I had been heads-down inside working.

I stepped outside on a break and found my tools spread out on the ground. Next to them was a pile of kickstands, racks, reflectors, and bags.

Harrison was bent over a bike, wrench in hand, pulling another reflector off. Miranda stood next to him like a surgical nurse, taking one tool and handing him another.

He caught my eye, then pointed to a sheaf of papers laying on the ground by the tools.

"There's a BMX race in the park in an hour," he said. "And the rules say all this stuff has to come off."

I had a couple of reactions.

First was practical dad.

I asked if there were entry fees. "Waived for first-timers," he answered.

I asked if our regular bike helmets were enough. "They're loaning us the right ones."

Fair enough.

Traveling homeschool dad reaction was next.

The kids saw an interesting opportunity and reacted. They found whoever was running the race, spoke to them, got a set of rules, figured out where they came up short and negotiated solutions.

They read the rules and figured out what modifications the bikes needed. They found the tools. They were working together to be ready in time for the race.

Traveling homeschool dad was proud. This is what traveling was all about - challenging comfort zones and doing new things.

I was also proud of Harrison for including his sister. The two got along well overall, but did have the normal brother-and-sister-living-in-a-small-space kinds of conflicts.

In a situation where he easily could have just thought for himself, Harrison was gracious. He got Miranda's bike ready with his, helped her get the bor-

rowed helmet on, and they went off to the race together.

My third reaction came from a much deeper, older place.

My gut ached. I wanted photos, but had a hard time watching.

Because I was scared.

I had BMX bikes growing up. We lived on them. Customized them. Made jumps for them. Did wheelies. Learned endos.

But I never raced.

Because I was scared to lose. Embarrassed to lose. Ashamed to lose.

And after all their "carpe dieming" and rule-reading and prepping and excitement?

My kids were going to lose. I wasn't being mean - they had never been to a BMX race. They had no idea how fast the other kids would be.

I worried for them.

And - selfishly- I worried for myself.

I had no idea how we were going to deal with the fallout from this.

GO!

The gate dropped.

The pack swarmed down the ramp. Harrison and Miranda were immediately behind. Literally left in the dust. By the first berm they were alone on the track.

The race ended. Sure enough. They came in last and second to last.

I walked over to them.

Their faces were hidden behind sunglasses and full-face helmets. I searched for consoling words as they fumbled with helmet straps.

The helmets popped off.

They were both beaming. Laughing. Saying words like "awesome" and "fun."

They didn't care one whit about winning or losing. They'd raced just to have fun. The loss held no embarrassment for them at all.

We talk about homeschooling like it's a one way street of learning. Parent to child.

But that day in Albany, I was the student.

According to statista.com, 3.8 million people ages six and up participate in BMX races. Learn more at usabmx.com.

Photos:

1. The Boyink kids (left) wait for the gate to drop.
2. Removing unnecessary bike parts.
3. Harrison helps Miranda with her helmet.
4. Already behind by the first berm.
5. Post-race smiles.

ALBANY, GA

78 Plains, GA

You'd think the name came from a description. Plains because it's on a plain.

And while that's true - the land around Plains, Georgia is relatively flat - it's not the source of the town's name.

In the mid-*1800s* the town was known as "Plains of Dura." That from Daniel *3:1*, as the name of the plain on which Nebuchadnezzar, king of Babylon, set up the great golden image which all his subjects were ordered to worship.

Why a bunch of ostensibly God-fearing people would name their hometown after a place of idol worship remains a mystery, but by the late *1800s* the settlement relocated to be closer to the railroad and took the opportunity to shorten its name to just "Plains."

And defined the town limits as a circle. Plains is one of a small number of circular-shaped towns located in Georgia and South Carolina.

But Plains isn't famous for being circular.

Plains is known for peanut farming.

And for one peanut farmer in particular.

Well, two peanut farmers really.

Brothers.

One famous.

One rather more infamous.

Both born to a poor family. Dirt roaders. Dad a farmer. Mom a nurse.

Junior was the older brother. A studious sort. Loved reading. But Junior was also enterprising. By his teens he was managing his own acre of peanut farm and renting out a house he had purchased. In high school he was a basketball player, woodworker, and FFA member.

Junior graduated high school, went off to college and entered the Navy. Things went well until Senior died, causing Junior - now a married father of three - to leave the Navy and come home to run the peanut farm.

Money was so tight the family had to live in public housing in Plains.

Then there's William.

The other brother.

He also graduated from Plains high school. Went off to college, but chose to enter the Marines before graduating. After a four-year stint he also returned to Plains to help with the family business.

William also married and started a family that would have six kids.

As the brothers worked the family business, Junior got interested in politics.

First, the local school board. Then State Senator. Then the Governor of Georgia.

And finally, in *1977*, James Earl "Jimmy" Carter Jr. was sworn in as the 39th President of the United States.

And William?

AKA Billy?

He'd mismanaged the family peanut business. Jimmy had to put the ownership and management of the business into a trust.

Billy quit and opened a gas and service station in Plains.

He tried the politics route too.

Lost an election to become the Mayor of Plains.

Billy went on to become something of a character during his brother's presidency. Newspapers considered him a "buffoon" good for an offbeat, colorful quote. He'd drink beer while reporters interviewed him. He bragged about smoking pot at the White House. He worked with a brewery to introduce "Billy Beer." He wrote a book entitled "Redneck Power" and charged $5,000 for personal appearances.

Jimmy once joked that he wanted to combine the FBI and CIA and find Billy a job in the new organization, but "Billy didn't want to join any agency he couldn't spell."

In *1981*, Billy had to sell his property in Plains to pay off tax debts. He moved away, taking a job with a manufacturer of mobile homes and outfitter of private airplanes.

In *1985*, Billy entered a guilty plea on behalf of his employer in a case involving invoice padding. The company was fined *$10,000*.

Billy Carter passed away in *1988* at age *51* from pancreatic cancer.

And former President Jimmy Carter?

Still alive and active in his late *90s*.

Maybe not considered the best President the USA has ever had.

But probably the best ex-president.

He's written over *30* books. Won Emmy awards for audio recordings of them.

Won the Nobel Peace Prize.

He and his wife Rosalynn have worked on *4,331* houses as part of Habitat for Humanity.

They still live in the only house they've ever owned.

In Plains, Georgia.

Where a beloved tradition recently came to an end.

For over *40* years, at the local Maranatha Baptist Church, former President Jimmy Carter would often teach an "open to the public" Sunday School class.

We were sad to have missed learning from the peanut farmer turned president.

Plains, GA is located approximately an hour southeast of Columbus, GA. The Jimmy Carter National Historic Park can be found online at nps.gov/jica.

Photos:

1. The former high school in Plains is now the Jimmy Carter National Historic Park visitor center.
2. Carter ran his presidential campaign from this former train depot.
3. Billy Carter's service station is now the only "Presidential Brother" museum in the country.
4. Cans of Billy Beer.

79 Fremont, MI

A little farm town. Middle of nowhere. One large employer.

High school sports. Hometown pride. Veterans Day parades. Farmers' Markets. Classic cars. Festivals. Summertime fishing. Fall hunting.

I could be describing Ava, Missouri, where we landed after our time on the road.

I'm not, but someone from Ava would be comfortable in Fremont, Michigan.

Until the snow flies, that is.

Fremont averages 63 inches of snow per year to Ava's 13 inches.

Not that we were there for winter.

The hardest season to RV full-time is summer. Summer is when all the "normal" people pull their campers out of storage and fill up the same campgrounds that full-timers want to be in.

Michigan has some state parks that are beautiful. And popular.

Other northern states are the same way - a short camping season means campgrounds book out months in advance.

As full-timers we didn't like to plan out that far.

Our kids were maturing. They wanted things like summer jobs and internships. We had medical issues that needed attention. We wanted to visit family.

And we were on a budget.

Buying nights in campsites is like buying anything else. The more you buy, the cheaper you can get them.

A campground that costs $35 per night for one night can be had for $18 per night if you buy a month at a time. And $13.50 per night if you buy a whole season (five months).

We bought the season in Fremont.

And became small-town residents. Fremont's city-owned campground is right on Lake Fremont.

We watched the sunrise while floating on the lake in our kayak. I fished from the shoreline. We walked downtown for half-price burger night at the local bar. We got to know our neighbors and pulled our chairs over to the community campfire at night. We got library cards and maxed them out. We went berry-picking and apple-picking in local orchards. We went to the free concert series in the local park. We volunteered for community events.

Our son found a job at Subway and umped in the Little League. Our daughter found an internship at the Humane Society.

We enjoyed Fremont so much we ignored our own "don't repeat an experience" rule and did it all again the next year.

Thinking about it makes me miss Michigan.

Especially in mid-August.

Something happens to the breeze in the middle of August in Michigan. I've never been quite sure what it is. Maybe it comes from a different direction. Maybe it's a degree or two cooler. Maybe it smells different. Maybe it knocks the first leaves off the trees.

No matter what the cause, the result is the same.

Summer becomes fall.

The nights get cooler. Apple trees get heavy with fruit. Cider goes on special. A bit of orange and yellow starts to appear in the trees. Beaches fill up with last-hurrah families. Ice cream stands limit their hours. Boats start to disappear from docks.

Don't get me wrong. We love our life in the Ozarks. Getting established here, finding jobs, buying a house - it has been as much of an adventure as traveling.

But I don't ever think I'll make it through August in the Ozarks without missing Michigan.

Fremont, MI celebrates its heritage with an annual Baby Food Festival. Learn more at fremontcommerce.com/national-baby-food-festival.

Photos:

1. A barn outside of Fremont, MI.
2. Sunset over Lake Fremont.
3. A train picks up grain outside of town.
4. West Michigan produces bumper crops of berries.
5. A merry-go-round lit up at night for the Gerber Baby Food Festival.

80 Fremont, MI

"Where are you?" It was 8 a.m. I was barely awake. Not expecting the phone to ring.

"Excuse me?"

"This is Child Protective Services. We need to speak with you in person. Where are you?"

CPS? I stammered out that we were camping, told them where, and hung up.

And may have said some not-so-nice words.

As homeschoolers, we already lived outside the norm. We had heard of Child Protective Services (CPS) being called on homeschool families simply because their kids were outside playing on a school day.

While living in an RV full-time is completely legal, it put us even further outside mainstream society.

My greatest fear while traveling was that someone who didn't understand why we weren't living like "normal people" would report us to CPS.

We'd traveled through dozens of states and stayed in hundreds of campgrounds over the course of several years with no issues.

Then it happened.

Why?

It wasn't travel-related. No one reported us just for living in an RV.

We had a family situation that led to CPS getting called.

It happened on a Monday. On Tuesday we had to move campsites. The call came on Wednesday morning.

Not that CPS wanted to call. They wanted to surprise us. They had gone to the address we listed as "home" on our driver's licenses. But we didn't actually live there.

It took them an hour to find us.

I used that time to research. I was terrified by heartbreaking stories of families being traumatized by CPS interactions.

But that time was also a Godsend. I bought a membership to the Homeschool Legal Defense Association (HSLDA).

And I learned more about CPS.

By the time the gray, nondescript government car pulled up to our site in the campground, I felt at least a little prepared.

I learned that anyone can call CPS and make an anonymous report. CPS is required to investigate. You are more or less considered guilty until proven innocent.

Public school students can be questioned by CPS agents at school without parental approval or knowledge.

CPS agents will not apprise you of your rights the way a police officer will. But you still have those rights - including the right to remain silent.

CPS may not be forthcoming about the purpose of their visit. I was not told what I was being investigated for and didn't think to ask directly. The CPS agent didn't read me his report nor did I think to ask to read it.

CPS needs a search warrant to enter your home without permission. I read stories about simple things like dirty dishes in the sink becoming evidence for an "unsuitable home environment."

I kept the agent out of our trailer and met him outside.

The interview may use verbal trickery. Our agent tried to get me to respond by claiming our child had said things they hadn't.

CPS has a list of things the agent is supposed to investigate. I asked for and received a copy of that list (it included things like "condition of the home"). After reviewing the other items on the list I ended the interview, saying I wanted to talk with our lawyer.

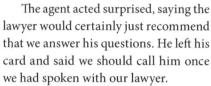

The agent acted surprised, saying the lawyer would certainly just recommend that we answer his questions. He left his card and said we should call him once we had spoken with our lawyer.

While we waited to hear back from HSLDA, we started family counseling with a local provider.

We heard from the HSLDA lawyer. He recommended we NOT answer the CPS agent's questions (they've been known to pass your answers on to law enforcement to use against you in court).

He also recommended we not contact CPS, but wait for them instead. If CPS returned, he said to tell them that we had started family counseling and then to stop talking.

About a week later the CPS agent came back. We again met him outdoors. I did what the lawyer had said to do. I said my piece and then shut up.

The agent acted surprised.

"If you have nothing to hide why would you not talk to us?"

I repeated that I was acting on advice of my lawyer.

He left.

After the second CPS visit I had several weeks of fear and dread. I watched every car that came in the campground.

Every time a siren sounded I had a momentary thought of "are they coming?"

We made efforts to keep the trailer cleaner and neater than normal. We didn't restock on beer or wine. We tried

to be up and dressed and busy earlier than normal.

We had a few hiccups trying to contact HSLDA for more advice, so this time dragged on longer than I would have liked.

We wanted resolution. The end of our seasonal campsite was coming. We were planning to head south. We didn't want to stay into the Michigan winter while a legal process dragged on.

We finally reconnected with HSLDA. They said CPS can be a hornet's nest that you don't want to poke. Best to just wait it out. CPS has a period of time where they need to act if they are going to. We were close to the end of that period.

HSLDA felt that if CPS was going to act they would have already. CPS budgets are known to be tight and the caseworkers overloaded. Our case didn't have any signs of needing further involvement on their part.

So we sat on our hands and tried to not think about things. We continued with family counseling. And made preparations to get back on the road.

We never heard another peep from CPS.

Fall eventually came. As fall does.

We emptied tanks. Coiled up hoses. Swept leaves off the roof. Pulled the slides in. Checked tire pressures. Then we hitched up the truck and pulled out of the seasonal campsite we'd called home for five months.

Counseling hadn't made us perfect. But we'd had some very real, bare-souled conversations. We addressed the root issues that caused all of this to happen.

And yes, we slipped, argued, apologized and started over.

But we headed down the road together.

As a family.

Photos:

1. Miranda volunteered at the Fremont Humane Society, because puppies.
2. Harrison umped in the local Little League, because baseball.
3. MsBoyink and I out for a sunrise paddle on Lake Fremont.
4. Daisy Creek and Lake Fremont turned pink at sunset.
5. Miranda walks in the Fremont Harvest Festival Parade.

81 Suffolk, VA

Drain the swamp!

A Trump campaign promise, yes. But another would-be president spoke those same words hundreds of years ago.

George Washington.

Washington wasn't slinging political insults. His time as president was still decades away.

Young Washington was a surveyor and land speculator. He joined a group of 11 others and bought land to clear and farm.

But first? They'd literally have to drain the swamp.

The Great Dismal Swamp.

Yes, there is such a thing. And - like our current political morass - your tax dollars support it.

The Great Dismal Swamp is actually many things.

It's public land.

The swamp straddles the Virginia and North Carolina state line. In Virginia, it's a National Natural Landmark and a National Wildlife Refuge. In North Carolina it's a State Park.

It's accurately named.

"Swamp" because its soils are 85-95% water. "Dismal" because it's hot, humid, soggy, thorny, and inhabited by federally protected varmints ranging from chiggers to bears. "Great" because it originally covered over 2,000 square miles.

It's mysterious.

Lake Drummond lies in the center of the swamp. One of only two natural lakes in Virginia, no one knows how it got there or where its waters come from.

It's home to the only presidential ditch.

To drain the swamp, Washington and his cohorts dug ditches. Many remain, and one is named the "Washington Ditch."

Trump would probably approve.

It's part of the Underground Railroad.

Slaves were used in the efforts to drain the swamp. Thousands escaped into it and settled in remote "maroon colonies." Other runaway slaves would find safe harbor in those colonies on their way to freedom.

It's the setting of a book by a famous author.

The next novel Harriet Beecher Stowe

wrote after *Uncle Tom's Cabin* was *Dred, A Tale of the Great Dismal Swamp.*

It was the road less taken.

Robert Frost once headed into the swamp to commit suicide because his lady wouldn't consent to marry him. He didn't go through with it. She later said yes.

It's part of the Intercoastal Waterway.

Initially proposed by Washington, the 22-mile Dismal Swamp Canal connects the waters of Chesapeake Bay in Virginia and Albemarle Sound in North Carolina. It remains the oldest continually operating man-made canal in the US.

It was the location of our longest kayak trip.

We weren't hardcore kayakers, pre-ferring paddles that didn't keep us out past mealtime.

But we survived the four-mile-long "Feeder Ditch" into Lake Drummond, had lunch, and paddled the four miles back. The only varmints we encountered were aggressive ducks.

At the Great Dismal Swamp, we had finally gone the extra mile to see more of a park than what was visible from the visitor center or scenic driving loop.

Not a dismal day at all.

The Dismal Swamp Canal Welcome Center off Highway 17 south of Chesapeake VA is the most accessible place to begin a swamp visit. Get directions and information at dismalswampwelcomecenter.com.

Photos:

1. Cypress trees in Lake Drummond in the Great Dismal Swamp.
2. The Boyink kids kayak on Lake Drummond.
3. Being chased by ducks in the feeder ditch heading towards the lake.
4. Miranda comments non-verbally about the length of the kayak trip.
5. The Great Dismal Swamp National Wildlife Refuge sign.

82 Kinston, NC

The CSS Neuse just couldn't catch a break.

One of 26 Civil War "ironclads" commissioned by the Confederate Government in 1862, construction of the ship was behind schedule before it even began.

The Navy wanted the wooden hull by March 1, 1863. They didn't get it until late that summer.

Then it was a matter of not having enough iron plating to cover the wood. Iron was scarce enough in wartime. When the Navy finally found some, they couldn't transport it because the Army was hogging all the trains.

Finding a crew was also a challenge. The Confederacy had naval officers. But enlisted men? Not so much. The Navy had to steal them from the Army. The resulting crew was described by an officer as "ridiculous, all legs and arms, always in the wrong place and in each other's way."

There were other labor issues. A new paymaster didn't understand an overtime agreement, and four carpenters walked off before the matter could be settled.

In spite of all the obstacles, construction continued. The boilers and propulsion systems went in. Her guns were installed. Ammunition was loaded.

As each step of the ship was completed, the hull sat lower and lower in the water.

Which was a problem.

Because the Neuse River, on which it was being built, was falling.

As much as one foot a day.

The CSS Neuse needed seven feet of water.

The channel in the Neuse River only had five.

Nevertheless, the war raged on. Orders came down. The ship was needed for an upcoming attack.

The Confederate Navy constructed wooden caissons designed to lift the ship higher out of the water.

And on April 22, 1864, still lacking some of the steel armor it was supposed

to have, the CSS Neuse steamed out of its construction moorings in Kinston.

And made it a half-mile before getting grounded on a sandbar.

She sat there a month before the river rose enough to float again.

The Navy returned the ship to its construction moorings, but by that time most of the supporting Confederate troops had been called away to more important duties.

The CSS Neuse remained in the Kinston area, essentially a floating fort that saw no active duty.

By 1865 the Civil War was ending.

Union forces were headed through Kinston to meet up with General Sherman.

Retreating Confederates crossed the Neuse River to escape the Union forces following behind.

The CSS Neuse waited for its own soldiers to pass by, then fired a few shells at the Union ranks.

Those shells would be the only shots the CSS Neuse ever fired in hostility.

Then the so-called "CSS Neuse-ance" was intentionally sunk by its own crew to avoid capture by the Union.

And laid right there, in the Neuse River, for nearly a century.

Most of the good stuff disappeared.

The cannons, anchors, propellers, and armor.

But in 1963, funded by Kinston businessmen, the lower hull of the ironclad was raised, loaded onto semis, and moved to an indoor facility in downtown Kinston.

Along with approximately 15,000 artifacts - sauce bottles, folding chairs, and grappling hooks. Even the ship's bell.

All of these items are now part of the CSS Neuse Civil War Interpretive Center and Governor Caswell Memorial.

Kinston didn't stop there.

The city also created the world's only full-size replica of a Confederate Ironclad ship.

Built from the original Confederate Navy plans, the CSS Neuse II is also in downtown Kinston, just a couple blocks from the museum containing the hull of the original.

Learn more about the original CSS Neuse at historicsites.nc.gov and the replica CSS Neuse at cssneuseii.org.

Photos:

1. The CSS Neuse II, the only full-scale replica of a Confederate Civil War Ironclad ship, located in Kinston, NC.
2. The CSS Neuse Civil War Interpretive Center has the original CSS Neuse hull overlaid with a skeleton of the original upper decks.

83 Kinston, NC

It all began over an ochoko (cup) of sake. An improbable drink. Which we were drinking in an even more improbable spot.

Kinston, North Carolina.

Land of tobacco sheds, cotton fields, and gospel music.

And, generally, more rum or whiskey than sake.

We came to Kinston for the cheap camping. At the time, the city-owned campground offered riverside sites with full hookups for $12 per night.

An old Willys pickup parked downtown led to a conversation with an art gallery owner. The conversation led to an invitation to a sake taste-testing event during a birthday celebration for the local brewery.

MsBoyink and I had never had sake, so were easily convinced to attend.

Two couples joined us at the bar - Warren and Jane, and "Little Warren" and Holly.

We made introductions all around. They asked us how we had come to be

there, and we filled them in on our travels.

Then we asked them. "What do you guys do?"

The Warrens were local farmers.

Jane was married to "big" Warren and helped out on the farm.

And Holly?

She was the personal assistant of a local chef. That chef and her restaurant were part of a PBS reality TV show called *A Chef's Life*.

Which we had never heard of.

Cue the awkward moment.

And it wasn't just that we had met someone "behind the scenes" of the show.

The Warrens - and their farm - were often featured on camera. They provided many of the fresh ingredients that the restaurant was known for.

We were sitting in the middle of reality TV celebrities.

But we didn't watch TV.

We had ditched broadcast and cable TV years earlier. While traveling we went to a few movie theaters and rented the occasional movie.

But otherwise?

No television.

I had to fess up.

I let them know we had never heard of the show. We were the oddballs who never watched TV.

The conversation found a pleasant

DRIVEN TO WONDER

detour, and after another sample of sake they got up to move on to another birthday party event.

Then Jane came back into the room.

She handed us a note with her name and number. She invited us to their house for Sunday brunch featuring green Bloody Marys.

We have tried to adopt a 'never say no' philosophy in situations like this. So we said yes.

And on the way home?

We lost the note.

Add sheepish to awkward.

Google to the rescue. We found the phone number for the farm and RSVP'd in the proper southern fashion.

Sunday was a couple days away. During that time we researched *A Chef's Life*. We learned that it told the story of Chef Vivian Howard and husband Ben Knight leaving New York City to come back to Vivian's hometown of Kinston and opening "Chef and the Farmer," a white-cloth farm-to-table restaurant.

We liked how the show treated the area and the locals with respect. It's common for "big city comes to the cotton field" shows to lampoon the locals.

Sunday came.

We found a large covered porch with food available on every surface. Jane brought out scrambled farm eggs, cinnamon toast, and green smoothies.

And yes, green Bloody Marys.

With full bellies we climbed into the back of a pickup for a tour of the growing areas of the farm. Warren was a fifth-generation farmer and with his southern style and quick wit was an excellent barefooted guide.

We fed some huge hogs. We tried fresh sorghum. I shot photos of ancient farm buildings.

Back at the farm house the sun was getting low in the sky. We grabbed some group photos, with all of us trying (and not quite succeeding) to find the spotlight between the shadows cast by the thick live oak trees.

The PBS TV show continued for a few years after our visit. Chef and the Farmer remains open in Kinston, serving "thoughtful, creative cooking rooted in this region's ingredients and traditions."

We hope Warren and Jane Brothers continue to be the farmer in that equation. We're grateful for the hospitality they showed to some awkward out-of-towners.

And for giving us a brush with celebrity.

Kinston, NC is located approximately an hour and a half southeast of Raleigh, NC. Learn more about Kinston at visit-kinston.com.

Photos:

1. A scene from the Brothers Farm close to Kinston, NC.
2. Asking a question about this Willys truck led to our brush with celebrity.
3. Inside a greenhouse at the Brothers farm.
4. This old tractor was put out to pasture.
5. Some pig!

84 Columbia, SC

"Sesquicentennial State Park"

I love words. And it's cool that there is actually a word for the hundred and fiftieth anniversary of something.

But, knowing the word "sesquicentennial" is like what they say about tomatoes. Knowledge is knowing they are a fruit. Wisdom is not putting them in a fruit salad.

Wikipedia says the locals "affectionately" call the park *Sesqui* instead. I'm guessing it's less with affection than contempt for whatever government committee gave the OK to a six-syllable name.

With a "q" thrown in out of pure spite.

Anyway, while "Sesqui State Park" was still showing pretty fall color during our mid-November visit, it wasn't the reason we stopped in Columbia, South Carolina.

We were there to pitch, create, and present a business.

In a weekend.

Impossible? Maybe.

Yet, dozens of other people were there to either try and get an idea of theirs off the ground, or help someone else with their business idea.

The event was a Startup Weekend. Founded in *2007* in Boulder, Colorado, Startup Weekend is a *54*-hour event that attracts entrepreneurs, software developers, graphic designers, coaches and speakers who gather at a bootcamp-type event and attempt to create a fully operating startup company.

The group gathers on Friday night for a "pitch session" where people with a business idea get up, tell the crowd about it, and try to convince people to help them.

Once all the pitches are done, the crowd votes. Winners move forward in the process. Each attendee joins the project team of their choice.

I didn't intend to pitch an idea. I had attended Startup Weekends in the past and realized they were a perfect way for homeschool students to get a business education in a weekend.

Plus, it would give our kids a chance to interact with other students in a way that was different than a campground football game.

But on the long drive to the event?

I hatched an idea on my own.

For a board game.

Which MsBoyink still laughs about.

Because I don't like playing board games.

Nevertheless, I got up in front of the crowd and nervously pitched the idea

DRIVEN TO WONDER

for a board game that encouraged players to earn experiences by getting rid of posessions.

And the crowd voted us in.

I wanted our kids to get experience working with other people, though, so didn't let them join our team.

They didn't seem heartbroken.

Being bookworms themselves, they found a team looking to improve library circulation.

We found people to help us. We identified target customers. Created a brand. Did competitive research. Researched pricing. Roughed in a design. Got input from several provided coaches from the business, legal, and accounting worlds.

Somewhere else in the same building, the kids were doing the same.

Trying to get as much done by Sunday as possible.

Because on Sunday afternoon, the entire group gathers back to give presentations showing what you accomplished over the weekend.

And not just to the other teams.

Sitting in that audience would be local business leaders and - quite possibly - a venture capitalist looking to fund the next big thing.

That group would vote on the presentations, giving prizes to the business ideas they felt showed the most promise. Prizes included office space, software licenses, additional coaching, etc. - all with the intent of helping the business come to fruition.

Our board game business idea did... okay. We had a unique idea within the board gaming world and had created a decent looking prototype game to display.

In hindsight, however, I think we got bogged down too much with the rules of play for the game.

We should have focused more on the business model, making sure that we could overcome the irony of trying to sell a game that taught players how to stop buying stuff.

The kids though?

Their team designed a web browser add-on that would tell you if the book you were looking for on Amazon was available at your local library.

Their team won.

Ultimately the business didn't end up taking off. Most startups don't. It probably wouldn't have gotten past Amazon's lawyers anyway.

Profit, intellectual property, and all that.

But after a weekend that included thinking, talking, researching, and making public presentations?

The kids still won.

According to its website, Startup Weekend is a "creative and collaborative three-day educational event where anyone can develop and pitch new startup ideas." Learn more at techstars.com/communities/startup-weekend.

Photos:

1. The Boyink kids with their winning team.
2. Our board game concept.
3. Harrison won a group-wide rock/paper/scissors contest.
4. Miranda keeping track of her notes at StartupWeekend.

85 Brunswick, GA

We weren't, as a general rule, epicureans.

If you haven't heard that 50¢ word before, Dictionary.com defines an *epicurean* as someone who is:

"fond of or adapted to luxury or indulgence in sensual pleasures; having luxurious tastes or habits, especially in eating and drinking."

We didn't eat like we were on vacation all the time. Food was a budget item that had to be kept in check, especially since we had two growing teenagers on board.

We ate lots of canned soup. We had homemade turkey wraps so often I still get a bit ill thinking about them. Box meals weren't uncommon. Our go-to family meal was a Walmart rotisserie chicken served from the truck tailgate out in the parking lot.

And yet, it didn't make sense to only indulge our eyes as we traveled. Might as well let the taste buds in on the action too.

We had Philly cheesesteaks while walking the streets of Philly. Fresh seafood while in the Outer Banks. BBQ in North Carolina, South Carolina, and Texas. Boiled peanuts in Georgia. Tex-mex in San Antonio. Cracklins in Louisiana. Smoked salmon in Washington.

And a pork sandwich in Brunswick, Georgia.

I don't recall setting out to have a food adventure. It was suppertime. We were hungry and the RV was low on groceries. MsBoyink said "just go get something."

Thinking pizza, I came across online reviews of Willie's Wee-Nee Wagon. The business looks like just a hot dog stand, but most of the reviews mentioned a to-die-for porkchop sandwich.

That sounded more memorable than a franchise pizza.

Add in a gutsy business tagline of "we relish your bun" and I couldn't punch the Wee-Nee Wagon's address into our GPS fast enough.

Don't go to Willie's expecting ambiance or presentation. Willie's is what it looks like - a hot-dog stand that expanded its offerings.

Bring cash, know what you want, order at the window, pick up at the window. There are a few seats indoors but it's mostly outdoor seating at painted picnic tables.

The porkchop sandwich lived up to

the hype. Deboned, melt-in-your mouth tender pork simply presented with a bit of mustard, mayo and some onions on a hoagie bun.

Even now, a few years later, my mouth starts to water just at the mention of Brunswick, Georgia.

We did more than just eat in Brunswick. We biked some campground trails. We explored Fort Frederica National Monument. We walked under some of the tallest live oak trees we'd ever seen, with giant smears of Spanish moss hanging from the limbs. I photographed boat launches on pretty waterways.

But it's that porkchop sandwich I'll always remember.

Learn more about Willie's at williesweeneewagon.com, and more about Brunswick, GA at exploregeorgia.org/city/brunswick.

Photos:
1. Exploring nearby Fort Frederica National Monument.
2. Willie's Wee-Nee Wagon sign in Brunswick, GA.
3. A pork sandwich from Willie's.
4. A boat launch stretches out over the Brunswick River.

86 Palatka, FL

I've never written about what happened that night. It's rarely come up in family conversations. Once mentioned, the subject quickly changes.

It was dark. It was late.

We were stopped in the middle of a secluded road on the outer edge of the Ocala National Forest.

The truck high beams lit up the road. The view was symmetrical. To the right and left was a mowed shoulder, a shallow ditch, and an unbroken line of pine trees.

But we weren't looking right or left. We were looking straight ahead.

Like diamonds laying in black silk, the surface of the road glittered with a thousand specks of light.

Moving.

Blinking.

Jumping.

It took a minute to comprehend. I rolled down the truck window for a better look.

Toads.

As far as we could see, to where the truck's lights faded into darkness, the road was teeming with toads.

They were between us and home. We'd setup the RV in a state park campground, then left to visit friends.

We looked for alternative routes home. The only suggestion from our GPS was *17* miles of unpaved National Forest roads. We didn't have four wheel drive. And Florida has mud.

We talked about clearing a path ahead of the truck. Lacking some kind of toad-plow, there were just too many to even step between.

Plagued by a growing sense of dread, I looked over at MsBoyink. In the glow of the dash lights, I could see that she had reached the same conclusion.

I prayed a quick prayer of forgiveness. I rolled up the window. I turned up the radio. I shifted the truck into drive.

And I let my foot slip off the brake.

A mile later, it was over. I let out a breath I didn't realize I'd been holding.

Sleep didn't come easy that night.

And the next day, as much as I could, I washed that truck without looking at it.

The Ocala National Forest has 607 square miles of sand pine scrub forest and water features. Learn about the park at fs.usda.gov/ocala.

Photo:

1. Silver Springs, FL is located in the Ocala National Forest.

87 Apopka, FL

We were once kicked off the doorstep of a church that had the word "outreach" in its name.

By the pastor.

It was a dramatic illustration of how our traveling lifestyle and the traditional North American model of doing church were at odds with each other.

A low point, for sure.

But only one stop on a journey.

Other stops on that journey included:

- Visiting multi-location churches so big the pastor flew by helicopter to one campus and video-streamed his sermon to the others.
- Visiting churches so small when our family of four walked in we doubled the size of the congregation. MsBoyink volunteered to "play the pianer" - but first someone had to get the key from the laundry room to unlock it.
- Trying an online church.
- Awkward attempts at home church.

Along the way, we met other people with the same struggle. They were Christian families, enjoying exploring the USA on long-term road trips, longing to gather with other believers, but not feeling served by traditional churches.

There's a rhythm to RV travel in the USA.

An ebb and flow.

During the summer months the big boxes on wheels mostly disperse north. With a greater range of comfortable temperatures to be in, there's more of the country available to the traveler.

Come winter?

Find I-10 on the map.

And look south of that.

From Los Angeles to Phoenix to San Antonio to New Orleans to Mobile to Jacksonville, I-10 and all points south.

That's where you'll find most RVers.

One winter found us at the eastern end of I-10 in Florida.

Along with five other traveling families of faith.

We all managed to reserve campsites

close to each other at Wekiwa State Park in Apopka, Florida.

And our church service began.

It didn't look like you'd expect.

Tents over there. A bus over here. A couple of fifth wheels mixed in.

A campfire ring surrounded by an audience of bag chairs holding an ever-changing cast of occupants.

Men talking around trucks. Women just back from a hike through the woods. Kids running free-range.

Plans being made for a morning kayak run.

Guitars coming out and campfires turning into worship.

Group potlucks coming together last minute and (with a recklessness that might get one kicked out of some churches) without sign-up sheets.

All a bit chaotic, yes.

But also?

Church.

Like we'd never experienced it before.

People talking openly about their faith. Their struggles with it. Or how traveling strengthened it.

The New Testament uses the phrase "one another" *100* times.

We are to love one another (John *13:34*).

Be devoted to one another (Romans *12:10*).

Honor one another (Romans *12:10*).

Live in harmony with (Romans *12:16*).

Build up (1 Thessalonians *5:11*).

Accept (Romans *15:7*).

Greet (Romans *16:16*).

Don't grumble against (James *5:9*).

Stop passing judgment (Romans *14:13*).

The Florida group was in no way perfect.

But for that magical, warm December in Apopka, Florida?

We one-anothered.

For more about the hiking, kayaking, swimming and biking available at Wekiwa Springs State Park, visit floridastateparks. org/parks-and-trails/wekiwa-springs-state-park.

See all of the "one another" Bible passages in an infographic at overviewbible. com/one-another-infographic.

Photos:

1. A rustic amphitheater at Wekiwa Springs State Park in Apoka, FL.
2. Kayaking church in the Wekiva River.
3. The "Mens Ministry" having a board meeting in the campground.
4. Spontaneous group meals always provided enough food for the crowd.
5. The "Women's Ministry" enjoyed several walks on the campground trails.

88 Melbourne, FL

We had reservations. Because it was winter and it was Florida. And we wanted adjacent sites for an extended stay with friends who were also RVers.

We arrived first. I wanted to check out the campsite before backing the RV in. And?

I wanted to check out the neighbors. Colored hair and odd clothes. A tent with TV, VCR, and desk with computer and printer. A piled-up picnic table. An overflowing trash can.

This wasn't camping. This was one step away from homelessness.

I had reservations.

But it was winter. And it was Florida. Our friends were on their way.

I backed the RV in.

One of the "tent-camping" neighbors watched closely. "Nice job," he called out.

I thanked him. And wondered if it would be money or food he'd ask for next.

Our friends rolled in and set up. I was glad their tall converted bus blocked our view of the tenters.

We went over to visit. From inside the bus, I looked down - both literally and figuratively - on the people next door.

How much of our gear could I safely leave outside?

"Want some tea?"

Hannah wasn't asking us. She had her bus window propped open and was talking to them.

I saw risk.

Hannah saw a ministry opportunity.

They accepted. Tea became dinner. Dinner became a campfire. A campfire became a raw conversation about faith and God.

Before we knew it, two conservative, Christian families were friends with a homosexual male couple, a blue-haired American Indian woman, and an out-of-work actor from LA in the middle of a road trip to "find himself."

The actor soon started asking odd, personal questions. After we answered he'd disappear back into his tent.

And I'd google "identity theft."

Then a small, padlocked wooden treasure box appeared on our picnic table. It had a leather pouch with a paper clue and key attached.

We gathered around it - four skeptical adults and six excited kids.

Unlocking the box, we found compasses inside. We decoded a clue, got our bearings and started walking.

We ended up in the park laundromat. We found another clue hidden there, coiled inside a corked glass bottle.

That clue led us to another in the park amphitheater. From there to the senior center. Then the horseshoe pits, the dog park, the archery range, and finally the volleyball court.

The final clue also had a leather map and key. It led us to a marked path in the woods and an "X" of branches laying on the ground.

The kids dug barehanded. They unearthed and unlocked a pirate captain's treasure box.

Inside?

All those odd questions finally made sense. Small boxes disguised as ancient books held knitting needles and yarn. Or a journal and art supplies. Or a $50 gift card. Each gift was tailored to that person's interests.

Yes, there was also a generous gift for me in that buried chest.

But pirate booty wasn't my treasure that day.

My treasure was what I learned those weeks. About being too judgmental. Too selfish. Too safe.

About what the command to love your neighbor really looks like.

Melbourne is on the "Space Coast" of Florida, just 25 miles south of Cape Canaveral. Learn more at melbourne-florida.org.

Photos:

1. Pirate's treasure hunt clues and booty created for us by a campground neighbor in Melbourne, FL.
2. The group sets off treasure hunting.
3. Digging in a volleyball court for clues.
4. Successful seekers pose prettily with bountiful booty.

89 Ocala, FL

"The mind, once stretched by a new idea, never returns to its original dimensions."

-Ralph Waldo Emerson

Experiences are the same. Once you go through a new and different experience, you aren't quite the same person as before.

Once people learned about our full-time family travel adventure, they'd often comment along the lines of "that's a great experience for your kids."

And it was.

But it was pretty good for the adults too.

We took jobs doing things we had never done before. We had conversations and meals with people from (far) outside of our normal circles. We did some public speaking about our mobile lifestyle.

Granted - one of the reasons we decided to travel was to do exactly this. We wanted to shake ourselves out of middle-class suburban existence that was starting to feel a bit too much like the movie *Groundhog Day*.

Once on the road we intentionally sought out many new experiences and tried to always say yes to anything that came up unexpectedly.

It worked.

But other experiences were thrust on us without giving us a choice.

Stressful experiences.

A truck accident in rural Kentucky. Dealing with CPS in Michigan. Putting a new roof on the RV in Utah.

There was one experience we worried about being thrust on us, and we wanted to prepare for it.

We knew many full-time RVers where the couples shared driving duties.

That wasn't the case for us. While MsBoyink - and eventually the kids - could do all the work of hitching and unhitching the RV from the truck, once it was time to roll down the road, I always drove.

We didn't really think much about it. I had experience with trailers and MsBoyink didn't. I liked driving more than she did. She dealt with cataracts that made driving harder. And growing up, her dad taught her to read maps so she made an excellent navigator.

But we heard stories.

Stories from other mobile couples where one always drove and then suddenly couldn't.

The worst was from a couple we met in Washington state. They traveled in a Class A motorhome and he always drove.

Then he had a heart attack.

While behind the wheel.

While towing a smaller car.

She pulled him out of the seat enough to get behind the wheel and get the rig stopped on the shoulder.

Once he was bundled off in an ambulance, she then had to drive the rig to a nearby RV park and do all of the disconnecting and setup by herself.

We needed to make sure MsBoyink could do something similar if anything ever happened to me.

But we procrastinated. Moving days can be stressful. It was easier to stay in our normal roles.

Then the experience more or less thrust itself on us.

I didn't have a heart attack. It was allergies. I'm still not sure what set them off in Florida in March, but I woke up sneezing that day and never stopped.

Eyes watering, nose dripping, coughing, face itching - I was miserable and in no shape to drive.

We tried to extend our stay in the campsite we were in, but Florida. In March. Enough said.

It was time.

MsBoyink and the kids got the RV disconnected from the campsite and hitched up to the truck.

Then MsBoyink got behind the wheel.

Have you driven in Florida during the winter? We saw crazier stuff on the roads there than anywhere else in the country.

Nonetheless, MsBoyink drove us out

of one park, down busy Florida highways and to the next campground in Ocala.

Where, for reasons that were never clear (except maybe divine intervention),

the park assigned us to a handicapped campsite.

Which was about twice as wide as a normal campsite.

Her first attempt at backing the RV in didn't go well. Not that I ever always got it right the first time either.

We learned early on - sometimes it was best to just pull back out, drive around the loop, and start over.

Her second try was successful - with the RV nice and straight and placed in the middle of the spot with room for all the slideouts.

The smile on her face as she got out of the truck made the allergies of that day worthwhile.

I know. Maybe you back up large trailers every day and it ain't no thang.

But for MsBoyink it was a new experience. An obstacle overcome. A victory.

The day never came where she had to tow and setup the RV again.

But it was no longer a worry. She wasn't that person who couldn't tow an RV anymore.

Ocala, FL was recently named one of Americas 50 worst cities to drive in by USA Today. See who else made the list at usa-today.com/story/money/2020/11/27/americas-worst-cities-to-drive-in/114973914/

Photos:
1. The Boyink kids kayaking outside of Ocala, FL.
2. What you can't see is the 34 feet of RV she's towing down a Florida highway.
3. MsBoyink's smile of triumph after successfully backing our RV into a campsite.
4. MsBoyink kayaking outside of Ocala, FL.
5. The swamps of Florida have their own kind of beauty.

90 Marshall, IN

Unlikely. An unlikely reality. And an unlikely history.

Say you were wanting to do some hiking. Something with canyons, gorges, bluffs, waterfalls, and rock scrambling.

You'd think Colorado. Utah. Montana. Idaho, maybe.

But Indiana?

Like an hour outside of Indianapolis? Not so much.

And yet, in the middle of the flat agricultural landscape that represents most of Indiana, Turkey Run offers an out-west outdoors experience.

The geological features are a result of a familiar formula.

Water + rock + time.

The water is Sugar Creek (and yes, if you were a young reader of *The Sugar Creek Gang* series by Paul Hutchens, it's that Sugar Creek).

The rock is sandstone. Specifically Mansfield Sandstone.

Let the water run against the sandstone. Add time. Time enough for high waters, floods, and erosion.

And you end up with the reality of Turkey Run State Park. A series of canyons cut into the sandstone. Trickles of snow melt over rock. A waterfall. Gorges. Hollows. Ladders. Mud.

A western experience in the midwest.

One we can thank, of all things, a newspaper columnist for.

Juliet Strauss, who in *1915* was writing for the *Rockville Tribune*, the *Indianapolis News*, and the *Ladies Home Journal*. In addition to being a columnist, Strauss was an author, editor, and public speaker covering "country life, rural traditions,

motherhood and a woman's role as a homemaker."

The land now known as Turkey Run had been privately owned. But the owner had passed away, and the land was going up for public auction.

Which meant that, most likely, a timber company would buy the land and harvest the wood from it.

Juliet Strauss wanted to preserve the land, so she wrote a letter to the Governor. The letter led to a Commission. The Commission recommended the creation of a new state park system in Indiana, with Turkey Run being the first park.

DRIVEN TO WONDER

A great idea, but there wasn't funding for it.

A private fundraising effort began. The state park advocates raised enough to bid $30,100.

And the Hoosier Veneer Company of Indianapolis bid $30,200.

Strauss and the other state park folks didn't give up.

They offered the Hoosier Veneer Company another $10,000 for the land if they could buy it a few months later.

And the company agreed.

But the extended negotiations caused Turkey Run to miss out on being the first of Indiana's new state park system.

During the negotiations for Turkey Run, McCormick's Creek State Park was established as Indiana's first.

Turkey Run was a sentimental visit for us. I had camped there when I was younger, and couldn't forget the hiking trails that required climbing ladders up bluffs.

We visited in early May, before the busy camping season kicked in. We hiked some of the trails. And we kayaked down the river, taking turns playing photographer and livery service for each other.

Traveling on sentimentalism can be risky. Places change. People change. Favorite items on restaurant menus change.

There were some sentimental places I wish we hadn't revisited. Memories were sullied.

But Turkey Run wasn't one of those places. It was as special as I had remembered.

Turkey Run State Park has over 200 campsites, historic home tours, ecology hikes, kayaking, fishing, horseback riding, a covered bridge, and more. Learn more at turkeyrunstatepark.com.

Photos:

1. MsBoyink and Harrison kayak on Sugar Creek.
2. Harrison and MsBoyink stand on a waterfall in Turkey Run State Park.
3. Some of the hiking trails require ladder climbing.
4. Miranda kayaking on Sugar Creek.

91 Holland, MI

What becomes a traveling teen? Our kids were *12* and *13* when we hit the road. We were only planning - at that point - to be gone for a year.

But I wanted to know. If we traveled longer, how would the kids launch off on their own?

Would they just choose a town and jump? Would a college admissions officer wonder if we'd been on the run from the law?

Were we going to somehow screw up our kids' future by doing this?

I googled for answers.

I found plenty of other families traveling full-time. But all with younger kids.

I couldn't find any stories of launching kids-turned-adults from a moving vehicle.

But that was all at least five years away. We set it aside and left on our big adventure.

The year went quickly. We came home, sold the house, and returned to the road. Two years gone stretched to three.

Three years became five. Somewhere in another state, our *13*-year-old turned *18*.

A man.

With his own thoughts. His own ideas. His own dreams.

Which didn't include staying with us. He wanted the freedom that independence promised.

Harrison was a fan of acapella music and the unexpected geographical hotspot for it was Dayton, Ohio. He'd attended an acapella summer camp there, the college had singing classes, and there were several singing groups.

Harrison wasn't ready to enroll in college, but wanted to locate to Dayton and try to plug into the scene while working.

But it was tough finding work and lodging in a town six hours away from where we were summering in Michigan. He and MsBoyink drove to Dayton, but weren't able to find a situation that felt right.

Meanwhile, summer was slipping away. Our seasonal spot timed out in October. We made plans to get mobile again.

Harrison didn't like his options. He was done sharing an RV bunkhouse with his sister. He was tired of traveling. Dayton wasn't working out. Holland was boring after seeing over *30* other states. And it had no acapella scene.

On the other hand, Holland had

industry. Manufacturers were aggressively hiring.

And we still had a network of contacts.

We sat down with Harrison and a calendar. He didn't have months to figure this out anymore. He had weeks.

He had to make concessions, otherwise we'd be forced to drop him off at the rescue mission on our way out of town.

I mentioned the available jobs in Holland. And said we could reach out to our old church network for a lead on housing.

We all have these moments. Caught between what we want and what life is offering. It's never easy.

But Harrison stepped up. He chose to locate back in his hometown of Holland.

We brought him to a job interview. While we waited, I posted a housing request on our former church's Facebook group.

I'm probably remembering it wrong. But I swear, after a summer of angst, of indecision, of roadblock after roadblock, once Harrison decided Holland was okay?

A few hours later he had a job offer and a room to rent.

And both of them were solid.

The job was with a Fortune 500 office furniture manufacturer. Harrison suddenly had better benefits than we did.

The room was with a young homeschooling family that we knew. It included laundry, wifi, and a kitchen. He could eat with the family if he wanted. And it was cheap.

All great, but.

The room and the job were six miles apart. We didn't have the money to buy Harrison a car. He didn't either.

We could spare a bike. And I knew Harrison could probably find a coworker to ride-share with.

We had often parted ways with friends while traveling. We learned to say "see you down the road" instead of "goodbye." But we'd never left one of our children behind with no intention of them rejoining us.

The day approached. I'd scripted it all out in my head. The script fell apart in a flurry of last-minute repairs, road-prep, family visits, and emotions.

The moment came. The hugs. The tears. The family photos. Plans for phone calls and text messages.

I felt Harrison's absence when it took longer to get the trailer hitched up to the truck. My right hand was gone. Moving again, we headed towards the Mississippi River. The empty space in the back seat silently spoke the words we couldn't say.

Harrison stuck his landing. For weeks he faithfully biked to work in the wee hours of the morning. A ride came along. Then a cheap car.

And, as it turned out, he wasn't done traveling. Just traveling with us. He went to Australia on a missions trip. Germany to visit friends. New York City to see a show. LA for a spell. Florida for a mid-winter break.

The years brought different cars, new friends, a real apartment, a better job, and a girlfriend.

What becomes a traveling teen? In Harrison's case, a traveling teen turned into a young man that we are proud of.

Photos:

1. Our travel blog was DitchingSuburbia.com - we joked that Harrison had been "ditched in suburbia."
2. Harrison heads into a job interview.
3. Harrison and MsBoyink move his stuff into a rented room.

92 St. Ignace, MI

Michigan - our home state - has the City of Marquette, Marquette County, the Pere Marquette River, the Pere Marquette State Forest, and the Pere Marquette Beach.

Missouri - our adopted state - has Marquette High School in Chesterfield, Marquette Park in St. Louis, and Marquette Island near Cape Girardeau.

The common names have a common source.

Jacques Marquette.

Aka Pere Marquette.

A Frenchman.

A missionary.

Assigned to New France (now Canada) in *1666*.

Marquette helped found Catholic missions in Sault Ste. Marie, Michigan and St. Ignace, Michigan.

We happened upon the Father Marquette National Memorial in St. Ignace, Michigan.

Mainly what caught our interest was what Marquette headed off to explore.

Because we were headed west to explore the same exact thing.

The Mississippi River.

But we knew what Marquette didn't.

Where the river ended.

In *1673*, French Expansionists wanted to establish a French presence in the western territories.

And rumor had it that the great "Michissipi" flowed all the way west.

Into the "sea of California."

But no one knew for sure. Marquette and another explorer named Louis Jolliet decided to find out.

They left St. Ignace, Michigan with five men in two canoes on May *17, 1673*.

Their route took them from the Great Lakes, to Green Bay, to the Fox River, to the Wisconsin River, then into the Mississippi near present day Prairie du Chen.

Marquette and Jolliet watched the direction of the river's flow.

And met Indians.

Illinois. Quapaw. Michigamea. All friendly.

After paddling south for hundreds of miles and getting as far south as the confluence of the Arkansas and Mississippi Rivers (about *100* miles south

of present-day Memphis), the explorers knew three things.

First?

The Mississippi River didn't go west to California. It went south to the Gulf of Mexico. But there was another river - the Missouri - that looked to lead off in the right direction. Two fellas named Louis and Clark would follow that one *130* years later, still hoping to find that highly-desired water route to the Pacific Ocean.

Second?

It was possible to travel from the Great Lakes south to the Gulf of Mexico entirely by water. Later explorers would build on their accounts and create a network of trading posts along the route.

And third?

It was time to head home. Marquette and Jolliet started spotting Indians carrying Spanish-made trinkets. And the Spanish weren't friendlies.

Rather than risk being captured and forced into slavery, Marquette and Jolliet headed back north.

They arrived in Illinois Territory in late *1674*. The duo parted ways, with Jolliet returning to Quebec, and Marquette heading back to St. Ignace, Michigan.

He didn't make it.

On May *18*, almost exactly two years after embarking on his Mississippi exploration, Jacques Marquette died of dysentery near modern Ludington, Michigan.

He was buried near where the river that now bears his name empties into Lake Michigan.

He was *37* years old.

Learn more about the Father Marquette National Memorial at michigan. gov/marquettememorial.

Photos:

1. Miranda enters the Father Marquette National Memorial in St. Ignace, MI.
2. The Mackinac Bridge connecting the Upper and Lower Peninsulas of Michigan is visible from the memorial.
3. The marker in Ludington, MI, where Father Marquette died.

93 St. Paul, MN

Curling. You know, that funny Olympic winter sport with the brooms and big pucks on ice.

YouTube comments on curling videos can be harsh:

"LOL curling is the biggest joke ever... worst thing is that they call this a sport."

"This sport is for ppl who cant play any athletic sport."

A popular cartoon character was a bit less caustic, saying to his wife: *"This is perfect for both of us! It's got bowling for me and sweeping for you!"*

And I have to admit.

When we drove through Bemidji, Minnesota (which I don't know how to pronounce either), and saw that it was the "Curling Capital of the United States," I might have smirked.

And I may have had a little of my tongue in my cheek when I suggested we should try curling.

We were, after all, in Minnesota. Besides listening to *A Prairie Home Companion* and going to a church potluck,

what could be more Minnesotan than curling?

We were headed south, following the Mississippi River. I looked downstream and found there were curling clubs in the Minneapolis/St. Paul area.

One of them was offering lessons. *Free* lessons.

I signed us up.

We started in a classroom learning the basics of the game.

Each curling team has four people. The lead is called a "Skip" and they are the team strategist, showing players where to aim their shots.

To curl, you put a broom under one arm, crouch down, and grab the "stone" with your other hand.

You then push off against a "hack" with one foot and slide on the other foot.

You release the stone, both aiming and twisting so it rotates (or curls) as it slides over the ice.

Your teammates influence the speed and direction of the released stone by sweeping in front of it. But no touching

- that's called "burning the stone" and is an infraction.

At the other end of the rink is the "house" - a giant bullseye. A team scores one point for every stone that it has closer to the center of the house than the other team.

The Skip may want you to try and score, or knock an opponent's scoring stone out of the house. Or both.

Each game of curling has eight or ten "ends" - much like an inning in baseball.

It all made sense in our heads. Kinda. We headed onto the ice to put our new-found curling knowledge into practice.

I had skated as a kid. At times the creek behind our house would overflow in winter then freeze and we'd have fun for a couple of days.

But I'm no Scott Hamilton.

And it showed.

Trying to balance, slide, aim, spin and release a curling stone successfully without ending in a faceplant is hard.

We looked like newborn giraffes learning to walk.

We all had delivery attempts that ended with us splayed out on the ice before getting the stone released successfully.

But we had good coaches and understanding teammates. We kinda-sorta got the hang of the stone delivery (although one of us may have started pinch-hitting for the others).

The game strategy was engaging. The banter between teams was playful.

And after a few minutes?

I had to shed a layer or two. I was getting overheated from the physical effort required to play the game. I don't care what the YouTube haters say - curling raised my heart rate.

And - I have to confess - while we signed up for curling lessons with intentions to lampoon the sport on our blog, curling had the last laugh.

Because we enjoyed it.

Find a curling club near you at usacurling.org/find-a-club.

Photos:
1. MsBoyink (left) gets instructions before delivering a curling stone.
1. Michael in mid-delivery.
2. Curling stones waiting to be pulled into play.

94 Wabasha, MN

Superman. Popeye. Kermit the Frog. Johnny Cash. BB King.

All united.

All have common roots.

They were all born on or close to the Mississippi River.

But the river has contributed to America in other ways besides generating movie and music stars.

Bald eagles.

Maybe you are old enough to remember when seeing one was like hitting the lottery?

Despite the *1940* Bald & Golden Eagle Protection Act, in the early *1960*s there were just *417* nesting pairs in the lower *48* states.

Quite a disgrace for the bird first chosen to symbolize America in *1787*.

The founders were inspired by the bald eagle's majestic beauty, great strength, long life, and North American nativity. At that time there were between *25,000* and *75,000* birds in the lower *48* states.

Farmers didn't find the birds as inspiring as the politicians. They considered bald eagles pests and shot them on sight.

But it was something else farmers (and residential gardeners) were doing that had a far greater impact on bald eagle populations.

Applying DDT for insect control.

It was a trickle-up problem.

Small animals ate the DDT-treated bugs. Bald eagles ate the small animals. DDT caused thin walls on bald eagle eggs, and the eggs were crushed or didn't hatch.

DDT was banned in *1972*.

Things didn't improve overnight. Eagle populations were still in jeopardy.

The birds were added to the Endangered Species list in *1978*, which provided further protections.

Sometimes "time heals all wounds" proves true.

By the mid *1980*s, the residents of Wabasha, Minnesota took note of a number of bald eagles coming to feed on the open waters of the Mississippi during the winter.

So many birds were showing up that in *1989* Wabasha volunteers built a riverfront viewing deck and began to promote the spot to visitors.

Bald eagle populations kept growing.

In 2000, the US Fish & Wildlife Service proposed that the bald eagle be declared fully recovered. Moving with typical governmental speed, the Department of Interior agreed and took the American bald eagle off the Federal List of Endangered and Threatened Species in 2007.

That same year, the National Eagle Center opened their 15,000 square foot interpretive center on the Mississippi River.

The Center provides a home for non-releaseable bald and golden eagles. In addition to care and feeding, the birds are shown up close and personal during programs hosted by the Center.

But chances are, you don't need to travel to Minnesota to see a bald eagle in the wild.

By 2009, there were 72,000 bald eagles in the lower 48 states.

That number has now more than tripled.

The U.S. Fish and Wildlife Service said there were an estimated 316,700 bald eagles in the lower 48 states during the 2019 breeding season.

United States Secretary of the Interior Deb Haaland said in a press conference that the bald eagle represented "a historic conservation success story."

If the iconic bird that represents our nation can make a successful comeback from a period of suffering, maybe our nation can as well.

Check current hours and restrictions at the National Eagle Center at nationaleaglecenter.org.

Photos:

1. Ambassador Was'aka flaps his wings during a presentation at the National Eagle Center in Wabasha, MN.
2. A statue of Chief Wapahasha II outside the National Eagle Center.
3. Ambassador Angel enjoys a widescreen view of the Mississippi River.
4. Looking up while inside the National Eagle Center.

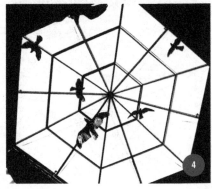

95 La Crosse, WI

People were looking. People were pointing. There may have even been a phone aimed at us, recording video.

A young mom leading her kids down the hiking path saw us, stopped short, and kept watching. The scenic view, evidently, could wait.

We had been following the Mississippi river from top to bottom. The river had taken us to La Crosse, Wisconsin. Grandad Bluff was said to offer a great view of La Crosse and the river.

So we found the park on our GPS and headed up.

While towing.

The reviews said the park was popular. And on this clear, crisp, peak-color fall day, it was busy.

Like "Atlanta during rush-hour busy."

But a popular park would have a way to manage traffic, right? A loop drive? A large parking lot? Dedicated large rig spots? Police?

Right?

Grandad Bluff is a linear park. One way in, one way out.

And no traffic control.

We drove until the road ended in a small, tadpole-shaped parking lot ringed with dozens of cars. The scenic view was a short walk away.

There was no way out.

I stopped. I put our emergency flashers on.

Traffic didn't stop. Cars zipped around us, careening into any open parking spot. People would jump out of them and walk right past the nose of our truck.

Without making eye contact.

I wasn't new at towing a large trailer. We had been on the road a few years.

We'd set up camp dozens of times. We had even traded up to a longer RV.

But I still didn't like backing up if I didn't have to.

Especially with an audience. And moving cars not paying attention.

They say highly stressful situations can trigger a "fight or flight" response.

It's true.

I wanted out.

I noticed an opening by the trail-head kiosk right ahead of us. Looking in my mirrors I saw an open parking space off one corner of the RV.

It would have to do.

MsBoyink jumped into the fray. She dodged incoming traffic, got to the open parking space, and started waving cars away from it.

I pulled forward as far as I could, cranked the steering wheel, and began backing up. More than once I had to stop and wait as a clueless driver scooted around the rear of the RV.

I pushed the trailer into that open spot. MsBoyink watched to make sure I didn't scrape any parked cars.

A three-point turn became six. Six points became nine.

And with a miraculous break in oncoming traffic, we escaped.

To the only applause I've ever gotten while driving.

We found parking further back down the road. Had lunch. Let the white disappear from our knuckles.

But we couldn't leave without seeing the view. So we walked back up to that parking lot.

And may or may not have made loud comments about those clueless Michigan tourists who drove up here while towing their big RV.

Voted the most scenic view in the state, you can see the Mississippi River, Wisconsin, Minnesota and Iowa from the top of the 600-foot tall Grandad Bluff. Learn more at explorelacrosse.com/project/grandad-bluff-la-crosse.

Photos:

1. La Crosse, WI streets and houses viewed from Granddad Bluff.
2. The Mississippi River viewable in the distance from Grandad Bluff.
3. Michael and Miranda taking in the view.
4. The University of Wisconsin at La Crosse as viewed from the bluff.

96 Dickeyville, WI

Matt was *31* years old. Living in Germany. Training to become a priest.

He decided to move to America.

Not New York. Not San Francisco. Milwaukee.

Resourceful, somehow, Matt managed to reengage in his training. He earned ordination as a Catholic priest three years later.

Then he disappeared. Eleven years later, he popped up *160* miles east of Milwaukee. In Dickeyville.

Dickeyville wasn't much - maybe *150* souls called it home.

The town had one of most things. One hotel, one store, one saloon, one shoe shop, one cheese factory.

It had two of a few things. Two schools, two carpenter shops, and two churches.

Matt became Father Matthias Wernerus at one of those churches.

And at *45* years old, he began the work most would remember him for.

He started small. Little projects around the church and graveyard. But a vision for something bigger developed as he worked.

That vision formed around two passions - God and his adopted country.

Where Father Matthias got the skills is anyone's guess. Certainly the Catholic Church didn't teach them.

He didn't ask the church for help in either the form of money or labor. Working with his own funds and his own hands, he began his bigger project.

It took rocks and stones, both local and imported.

It took gems from all the U.S. states and some foreign countries.

It took sea shells, colored glass, fossils, coral, bits of iron, copper and lead, fool's gold, pottery, porcelain, door knockers, figurines, and anything petrified.

It took cement to give it shape.

It took all year. He worked in the church basement during the winter and outdoors during the summer.

For five years, the rocks keep coming. Thirty-ton truckloads at a time.

Finally, in September of *1930*, Father

Matthias Wernerus laid down his tools. The truckloads of rock stopped coming.

The completed portions of the Grotto include statues of Christopher Columbus, George Washington, and Abraham Lincoln.

It has a replica of the Liberty Bell, and names the fruits of the spirit and the seven virtues.

There are shrines to the Holy Eucharist, the Sacred Heart, Christ the King, Fatima, and the Stations of the Cross.

And much more.

People started to visit. Lots of people. Fifty thousand on one Sunday alone.

On dedication day, High Mass was conducted. The Governor gave an address. The Grotto was consecrated. Fireworks were set off while a brass band played.

After all the time, all of the work, and all of the attention, one aspect of the project remains a mystery.

Why?

Did Wernerus want to help the church heal from losing young men during the wars?

Did he want to inspire viewers to better appreciate their country or faith?

Did he want more people to know about his church?

"Why it was done I could not reveal," Wernerus said. "The last day will tell you more about that."

A year after the Grotto was dedicated, another stone marker was added nearby. No gems, shells or coral adorn this one. It's a modest, gray stone that reads:

Builder of the Grotto
Ordained June 23, 1907
Rev. Matthias Wernerus
1873-1931

Matthias is gone. But one rock by one piece of glass by one bit of pottery, he built a legacy that thousands of people still come to see each year.

The Dickeyville Grotto has been featured on Atlas Obscura, Travel Wisconsin, Roadside America, PBS, and countless travel blogs. Learn more at dickeyville-grotto.com.

Photos:

1. A closeup of rocks and gems embedded in cement at the Dickeyville, WI Grotto.
2. The visitor center was closed on the day of our visit.
3. The Boyink girls study the handiwork of Rev. Matthias Wernerus.
4. A shrine in the Grotto.
5. "Fortitude" - a display in the Grotto.

China has the Great Wall. Greece has the Parthenon. England has Stonehenge.

Ancient structures from previous civilizations.

Clues to those who came before. How they thought. How they lived. Where they traveled.

My recollection of Michigan public school Early American History is that the first settlers to America mainly found two things: Indians and wilderness.

The Indians were tent-dwellers, living off the land and moving with the seasons.

The wilderness remained because the Indians didn't clear fields, cut down trees, or make permanent homes.

But it wasn't just wilderness. North America does have ancient structures. They aren't brick edifices. They aren't ornate temples. They aren't monolithic rock formations.

They're mounds.

Piles of dirt, really.

Found in Minnesota to Louisiana. Oklahoma to South Carolina. Mounds are mostly found close to rivers and other bodies of water. Shapes vary from round to conical to animals including bears, birds, and reptiles. Sizes range up to *100* feet tall, *1,000* feet long and *800* feet wide.

The story of the mounds is arguably more fascinating than the mounds themselves.

I'm simplifying, but basically it goes like this:

White settlers find some mounds. "Hey, Indians - what are those?"

"Not sure, really. They've been there a while and no one remembers."

"Well, you guys certainly couldn't have built them, so it must have been a race of people who are gone now. Like Vikings. Or Romans. Or Hindus. Or maybe it was survivors of Atlantis. Or a race of giants. No, it was aliens. Definitely aliens. They could land space ships on them."

Mound-builder theories abounded for several decades, until the then-new Smithsonian Institute got involved.

Its researchers determined that there was no so-called single lost race of mound builders. Rather, the mounds were created by the ancestors of the current Native Americans, and there were multiple cultures and tribes involved.

But for all the efforts of the Smithsonian and other researchers since, we don't know much about the mounds, who built them, and why they built them.

National Park Service accounts of the

LITTLE BEAR MOUND

mounds include more weasel words and hedging phrases than a politician's press conference:

...may date from as far back...
...there remains the possibility...
...may have contributed...
...likely popularized...
...scholars believe...
...it is reasonable to project...
...most likely...
...some believe...
...may also indicate...
...evidence suggests...
...shapes were most likely...
...some mounds may have had...
...some have speculated...
...the data is inconclusive...
...perhaps size and shape...
...hence the assumption...

The uncertainty leaves fertile ground for conspiracy theories. There are still those who believe a race of giant Homo Sapiens were responsible for the mounds, and that discoveries of their seven-foot-tall skeletons have been covered up by the Smithsonian Institute.

As for us?

We usually enjoyed visiting National Parks and Monuments.

But I won't lie. We found the mounds themselves unremarkable, and the interpretive center a little too...interpretive.

But.

The fall color was in full rage. The weather was crisp and glorious.

The views of the Mississippi River were some of the best we'd seen.

And we learned, again, that science can't always provide all the answers.

And that was worth a stop.

Effigy Mounds National Monument is approximately an hour and a half north of Dubuque, IA. Learn more about Effigy Mounds National Park at nps.gov/efmo.

Photos:

1. This mound looks like any suburban backyard.
2. The Boyink girls look across the Mississippi River to Wisconsin.

98 Hannibal, MO

I was wrong. I've read almost everything the man ever wrote.

We listened to *Life on the Mississippi* while driving the entire length of the Mississippi.

I named our GPS after one of his characters.

I've tried to internalize his sarcasm, cynicism, irreverence and deadpan humor.

After visiting Twain's boyhood hometown of Hannibal, Missouri, I asked myself.

What would Mark Twain think of it?

I mean, really.

Statues?

Sure.

Parks and monuments?

Certainly.

A tourist bureau?

Yes.

A classic Mississippi riverboat? Unavoidable.

But Hannibal doesn't stop there.

A book and gift store named after one character. A store of "treasures" named for another character. You can probably guess who the bar is named after.

And Mark Twain's name on a gift store, wax museum, and bookstore.

My favorite?

Fried chicken sold under Twain's name.

I'm not sure what one has to do with the other (frog legs I would have understood).

I was convinced that cynical, sarcastic old Samuel Clements would roll his eyes at the crass, opportunistic commercialism found in current-day Hannibal.

And I was wrong.

Turns out?

Cynical sarcastic Samuel Clements would have broken into a smile behind that big droopy mustache of his.

Twain was actually one of the first celebrities to take advantage of his fame to make money by putting his name on products.

Mark Twain fountain pens. Mark Twain cigars. Mark Twain whiskey. Mark Twain pocket watches. Mark Twain self-pasting scrapbooks. Mark Twain flour. Mark Twain lemons and oranges. Mark Twain shirts. Mark Twain pants. Mark Twain pen knives. Mark Twain shoes. Mark Twain Hotels.

If it wasn't his name on it, it was his

endorsement of the product. Sheet music. Pullman cars. Oldsmobiles. Hotels. Political candidates.

It would be easy to dismiss Twain as the ultimate huckster, able to get us to paint his white picket fence while he sits on a nearby milk jug, counting the possessions we've given him for the privilege.

But as Twain wrote in the *Personal Reflections of Joan of Arc*:

"To arrive at a just estimate of a renowned man's character one must judge it by the standards of his time, not ours."

Twain came from a troubled family. His many business ventures were often as big of a failure as his books were a success. He went bankrupt and had to complete a *122*-show world tour to earn enough money to pay back his debts.

If nothing else, Hannibal's commercialism may be the most accurate tribute possible to Mark Twain's life.

As long as there's a little tongue in the cheek.

Check Hannibal weather forecasts, flooding status, and COVID-19 closures at visithannibal.com.

Photos:

1. Letting my youngest buy into an opportunity of a lifetime by paying me a couple dollars for the privilege of painting the Tom Sawyer fence in Hannibal, MO.
2. A statue of Twain behind the wheel of a Mississippi Steamboat on the waterfront.
3. Downtown Hannibal has a variety of Twain-related shops.
4. A Mississippi Riverboat offers river tours to visitors.
5. A statue of Tom Sawyer and Huck Finn.

99 St. Louis, MO

The hardest part about the City Museum is trying to describe it.

Take a Makers Faire, Carlsbad Caverns, a junkyard, an abandoned building, a Tim Burton movie, a county fair, a movie prop warehouse, an on-the-take OSHA inspector, Willy Wonka, and Mad Max. Mix them up, multiply by a gadjillion, and you start to describe the City Museum.

There's no linear experience at the City Museum. Every attraction has a dozen distractions. There is no narrative retelling.

A stream of consciousness is more appropriate:

Serpent fence, junkyard bike, fire truck, suspended school bus, stepping stones over water, dog made from gears and wrenches, giant grasshopper, two-story slide, covered climb, ferris wheel, water towers, run-up ramp slide, wire mesh climb-inside snowman, ten-story slide, empty building core, ancient pipe organ, yellow crane, fire pit, roasting marshmallows, ball pit, skeleton plane,

slinky climb, another plane, pelican, icicle ceilings, opera posters, graveyard cupola, amusement park trams, cement whales, cement frogs, gargoyles, tree nests, crawl-through caves, giant sewing machine, skate park, theater seats, rope swings, giant pencil, miniature train, glowing crystals, conveyor-belt stair rails, cement dolphins, climb-inside springs, escape holes in floor, Big Boy statue, shoelace looms, giant hamster wheel, doorknob collection, mounted insects, ancient bank safe, building cornices, stained-glass windows, robots, electronic test equipment, vampire, pinball machines,

rubber Legos, toy dump trucks, wooden blocks, giant propellers, sumo warriors, mounted eagles, stuffed squirrels, rooftop sharks, cardboard castles, snowflake story tellers, painting station.

Whew.

Behind great artwork there is often tragedy. Such is the case with the City Museum.

Artist Bob Cassilly founded the museum with his second wife, Gail, who was a former nun. They bought the former International Shoe Company building in 1993 and began transforming it. The public got a first look in 1997.

In *2000*, the always-creating Cassilly began work at a former cement factory in north St. Louis, calling it "Cementland." His ever-changing vision was another weird place with castles, bridges, ponds, water slides, obsolete machines, and smokestacks.

In *2002*, Cassilly bought out his wife's share of the City Museum and changed it from being a non-profit to a for-profit.

In *2011*, Cassilly suffered a fatal accident while working in his bulldozer at Cementland. Initially ruled an accident, further investigations initiated by his third wife alleged the cause of death wasn't natural and that the scene was staged to look like an accident.

After years of probate proceedings, Cassilly's widow and children inherited Cementland. They had hoped to continue construction, but fires, thefts, vandalism, continuing litigation, and financial issues have kept any progress from being made at the site.

While Cementland may never be realized, the City Museum remains an ongoing concern, attracting over *700,000* visitors yearly. New attractions continue to be installed by resident artists.

If you've never been, you need to go.

The City Museum is open with COVID-19 safety factors including limited attendance, one-way traffic, extra cleaning. Learn more at citymuseum.org.

Photos:

1. A school bus hangs over the edge of the City Museum building in St. Louis, MO.
2. Visitors can crawl into the cockpit of this airplane installed on a lower roof section of the museum.
3. Crawling through a wire cage suspended *30* feet above ball pits.
4. A Ferris wheel on the roof? Sure, why not?

100 Arlington, KY

*Two roads diverged
in a yellow wood, and I—
I took the one less traveled by,
And that has made
all the difference.*

-Robert Frost

Most people read these famous words by Robert Frost and apply it as a metaphor to their lives.

One fall day in Kentucky we found it had a practical side as well.

We were following the Great River Road (GRR). The GRR isn't one road. It's a route mapped over existing roads, all designed to keep you as close as possible to the Mississippi River.

Starting in Minnesota and ending in Louisiana, the GRR travels through ten different states. Each of them is responsible for GRR marketing and signage within their borders.

Some are better at it than others.

We didn't always explore with the RV hitched up, but today we were in full-on moving-day mode.

Two roads diverged in a yellow wood. And neither one had a GRR marker. We stopped, deliberating.

Then chose the road that looked like it would take us closer to the river.

It was a good road.

For a few miles.

We passed a man, working in his front yard.

He did that thing where you take a quick look, then put down what you are doing, straighten up, and then full-on stare.

A portent.

The road took us around a corner. And down a hill.

And got narrower. The shoulders disappeared. There were no driveways or intersecting roads.

We saw a sign on a tree.

"ATV Route."

Then another sign.

"Water over the road."

I stopped again.

You'll probably laugh at what stopped us.

A creek.

But the road didn't have a bridge spanning over the creek. Instead, the road had a paved low-water crossing that the creek flowed over.

We had never encountered one before.

I got out and looked at it.

I saw only two options.

Don't cross the water. But that left me no room to turn around. I'd have to back up the trailer, uphill and around a corner. With trees close to the road there was little margin for error.

Cross the water. The low water crossing had short and steep sections leading into and out of it, but our fifth-wheel had good ground clearance.

On the other side of the crossing was an open field large enough to turn around in.

But we were close to the Mississippi River. The field was rich, muddy river-bottom land. My truck needed new tires. And it was only two-wheel drive.

The challenges didn't end there.

I was low on gas.

And the sun was getting low in the sky.

A wrong move might mean spending the night.

Rock, meet hard place.

I decided to try the water crossing.

Going through it, the truck dipped down then back up. The trailer followed suit, angling up as its wheels climbed out of the water crossing.

It all cleared. I was through.

Or not.

The trailer spare tire was mounted on the rear bumper. It hung down just low enough to drag on the cement of the water crossing. It made a sharp screeching sound. MsBoyink then made a similar sound.

Now I had to turn around. And not get stuck.

I knew if I spun the tires, they'd cake up with mud and we'd be dead in the water. Then I'd need a tow truck.

I imagined an egg on the gas pedal and eased the trailer back into the muddy field. Shifting from reverse to drive was the moment of truth. Would we leave this spot under our own power?

The truck left ruts. The trailer left ruts. The trailer tires skidded as much as they rolled out of that field.

But I never spun a tire. The weight of

the trailer on the truck's rear tires gave us the traction we needed.

I went back through the water crossing - again dragging the spare tire mount down the cement.

I stopped on the other side and assessed the damage to the RV's spare tire mount. The dragging bent it, angling the tire forward. The top of the tire just missed puncturing the rear fiberglass wall of the RV.

We'd need a new tire mount, but they cost a lot less than a tow truck would have.

We took a deep breath, got back in the truck, buckled up, and headed back up the hill.

We had taken the road less traveled.

And it certainly made all the difference.

But in this case, we were quite happy to backtrack and choose the other option at the "Y".

And stay on the road more traveled by.

Learn more about Kentucky's portion of the Great River Road at kygrro.com.

Photos:

1. A water crossing on a road we shouldn't have been on in Kentucky.
2. Our bent spare tire mount.
3. Kentucky could have used at least one more of these Great River Road signs.

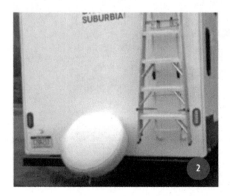

101 Dyess, AR

Times were hard. The flood of *1927*. The stock market crash of *1929*. Bank failures after that. Arkansas was especially hard hit. Most folks who had anything lost it.

Hard times called for hard-working men

Nick worked hard.

Cotton was king, and Nick picked it for money when he could. If cotton wasn't in season, Nick would walk or sneak onto a train to get to where the work was. If he was lucky he could make two dollars a day.

Two dollars a day to support a family.

It was *1934*, and Nick had to make a hard choice. He could stay where he was. And keep doing what he'd been doing.

Or he could take the offer in front of him. The offer was from the government, one of Franklin Roosevelt's "New Deal" programs.

It all sounded a bit radical. The government had purchased a big chunk of Mississippi bottomland in Arkansas. The federal government had pulled men off the relief rolls in Arkansas and used them to build roads and houses.

Houses for destitute people like Nick.

And now the government was offering one of those houses to Nick. Along with *20* acres of land. And a mule, a cow, groceries, and other supplies.

At no cost.

The land would be close to town. Town had a bank, beauty salon, library, theater, garage, school, and newspaper.

The catch?

It was a cooperative community. The community would pool money to buy seeds. Crops were to be sold collectively. Nick and his family would have to volunteer time for community tasks in the store, cannery, or cotton gin.

They would only see income when the community was profitable as a whole.

The pay wasn't in United States Dollars, but rather a local currency called "doodlum."

The government thought it would take them about three years to clear the land and make money farming. Then Nick could repay the initial advance and get a deed to the house.

Along with a fresh mortgage.

Nick was lucky to get the offer. Thousands had applied. Besides being dirt-poor, they had to show good moral background and the physical ability to clear the land.

He looked at his wife, Gail. Then across the faces of his kids ranging down to as young as three years old.

Some of Nick's friends called the offer socialism. Some even called it communism.

But the entire family was hungry.

What else could he do?

Nick signed the offer.

A few weeks later a flatbed truck came to pick up Nick, his family, and their meager belongings. The cost of the truck was added to Nick's bill.

A long, bouncy, dusty journey brought them to a plot of flat farmland in Dyess, Arkansas.

To Nick, the little whitewashed five room house looked like a mansion. Even if it didn't have running water or electricity.

He knew all too well the hard dirt-scrabble work that waited to earn it.

But at least now there was hope. Hope for a home. Hope to own his own fields.

The years weren't easy. They had to evacuate for a horrible flood. Accidents in the community claimed lives. Another World War fired up.

During that war the government stopped funding Dyess. Many of the residents left, either selling or abandoning their homes and fields.

But Nick and Gail held on. They had worked hard for what they had.

By *1950*, the Dyess colony had been around long enough that some of Nick and Gail's kids were now adults. They joined their classmates in deciding what to do with their lives.

Some stayed, starting families of their own. Some left farming to be part of the growing industrial revolution. Others went on to college. And some went into the military.

One of the Air Force-bound Dyess graduates filled in the recruitment paper work with the only name he knew.

J.R.

Initials, because his parents never did agree on an actual name.

But the Air Force? They didn't accept initials. It went against policy.

So J.R. told them his name was John. John R. Cash.

You probably know him better as Johnny.

Dyess, AR is home to the restored Johnny Cash boyhood home and other buildings and exhibits from the Dyess Colony. Learn more at dyesscash.astate.edu.

Photos:

1. The restored Johnny Cash boyhood home in Dyess, AR.
2. Inside the restored Cash house.
3. The Dyess master plan.
4. The Dyess community movie theater.

102 Memphis, TN

For some visitors to Memphis, it's Graceland. For others, the National Civil Rights Museum.

Or maybe Giant Pandas.

Or the 3/4-mile-long scale model of the Mississippi River.

We were after ducks.

Mallards.

The most common duck in the USA. Found in every state.

Mallards live in fresh water. In salt water. In parks, ponds, rivers and lakes. Estuaries, inlets and the open sea.

And in Memphis?

Ducks live in the Peabody Hotel.

Before Duck Dynasty - or anyone else - created duck calls, hunters raised what they called "call ducks." Live call ducks were used as lures for the ducks being hunted.

In the 1930s Frank Schutt was a duck hunter. He used call ducks. He was also the General Manager of the Peabody Hotel in Memphis.

As a gag, Schutt put his call ducks in the hotel fountain.

And stars were born.

A former circus animal trainer turned bellman volunteered to care for the ducks. He trained them to march from the hotel elevator through the hotel lobby and into the fountain.

Add a rooftop suite, red carpet, costumes, and music and the daily march of the ducks at the Peabody has become a public relations dream for the hotel.

Visitors crowd the lobby and surrounding balconies each day.

Celebrities like Oprah, Paula Deen, Molly Ringwald, and Patrick Swayze have lined up to be "Honorary Duckmasters."

The ducks have been on the *Tonight Show*, *Sesame Street*, and in *People* magazine.

We wanted to see them for ourselves.

We arrived early at the Peabody Hotel. Not early enough for front-row spots, however, so found a view from one of the surrounding balconies.

11 a.m. came.

We heard the music.
Saw the crowd shift in anticipation.
I readied the camera.
And waited.
Something distracted me.
I looked away.
Big mistake.
Those ducks don't march.
They don't waddle along, begging for handouts.
Once that elevator door is open?
They RUN.

I looked back, and they were already in the fountain.

People gathered around, dozens of phones taking photo and video. Kids posed. Adults took selfies.

Looking around, I realized.

It wasn't really about the ducks.

They are, after all, just Mallards.

Coming to the Peabody in Memphis was more about how uncommon the common can be.

And it was to see the other people who showed up to witness the same.

Roast duck is not on the menu at the Peabody Hotel. Learn more at peabody-memphis.com.

Photos:

1. The exterior of the Peabody Hotel in Memphis, TN.
2. Visitors crowd around the ducks in the fountain in the lobby of the Peabody Hotel.

103 Memphis, TN

"I don't sound like nobody."

That's what the 18-year-old man standing in the lobby of the recording studio told the receptionist.

The sign on the door said "We Record Anything, Anywhere, Anytime."

And the young man was there to record himself singing.

A gift for his mother, he said. But that wasn't the only reason.

He was also hoping to be "discovered."

After recording two songs, the receptionist noted his name and included the note "Good ballad singer. Hold."

The studio owner heard something he liked. He had the young man record a few more songs.

Not much came of it.

The owner was undeterred. He had previously recorded what many claim was the first rock and roll record. It had gone to number one on the charts. The owner had launched his own label based on the success of that song, but was finding it hard to keep profits up.

He needed a fresh new voice to keep the business afloat.

He found musicians to back the young man up. They launched into a jam session that lasted until late in the evening.

Again, nothing.

The band was ready to pack it in and call it a night.

In a last ditch effort, the young man grabbed his guitar and launched into a four-year-old blues number.

"I can't dance," he had told his prom date a few weeks earlier.

But he could.

And he was.

Band members recall him "jumping around and acting the fool."

The singing and dancing caught the attention of the studio owner.

He poked his head out of the control booth. "What are you doing?"

"We don't know."

"Well, back up, find a place to start, and do it again."

The owner - Sam Phillips of Sun

Studio in Memphis, Tennessee - pressed "record."

And the singer - Elvis Aaron Presley - launched again into the first song most people would hear him sing.

Called *That's All Right*.

People couldn't get enough. The local radio station played the song repeatedly and interviewed Presley.

Phillips sold so many Presley records he ultimately realized Presley needed to be on a national record label. Phillips sold his Presley contract to Colonel Tom Parker and RCA for an unheard-of *$40,000* (*$386,435* in today's dollars).

Presley went on to international stardom.

Phillips stayed in the recording business for a while, then lost interest and got into radio station ownership instead.

And the building at *706* Union in Memphis?

Sold to a plumbing company. Then an auto parts store.

In *1987* it was reopened as a combination tourist attraction and functioning recording studio. Acts including U2 and John Mellencamp have recorded there.

The highlight of the tour was a classic Shure *55* microphone, said to have been used by Elvis himself.

Not locked behind glass.

Out on a microphone stand in the studio, available for anyone to ham it up with.

We may or may not have taken photos of ourselves channeling our inner Elvis.

You'd probably ask us what we were doing too.

Sun Studio remains open for tours. Masks and temperature checks are required. Find more information online at sunstudio.com.

Photos:

1. A neon sign for the Memphis Recording Service at Sun Studio in Memphis, TN.
2. The classic guitar sign at Sun Studio.
3. A *1950s* radio station DJ booth replica - complete with smashed records.
4. Mic, mic, mic, mic, mic, mic and Mike.

104 Helena, AR

He shuffled in supported by a walker. He was the same height as my grandfather - coming just up to my shoulder.

He wore large, thick glasses and a green sweater over a blue button-up shirt. He wasn't quite bald, with some streaks of darker hair still showing through the gray.

We made small talk. He was a bit hard of hearing, but if you spoke up he was right there with you. He could serve up playful banter with a wry twist.

He kept an eye on the clock as we chatted. When the time came, he excused himself, made his way over to his desk, and sat down to do what he'd been doing every day for the last 64 years.

John William Payne, better known as "Sunshine Sonny Payne" put headphones on, adjusted the boom microphone attached to the desk in front of him, waited for his cue, then called out the words he opened every radio show with: "Pass the biscuits! It's King Biscuit Time!"

Payne played the blues and people listened. Muddy Waters listened. B.B. King listened. Robert Plant and Elvis Costello listened.

Payne started his radio career sweeping the radio station floors and learning to read and announce at night.

His big break came when the previous host couldn't make it back in time for the show, which had Sonny Boy Williamson and Robert Lockwood, Jr. waiting to play live. Payne stepped in and the rest, as they say, is history.

The Army called him away for a while. After his service Payne toured for a while, playing bass with jazz and big band groups.

1951 found him back at KFFA hosting the King Biscuit Time show. It was one of the first to feature blues musicians and led to the annual multi-day King Biscuit Blues Festival held in Helena each fall.

Payne's on-air work won several awards, including the George Foster Peabody Award for outstanding achievement in radio & TV journalism, the Blues Foundation's Keeping the Blues Alive

Award, and the Arkansas Broadcasters Association Pioneer Award.

He was also a *2010* inductee into the Blues Hall of Fame.

On the day of our visit Sonny hosted show number *17,381*. We weren't the only ones who had traveled to see him in action. We shared guest chairs with a group of Polish motorcyclists and a musician from New Mexico.

Once the show was over, we posed for a few photos, shook hands, and said our goodbyes.

We left grateful to have met Sonny.

We also left challenged with our culture's current views on retirement.

If Sonny had hung up his headphones at the age when society said he should have, we would have missed out on over *25* years of his work.

And would it have been the best thing for Sonny? His love for the music and a daily responsibility kept him active, engaged, and contributing to the world.

We can only hope for a similar "retirement" for ourselves.

John William "Sunshine Sonny" Payne passed away on February 9, 2018 at age of 92. The King Biscuit Time radio show continues on and can be heard at kffa.com.

Photos:

1. John William "Sunshine Sonny" Payne waits for his cue to speak during his *17,381st* show on KFFA in Helena, AR.

2. A vintage bass drum advertises the King Biscuit Flour show in the KFFA studio in Helena, AR.

3. Autographs from previous visiting blues players in the KFFA studio in Helena, AR.

105 Venice, LA

"There is no there there."

American novelist Gertrude Stein once said that of Oakland, California.

We found it to also be true of Venice, Louisiana.

I wanted to drive the entire length of the Mississippi River. We started at the headwaters in Lake Itasca, Minnesota.

The fall colors in Minnesota were stunning. The park was well-marked, with a designated place to rock-hop across the Mississippi at its source.

Driving south, we found adventure all the way down.

We learned to curl in St. Paul, Minnesota. Watched river tows go through lock and dams in Moline, Indiana. Rode up into the Gateway Arch in St Louis. Almost ditched our truck and RV after a wrong turn in Kentucky. Visited Sun Studio in Memphis. Found the blues crossroads in Clarksdale, Mississippi. Visited Kermit the Frog's birthplace in Leland, Mississippi. Heard live jazz in New Orleans.

Venice was supposed to be the triumphant end of the trip. We made camp in New Orleans, and bundled off in the truck to complete the last 77 miles of the 2000-mile journey, take the photo, and buy the fridge magnet.

South of New Orleans, the Mississippi River is not scenic. Hidden behind earthen levees and cement flood-control walls, the surface of the river is actually at a higher elevation than the road.

We passed a few citrus farms. We stopped at Fort Jackson - still rebuilding from being flooded during a hurricane.

And then, into Venice.

Venice was the song that ends with an unresolved chord. The novel that peters out before concluding the plot. The amusement park that's closed for cleaning after you drive cross-country with your family to get there.

There was no "End of the Great River Road" sign. No dedicated turnaround. No scenic photo opportunity. No shop of Great River Road trinkets.

Venice was a collection of weedy fields surrounded by chain link fence,

storage tanks, radio towers, electric lines, and shrimp boats.

Without a soul in sight. It was like the rapture happened and we were left behind.

And the river? We couldn't tell where the actual Mississippi was. Or used to be. Or was supposed to be.

The shipping channel went on past where we could drive. It may have contained the river. Or not.

The satellite view of Venice shows the Mississippi fragmenting into what looks like the root system of a tree, with several outlets connecting into the ocean.

I really didn't even know what to point the camera at.

The Venice city sign seemed as good as anything.

The Great River Road gets described in lofty terms: *"America's most important scenic byway." "One of America's National Treasures." "America's Greatest Drive."*

After the fizzle-out ending in Venice, we weren't too sure about those descriptions.

In time we got over that. And were able to think about our experience of driving the Great River Road.

It may not be the greatest. Or the most scenic. Or the most important.

But the Great River Road slices through the heart of America. Physically and culturally.

And that makes it the most purely American road trip you can find.

The Great River Road is a collection of state and local roads that follow the course of the Mississippi River through ten states of the United States. Learn more at en.wikipedia.org/wiki/Great_River_Road.

Photos:

1. The Great River Road ends somewhere around Venice, LA.
2. Our truck at Fort Jackson, south of New Orleans.
3. A freighter heads down the Mississippi towards the ocean.
4. Each state on the Great River Road marks the route using similar signs featuring a Mississippi River Steamboat.

106 San Antonio, TX

It all sounded good going in. A ranch in San Antonio, Texas offered us "free RV parking with full hookups" in exchange for hours spent caring for animals and doing other chores around the property.

We'd save some money by not paying to be in a campground.

And our animal-obsessed daughter would get some experience with alpacas, llamas, sheep, goats, miniature donkeys, horses, pigs, cats, dogs and an emu.

I sent them our availability and asked for details about the RV spot. The last time we'd parked our fifth-wheel on a farm, we had to cut down trees to get out.

The ranch assured us they'd had an RV parked there before. They said it was a straight shot in and out without any clearance issues.

I was happy. They were happy. We made a rough schedule and started driving their way.

On arrival, they met us on a tractor at their pasture gate. They unlocked it, and we followed them in.

Downhill.

To the lowest point on the property. Just after a record-setting year for rain.

The green grass gave way to black, gooey Texas mud. Deep enough to have standing water on top of it.

They splashed through the mudhole on the tractor. Just past it, they stopped and got off.

And pointed back at the mudhole.

This was the free RV spot.

I'm still not sure why I didn't just turn us all around and head back up to the gate.

But we had committed. And Miranda was already oohing and aahing over all the animals.

So I pulled forward.

Or tried to.

Our truck was two-wheel drive. I made it about four feet before spinning out.

They hitched us to their tractor and pulled us into place. We shored up the trailer legs with wood to stabilize it in the soft mud.

Even with the trailer disconnected from the truck, I was still stuck. We again hooked the tractor up and dragged the truck to dry ground.

I asked about the RV hookups. Power and water were easy enough.

DRIVEN TO WONDER

Then I asked about the sewer connection.

Our host got a thoughtful look.

And I got worried.

In RV lingo, "full hookups" means water, electric, and sewer. Without a sewer connection, we could only stay for about five days. After that we'd have to hitch up the RV and tow it somewhere to empty the holding tanks.

Which meant dealing with the mud again.

Our host promised to figure something out.

We drove to town and bought muck boots. I scrounged up some pallets and made a rough deck to act as a buffer between us and the mud.

And, as expected, Miranda fell in love with the animals. Not usually an early riser, she was up and out the door every day for the 7 a.m. feeding. She repeated the process at 4 p.m. She learned to drive the farm tractor. She learned how to vaccinate pigs. She held two newborn lambs.

We did get a sewer solution figured out. Before the tanks were full, thankfully.

And eventually?

The mud dried up.

RVers can find work-camping opportunities in a number of places online. Some sites require membership. We used the free website workersonwheels.com to find this gig.

Photos:

1. Using a zoom lens keeps me out of this llama's spitting range.
2. Our free campsite in the Texas mud.
3. Digging a drainage channel in the mudhole outside our RV.
4. Miranda discovers that llamas have no sense of personal space.
5. There are no stress relievers quite like newborn baby lambs.

107 McGregor, TX

We had been through Texas a number of times. You kind of have to, if you want to see the USA on wheels.

Texas is too big to miss.

We'd driven that *857* miles of I-*10* across Texas east to west before.

We'd also driven Texas north to south *538* miles from Sanger to Brownsville.

But most of our Texas time was in the winter. We joined the other "snowbirds" looking for warmer climes.

Then, finally, we stayed into spring.

And were there for "The Bloom."

Wildflowers, that is.

And, in true Texas fashion, the wild-

flower bloom is a bigger deal there than anywhere else we've been.

The State of Texas has been formally managing its roadside wildflowers for over *80* years.

Famously supported by efforts from Lady Bird Johnson in the *1950*s, the Texas Department of Transportation buys and sows *30,000* pounds of wildflower seed every year, planting over *5,000* species of flowers on *800,000* acres of right-of-way.

It shows.

Drive the Texas Hill Country roads during the wildflower bloom and the shoulders become a rolling canvas of color.

Indian Paintbrush in red, orange, yellow, and purple. Yellow sunflowers. Goldenrod. Poppies in red, white, pink and orange. Horsemint.

And, of course, bluebonnets. Bluebonnets are the Texas State Flower and during the wildflower bloom, turn vast

stretches of Texas land into waving fields of blue.

Driving around Texas during the wildflower bloom is a bit like being around "leaf-peepers" in the north in the fall.

You gotta stay on your toes.

It's not unusual to come up on cars pulled over, occupants spilled out into the fields, taking pictures of the flowers. Or kids sitting in flowers. Or pets sitting in flowers. Or taking flower-framed selfies.

The bloom lasts about six weeks.

Then the colors fade away, leaving Texas draped in shades of brown and green for another year.

But still just as big.

The Lady Bird Johnson Wildflower Center at the University of Texas uses native plants to restore and create sustainable, beautiful landscapes. Learn more at wildflower.org.

Photos:
1. Indian Paintbrush blossoms at sunset in Mother Neff State Park, McGregor, TX.
2. Star of Bethlehem flowers in McGregor, TX.
3. A field of Goldeneye phlox blossoms in McGregor, TX.

108 Quitaque, TX

Some people look for restaurants everywhere they go. Others are all about antique shops.

For us, it was sunsets.

Especially when there was an interesting view for the sun to set over.

The gorgeous rock bluffs at Caprock Canyons State Park provided that.

The park also has bison. Wildflowers. And a campground.

But no cell coverage meant we couldn't stay there.

We day-tripped instead. Parked the RV up the road a ways and came back to explore.

And see the sunset.

We drove way back. Found a nice ridge to park on. Set up our chairs. Made tea on the tailgate.

And settled in.

The light went sideways. Ridges and hilltops became defined. The bright, early stars started to show. The spaghetti-yowling of coyotes echoed in the distance.

I'm not sure if I heard it or smelled it first.

The sound was a light scraping on pavement. A soft whoosh of air.

Then a new odor. Musky. Sweaty. Animalistic.

I threw a glance over my shoulder, back at the truck. And saw it.

A bison. Maybe 20 feet from the nose of the truck.

Nose down in the roadside grass.

Alone. Quiet. Oblivious.

But, coming our way.

Now, we weren't exactly experienced cowboys. But we had been around animals. We'd stayed on private horse ranches. And on a ranch with horses, alpacas, llamas, donkeys, goats and sheep.

But not so much around bison.

Free-range bison, even.

What was protocol here?

Speak gentle words of non-aggression? Stand up and appear tall? Back away slowly?

We'd read stories of bison attacking tourists in places like Yellowstone. We knew bison were fast runners. And are more likely to charge if provoked or cornered. Especially if there were calves around.

DRIVEN TO WONDER

This one was alone. And looking content.

But those horns.

And that bulk.

And our lack of anything other than a cup of Earl Grey for a weapon.

And the distance between us and help of any sort.

We decided safe was better than being tomorrow's viral news video.

We slowly got up and slipped back into the truck. Just for a few minutes. Long enough to let the bison walk peaceably off into the sunset.

We returned to our chairs, and watched the horizon blaze up in golds, oranges and yellows, then die down to just a thin band of blue light.

Pronounced "kitty quay", the town of Quitaque, TX and Caprock Canyons State Park are located about 100 miles southeast of Amarillo, TX. Learn more at tpwd.texas.gov/state-parks/caprock-canyons.

Photos:

1. MsBoyink in a front-row seat for the sunset at Caprock Canyons State Park outside of Quitaque, TX.
2. When this gal snuck up behind us we quickly realized how little we knew about bison temperaments.
3. The bison just ambled off into the sunset.

109 Canyon, TX

You'd think the phrase would have been coined by a Texan.

"Everything is bigger in Texas."

The history isn't 100% clear, but it's possible that the first person to write those words was a New Yorker.

A newspaperman, complaining about the expectations of Texas women.

"Unless a man has a chest as broad as a sugar barrel they cannot think of draping their fair heads upon him. Everything is bigger in Texas than anywhere else, it seems, so naturally New Yorkers are quite out of scale."

New York Tribune, 1913

He might have been scorned, but he had a point. Many things are bigger in Texas.

The state is geographically about the same size as France, or twice the size of Germany. The Texas State Capital is the tallest of any state capitals. Texas boasts the highest speed limit in the USA at 85 mph on State Highway 130. Texas has private ranches larger than Rhode Island.

When you enter the state on I-10 heading west, the first road sign tells you that El Paso is 857 miles down the road.

That's just bragging.

Drive 857 miles north from our home in southwest Missouri and we'd be at the headquarters of the Mississippi in Lake Itasca, Minnesota. If we drove 857 miles southeast and we could meet Forrest Gump in Savannah, Georgia.

But - truth be told - not everything is bigger in Texas.

Texas is second to Alaska in terms of geographical size. And second to California in population.

Texas is also second to Arizona.

The category?

Biggest canyon.

Arizona has the Grand Canyon, of course. Most years over six million people travel to visit it.

But the second biggest canyon in the USA?

Palo Duro.

In Canyon, Texas, as it happens.

Just outside of Amarillo.

Size-wise, this second-place canyon is no slouch. Palo Duro is 120 miles long,

DRIVEN TO WONDER

6-20 miles wide, and 800 feet deep (for comparison, the Grand Canyon is 277 miles long, 8-18 miles wide, and a mile deep).

At times referred to as "Texas' Best Kept Secret," Palo Duro Canyon sees only a fraction of the traffic recorded at the Grand Canyon. The numbers apparently aren't even enough to brag about - the most recent available statistics online show 188,000 visitors to the park in 2014.

We had planned to do some hiking during our time at the Canyon. Or possibly some mountain biking.

But you know what is bigger in Texas? Thunderstorms.

The night before our visit to Palo Duro we watched as a storm rolled across the plains visible from our campsite.

The winds picked up.

And kept picking up.

The RV started to wiggle in the wind - even though we had hitched it back to the truck for stability.

We heard gravel pelting the walls.

Better safe than sorry.

I pulled the slide-outs in to minimize our profile. We suited up in our rain gear, stepped outside, held hands, and booked it for the campground tornado shelter.

Otherwise known as the bathhouse.

We ended up sharing a shower unit with a retired naval meteorologist. He had a radar app loaded on his phone and kept us apprised, pointing out the potential spots for twisters that came and went as the storm passed over.

Once our new best friend proclaimed it safe, we went back to the RV.

We didn't suffer any damage to our truck or RV.

We couldn't say the same of the hiking and biking trails in Palo Duro.

They were solid mud.

Thick, red, gooey Texas mud.

I could almost have tolerated the mud to get some time on the trails, but the thought of having to clean all of that inevitable mess back out of the truck and trailer was a deal-killer.

We settled for a drive down into and through as much of the canyon as we could see from the paved roads.

Any thoughts of relocating the RV into the campground located on the canyon floor were canceled by more rain in the forecast.

It may be a big canyon.

But it was created by rain.

By erosion.

By flooding.

We turned tail and headed west for the elevations of New Mexico instead.

Learn more about Palo Duro State Park at tpwd.texas.gov/state-parks/palo-duro-canyon.

Photos:
1. A view from the visitor center at Palo Duro State Park in Canyon, TX.
2. Natural caves form in the rock formations.

110 Amarillo, TX

If you are of a certain age you might remember a song named *Dust in the Wind* by the rock group Kansas.

Younger readers may remember Keanu Reeves' character Bill S. Preston, Esquire quoting the song's lyrics to "So-craytes" (Socrates) in the movie *Bill and Ted's Excellent Adventure*.

The message of *Dust in the Wind* is rarely as clear as when visiting the Cadillac Ranch just outside of Amarillo, Texas.

Created in 1974 by the art group Ant Farm, the Cadillac Ranch originally served to show the rise and fall of the tailfin in American car design.

Ten used Cadillacs ranging from 1949 to 1963 model years were sourced and buried nose-first into land owned by Stanley Marsh 3, a local millionaire considered "eccentric."

What makes the Cadillac Ranch different from other large art installations is that graffiti by visitors is encouraged rather than prohibited.

And visitors, it seems, are more than willing to take up that offer.

There's no entrance pass. No guestbook. No way to track the number of visitors to the Cadillac Ranch each year.

But, like counting rings on a fresh-fallen tree, the dozens of layers of paint on each hulk of a car tells the story.

The attraction is so popular that each freshly-painted name, slogan, logo, or shoutout is only visible for a moment and then it's gone.

On the day that we visited, the frontage road parking was busy with RVs, classic cars on Route 66 trips, minivans from day-tripping families and - a surprise to me - rental cars driven by people visiting from other countries.

I couldn't count the number of different languages I heard as we wove our way through the row of upended Cadillacs.

We had come prepared. Not surprisingly, the local Walmart had a large selection of 99¢ cans of spray paint.

I chose the roof of a Cadillac in the middle of the pack.

I started with white, painting a large blank canvas to help my work stand out from the cacophony of paint on the rest of the car.

Then within the white frame, I painted a rough version of our travel blog name and logo in black.

I stood back, admiring my work. I shot a few photos as keepsakes.

A middle-aged couple had been watching. He caught my eye, said a few words in a language I didn't understand, but motioned towards my can of spray paint.

Understanding, I handed him the paint.

And danged if he didn't spray his mark right over mine.

Dust in the wind.

The Cadillac Ranch is located west of the Amarillo city line on the south side of I-40 (old Route 66). Take exit 60, and follow the frontage road back east. Enter through the gate. Don't paint anything but the cars.

Photos:

1. Visitors look at the buried cars at the Cadillac Ranch in Amarillo, TX.
2. The cars are all Cadillacs, ranging from a *1949* to a *1963* model.
3. Miranda adds a tag to a car at the Cadillac Ranch.
4. Starting a spray-bomb version of our website logo.

111 Tent Rocks, NM

We were never as good at hiking as we wanted to be.

We had friends that could do 15 miles in a day.

With their young kids.

They'd come back exuberant and glowing with praise about the trail. Their cameras would be loaded up with print-worthy landscape photos that we just couldn't get from the driver's seat while on the "scenic drive."

We'd mumble about needing to get into better shape.

And change the subject.

Then we visited the Kasha-Katuwe Tent Rocks National Monument.

Yes, it's a long name. We just called it Tent Rocks for short.

Tent Rocks made us feel like real hikers.

At least for a day.

Tent Rocks is a National Monument rather than a National Park. From a practical perspective, that means little in the way of visitor centers, interpretive trails, or ranger talks.

But we don't remember Tent Rocks for what it lacked. We remember it for what it had: stunning views of cone-shaped rock formations set into valleys and framed out with scrub pines.

To earn that view we hiked a twisty-turny mostly-uphill trail through valleys, around rock outcroppings, over boulders and through a slot canyon.

But only for three miles.

Round trip.

We came back exuberant. And glowing. With lots of photos.

With renewed hope in our hiking abilities.

After a nap, anyway.

The Kasha-Katuwe Tent Rocks National Monument is located about an hour west of Santa Fe, NM. Check park availability at blm.gov/visit/kktr.

Photos:

1. Tent Rocks from the top of a ridge.
2. MsBoyink hiking at Tent Rocks.
3. Miranda in the slot canyon at Tent Rocks.

112 Farmington, NM

Easy highway access. Paved sites. Full hookups. Campground stores. Pools. Hot tubs. Dog runs. Walking trails. Wifi.

RV parks, like hotels, like to advertise their amenities in hopes of enticing you to come stay with them.

It didn't take us long, living on the road, to realize that an advertised amenity didn't necessarily guarantee an available amenity.

Hot tubs were often long-since-closed. Wifi might be technically working, but not actually usable. Pools would only be open for six weeks out of the year.

And of course, the overnight rate would be the same, working amenity or not.

But most RVs are self-contained. Storage tanks for water. Batteries (or generators or solar) for power.

RV owners don't always need RV parks and their amenities.

If we were in travel mode, just making time to a new location, we'd often try to find ways to not spend $30 just to get a few hours sleep.

Maybe you've noticed RVs in Walmart parking lots at night. They're doing the same thing - parking there overnight to save the cost of an RV park.

We stayed overnight - for free - in a number of places that weren't RV parks.

Walmarts. Sam's Clubs. Cabelas. Cracker Barrels. Churches. Truck stops.

If a free option wasn't available, we'd look for something cheap instead.

Cheap options were casinos, county parks, and city parks.

And fairgrounds.

Most fairgrounds have accommodations for RVs and, if no big events are going on, can be cheaper than an RV park.

While a campsite at a fairground is usually just a parking space in a large field, the experience of staying at one can be more memorable than a RV park.

You probably wouldn't encounter Crossfit Games, Gay Rodeos, or Biker Weeks at an RV park. But we did while staying at fairgrounds.

Our stay in Farmington, New Mexico was probably the most memorable of our fairground stays.

We were on our way to a camphosting job in Durango, Colorado. We were running ahead of schedule getting there, so just needed a place to be for a couple days.

Farmington is just an hour from Durango, and the fairgrounds had openings for RVs. We booked on the phone and headed that way.

Along with about half of the town, it seemed.

Traffic in and out of the fairgrounds was nonstop. When we finally wove our way to the gate, we learned that, while the RV parking portion of the fairgrounds complex would be quiet, the rest would not be.

They were simultaneously hosting a horse race, car show, and wrestling tournament.

Oh, and that night would be a Beatles tribute band.

All of which we could enjoy at no additional cost. Unless we wanted to bet on a race.

We skipped the casino, but appreciated the cars, horses, athletes, and music much more than we would have any campground pool.

Farmington is located at the confluence of the San Juan, Animas, and La Plata rivers in the "Four Corners" region of New Mexico. Learn more at farmingtonnm.org.

Photos:

1. The beginnings of a horse race at the fairgrounds in Farmington, NM.
2. A jockey walks by after his race.
3. The car show included this Studebaker Silver Hawk.
4. A regional wrestling tournament took place in another fairground building.

113 Durango, CO

An old Ray Charles song asks *Do I Ever Cross Your Mind*? Old trains - like old memories - sometimes cross our paths uninvited.

If the memory is happy we'll throw an arm out the window and wave as it passes. If it's not, we'll distract ourselves while wishing it would hurry up.

Sometimes in trying to recreate a favorite memory we end up derailed.

My favorite childhood vacations were in the Durango area. I visited twice with my parents and siblings.

We parked our *1970s*-era Winnebago motorhome next to gurgling streams in National Forest campgrounds.

We jeeped and dirt-biked the San Juan gravel mountain roads. We hung hummingbird feeders and hand-fed squirrels. We hiked to crystal-clear mountain lakes.

I even remember the smell - clear mountain air with a hint of ponderosa pine.

When I hit the road with my own wife and children I knew we'd have to go back to Durango.

And we did. Twice.

The first time was a late spring visit. Not much was open. It snowed and we left.

A couple years later we accepted jobs at a Durango campground as seasonal

DRIVEN TO WONDER

"camp-hosts." Our hope was that with five months in the area I'd get to savor my childhood memories and pass similar ones to my family.

It didn't work out. The park was mismanaged. We worked too much to explore the area. MsBoyink had altitude-related health issues. We ended up leaving early.

Trains are a mixture of cars. Some cars are open-sided. Some are closed. Some carry coal.

I left Durango with a mixture of memories. Those happy childhood memories remain, yes, but muddied and conflicted from trying to recreate them.

Sometimes it truly is best to leave well enough alone.

Starting service in 1882, the Durango & Silverton Narrow Gauge 45-mile ride is considered one of the top ten scenic train rides in the world. Learn more at durangotrain.com.

Photos:

1. The historic Strater Hotel in Durango, CO.
2. The Durango & Silverton Narrow Gauge train heads north.
3. View of the train and the Animas River from the Durango Public Library.
4. Inside a steam powered locomotive at the D&SNG museum.
5. Sign at the D&SNG train yard.

114 Colorado Springs, CO

"A good place for a beer garden."

It was *1859*. Year of the "fifty-niners." Rallying with the cry of "Pikes Peak or Bust!"

Rallying for the same reason most folks rallied west in the *1800s*.

Gold.

Not the Clampetts' "Texas Tea."

The real stuff.

The wagon trails leading towards Colorado rumbled with the sounds of *100,000* wannabe gold miners.

Mr. Beach and his partner were mapping out what would become Colorado City.

The location was just to the east of Pikes Peak. The men worked amidst other-worldly sandstone rock formations, cinnamon-colored against the blue sky, green junipers, and whitecap peaks.

The spot was not unknown. Multiple Indian tribes were connected to the area. European explorers had recorded visits, commenting on the unusual beauty of the rock formations.

Yet Beach could think no higher purpose for the location than a beer garden.

Colorado City was filled with men like Beach. They filled the newly-created streets of the city with opium dens, bordellos, and saloons.

Sin City at *6,000* feet.

Then Rufus spoke up.

Rufus was Beach's surveying partner.

And was maybe just a bit more philosophical than Mr. Beach.

"Beer garden! Why, it is a fit place for the Gods to assemble. We will call it the Garden of the Gods."

The name stuck.

Ownership of the land is unclear for another *20* years.

Then Charles Elliott Perkins enters the historical record.

Think "railroad tycoon."

Perkins thought the spot would make a good place for a summer home.

In *1879*, he bought hundreds of acres of land, some of which included the present-day Garden of the Gods.

But he never built that summer home.

Falling in love with the natural state

of the land, he spent the next *30* years buying additional parcels in the area.

And kept it all "unofficially open" to the public.

In *1909*, Perkins passed away. In his honor, his family decided to donate his land holdings to the City of Colorado Springs.

With two stipulations.

One, that the land be set aside as a public park.

Two, that it would be perpetually free.

Four million people per year currently enjoy that free access.

We certainly did - along with friends who we met on the road. They were another RVing family that we first met in Arizona. We reconnected in Oregon, Kentucky, Washington D.C., and several other states.

They eventually got off the road and relocated to Colorado Springs to enter the ministry.

It had been a while since we had seen them. Garden of the Gods was our place to reconnect as families.

After a long absence, some relationships need recovery time to get back to where they left off.

With others, it's like calling back after a dropped phone call - you just pick right up where you stopped talking.

That's how our time in the Garden of the Gods was. We talked. We hiked. Took photos. And tried rock climbing for the first time. It felt like our long absence had never happened.

We didn't head west to find gold. And our finances certainly hadn't improved. But we struck it rich nonetheless.

Learn more about the various tours, hikes, crafts, and climbs in the Garden of the Gods at gardenofgods.com.

Photos:

1. The entrance road to the Garden of the Gods park in Colorado Springs, CO.
2. Joining friends on the park walking paths.
3. Miranda (pink shirt) rock climbs.
4. Michael tries rock climbing in dress pants.

115 Ouray, CO

"We got ourselves a convoy."

It was the Fourth of July. I was nine years old. We were just outside of Ouray, Colorado.

Parked on US 550.

The stretch of 550 coming into Ouray is known as the "Million Dollar Highway," either because it cost that much per mile to build it in the late 1880s, or because the fill dirt under it held that much in gold.

No matter the origin of the name, it's one of the most beautiful drives in America.

With constant turns, steep grades, no shoulder, no guardrails, and plunging drop-offs, it's also one of the most dangerous drives in America.

But we weren't there just to drive the road.

We were lined up to be in Ouray's Fourth of July Parade.

Along with hundreds of other four-wheel-drive vehicles.

It was approaching dusk. The driver of each vehicle uncapped and lit emergency flares on either end of their front bumper.

Sitting in our fire-engine red 1966 CJ5, we tuned the CB to the predetermined channel at the predetermined time and made sure the volume was up.

The voice came through the speaker.

"We got ourselves a convoy."

You may recognize those words.

"Convoy" was a 1975 hit by Bill Fries, singing under the character name of C.W. McCall.

In the song, the narrator uses the CB to lead a group of truckers in a protest of government regulations.

In 1978, the song became a movie starring Kris Kristofferson and Ali MacGraw.

Bill Fries was a multi-talented man who loved Southwest Colorado. He wrote other songs about the area. He settled in Ouray, running a scenic slideshow for tourists. He ended up becoming the town's mayor, serving for six years.

Bill Fries was at the head of the Ouray Fourth of July parade.

Using the CB.

As a nine-year-old, hearing his voice

live from our CB speaker became my first celebrity encounter.

The sun slipped behind the mountains. The road fell into dusky shadows.

The convoy moved out.

Viewed from below, the bumper to bumper vehicles with flares burning looked like a giant orange glow worm snaking down the mountain and oozing into town.

Twenty years later I told the C.W. McCall story to another off-roader from Canada. He was also a fan. The conversation led to another visit to Ouray, this time with MsBoyink and our newborn.

I brought the very same red CJ5 I'd sat in as a kid - I had purchased it from my dad. But no holiday convoys this time.

I still remember that trip well, however, because I rolled that Jeep on a mountain trail just outside of Ouray.

No one got hurt, but the CJ wore scars from that rollover for years. Right up to the day I tore it down to build a new rig.

I spent years working on that one.

Then we decided to travel full-time.

I was telling our kids that in order to have the adventure of long-term RV travel, they'd have to make some sacrifices.

They'd have to give up some toys.

And it struck me.

I couldn't ask them to give up some toys unless I did too.

So I sold the Jeep, the matching trailer, and all my spare parts.

We ended up needing the income from the sale to be able to afford the RV.

We might have driven a Chevy pickup into this visit to Ouray.

But it was still an old Jeep that got us there.

On our own cross-country convoy.

Bill Fries (aka C.W. McCall) passed away on April 1, 2022 at 93 years old. His song Convoy *found new life during recent trucker protests in Canada and the US.*

Photos:

1. Overview of Ouray, CO.
2. The Beaumont Hotel in downtown Ouray opened in *1886.*
3. Following a brave RVer down the Million Dollar Highway into Ouray.
4. Miranda views a waterfall on a hiking trail just outside of town.

116 Animas Forks, CO

The *Animas Forks Pioneer* in Animas Forks, Colorado stopped circulation in *1886*.

After only four years in print.

It's not that the paper wasn't a good one.

There just weren't enough people left to buy it.

The gold was running dry.

The local mines, which were never reliable or profitable to begin with, were shutting down.

And it was October.

Winter was coming.

At its peak, Animas Forks had somewhere between *450* and *1,500* people. Most were employed at one of the mines in the area.

The town boasted *30* cabins, three general stores, a boarding house, jail, blacksmith, butcher shop, post office, saloon, sawmill, and hotel.

And a newspaper.

Said to be printed by the highest-altitude press in the United States.

Then in *1884*, a 23-day blizzard buried Animas Forks in *25* feet of snow. The residents had to dig tunnels to get from building to building.

The blacksmith never came back. The butcher shop closed the following year.

The *Pioneer* held on to the year after that. In October of *1886*, with overnight temps already hitting the low *20s*, the owners made the decision to get out before winter arrived in full force.

Animas Forks, however, wasn't done. The town would manage to hang on until a local mine started to ship ore in *1889*. People moved back. Houses filled in.

Until *1891*, when a kitchen fire in the hotel spread and destroyed most of the business district. The post office closed again.

The town emptied out.

Animas Forks sat empty for almost a decade.

In *1903*, new action at a nearby mine brought it back to life. The post office reopened. The railroad in nearby Silverton extended tracks into town.

Saloons reopened in *1905*. Some of the burnt buildings were repaired. New houses were built.

And Animas Forks hummed along for another few years.

Then the mine went bankrupt. It operated sporadically until closing permanently in *1910*.

Another fire, mine closing, and post office closing emptied Animas Forks out for good.

By *1920*, it was a ghost town.

The remaining buildings languished, left to the mercy of locals and passing tourists until the BLM took ownership of the property in *2011*.

Since then the dozen or so remaining buildings have received stabilization and restoration work. Interpretive signs have been installed.

These days?

Animas Forks is a highlight of the 65-mile long Alpine Loop, a scenic mostly four-wheel-drive trail popular with off-roaders. The trail connects Animas Forks with Lake City, Ouray, and Silverton.

Visiting town, you can't help but marvel at the tenacity of its former residents.

No doubt, the views are stunning. But between the work, the remote location, the elevation and the weather, living in Animas Forks couldn't have been anything but hard. Only a certain type of person would even attempt it.

But I'm sure those types of people gave the newspaper men plenty to write about.

Animas Forks is at an elevation of 11,200 feet and is 12 miles northeast of Silverton, CO. Due to the elevation the incoming road is often snowed shut. Check availability before visiting at fs.usda.gov/ sanjuan.

Photos:

1. An Animas Forks house with the San Juan Mountains in the background.
2. This vintage Willys Jeep still gets used for off-roading.
3. Jeeps continue up the Alpine Loop, driving past an abandoned mine.
4. View of the San Juans while heading back to Silverton.

117 Las Vegas, NM

Mark Twain was a river pilot, prospector, reporter, and (generally unsuccessful) businessman before becoming an author.

Colonel Sanders was a farmer, fireman, insurance salesman, and streetcar conductor before making it big in the restaurant business.

Julia Child worked in advertising, developed a shark repellent for the CIA, and flunked out of cooking school before creating a wildly popular cooking show on television.

Walt Disney was fired as a newspaper editor because he "lacked imagination and had no good ideas" before beginning Disney Studios and bringing some of the world's most memorable characters to life.

I grew up in one house. My dad held one job my whole life. I attended one school system from K-12.

It was a stable upbringing. Not much drama. Not much change.

I'm thankful for that.

But I think it's also why I'm drawn to stories of people who have reinvented themselves. Imagine the repressed smile on Walt Disney's face when telling people around the dinner table that he was accused of having no imagination. Imagine Julia Child seeing a former teacher in the studio audience of her highly successful cooking show.

Transition. Reinvention. Rebirth.

We decided to travel full-time for a number of reasons.

One of them was reinvention.

I remember sitting with MsBoyink on the couch in the living room of our

first house in Holland, Michigan. The housing market had tanked. I had been laid off from my "safe" corporate job. Our kids were young.

"We're going to die here."

I don't remember if I said it or she did.

But we both felt it.

Trapped.

Wanting transition. Wanting reinvention. Wanting change.

And somehow - through a series of what we see now as divine conversations - we found it.

And radically so.

Deciding to live in an RV required rethinking every aspect of our day-to-day lives. What we could eat, and where that food would come from. Where our wastewater went. How clients would pay us. How we'd get our mail. How we'd do our laundry.

It was hard.

But we did it.

Turns out, once was not enough.

During our travels there were times when we had smaller transitional moments.

Some costly RV repairs had us getting off the road for a while to save money.

Changes in the demand for our web development services led to reinventing our business as a content studio.

A dip in our income had us looking at farm stays and camphosting instead of paying for campgrounds.

Those events are tied to places.

My memories are geolocated.

Las Vegas, New Mexico is one of those places.

Tied to a transitional event.

A "Plan B" place on our travels.

We only ended up there because Plan A had failed.

We had taken a camphosting job in Durango, Colorado. It was supposed to last the entire camping season. It was supposed to save us money. It was supposed to let us explore southwest Colorado.

But that didn't happen. The camphosting job became a liability rather than an asset.

Just like being in that house back in Michigan, we felt trapped.

So we gave notice and left early.

With the camping season still in full swing.

Like Florida in the winter, summer in Colorado is a tough place to be without camping reservations. And they are expensive when you do find them.

So we looked south until we found openings.

Our research took us to Vegas.

No, the other one.

Las Vegas, New Mexico.

On paper, the town sounds interesting. Teddy Roosevelt's Rough Riders held reunions there. The town boasts of having 900 buildings on the National Registry of Historic Places. Legend has it that Billy the Kid, Wyatt Earp, Jesse James, and Doc Holliday all gathered in Las Vegas. The town has appeared in movies including Easy Rider, Convoy, Wyatt Earp, Wild Hogs, and others.

But for us?

Nothing against Las Vegas, but it was just a place to be. A place to grieve the failure of one plan. And to hatch the beginnings of another.

A place to transition.

Las Vegas, NM is approximately an hour and 45 minutes northeast of Albuquerque on Highway 25. Learn more at lasvegasnm.gov.

Photos:

1. Campers park on the shores of Storrie Lake at Storrie Lake State Park in Las Vegas, NM.
2. A redundant sign on a dilapidated bridge by the lake.

118 Brush, CO

There are RV driving schools. They teach people used to driving small things how to drive big things. Navigating corners. Passing other vehicles. Following at a safe distance. Entering and exiting campsites. Watching clearances.

But I didn't go.

Mainly because I can be cheap. And I was cocky.

Our RV was a towable fifth-wheel.

I had towed things before. Starting with a lawn cart behind a garden tractor before I'd even earned a drivers license. Then utility trailers behind family cars. And Jeeps flat-towed behind motorhomes.

To figure out the fifth-wheel, I watched a few YouTube videos and hit the road.

And did OK.

Yes, I clipped a few curbs. And tagged the roof of a covered picnic table. And, at times, took more than one try to get into a campsite.

But we played it safe. We chose the smallest RV we thought we could live in. We stayed in places designed for RVs.

We used Google satellite view to preview routes for problems.

My main goal?

Don't back up.

If we had to turn around I'd look for circle drives. Or corner businesses with exits on two streets. Or just a big parking lot.

It's not that I couldn't back up.

I just didn't like to.

I didn't have a backup camera. The RV completely blocked the rearview mirror. Using my side mirrors, I could see alongside it when we were going straight but not when turning.

Most of my backing up was just to get the RV into a campsite. Many RV parks have pull-through sites, but they usually charge more for them.

And I'm cheap, remember?

But Brush, Colorado wasn't about camping.

We had just wrapped up a visit with friends in Colorado Springs and were headed back to Michigan.

Our plan was a day of interstate driving, overnighting in a truck stop, then another day of interstate driving.

Our interstate driving turned into interstate parking.

A nasty accident had traffic at a complete standstill.

After what seemed like an hour, an officer appeared at my window.

"There's an exit a mile back. Can you back it up that far?"

"Can I turn around?"

"No, too messy. Too many other vehicles."

He looked at me again. "So, can you?"

I looked at him.

My wife and daughter looked at me.

I did what any red-blooded American male would do.

I nodded.

The officer walked on to the vehicles waiting behind me.

It took a couple of minutes until I had room.

Then, like some slow motion backwards turtle race, we all started backing up. Semis. Cars. Trucks. And me, with 34 feet of RV hitched to the truck.

We all gave each other plenty of room. Especially anyone towing.

I was wobbly at first, overcorrecting when the trailer started to veer off.

But I got better. I learned to sight the centerline in my side mirror and use it as a guide. As long as the trailer was parallel to it, I was going straight. My corrections got smaller and smaller.

I traded a "isn't this ridiculous" look with a semi driver doing the same thing. MsBoyink stood in the middle of the interstate to take the photo you see on the previous page.

I spotted the exit.

I backed onto the overpass connected to the exit we were all aiming for.

Almost there.

And then, after a mile of driving backwards using only my mirrors?

The officer reappeared at my window.

"The accident's been cleared. Drive on."

All we could do was laugh. And be thankful for the practice backing up.

Looking back, occurs to me that while a photo may be worth 1,000 words, those words may not tell the whole story.

Or even the right story.

In the picture, it looks like we were driving normally, making good time down the expressway.

But the reality is just the opposite.

I keep that picture in mind while navigating this marketing-driven, social-media-promoted world. People, families, relationships, churches, businesses, careers - anything can appear successful at a quick glance.

But the reality might be just the opposite.

Located about an hour and a half northeast of Denver, Brush, CO is home to the world's largest amateur rodeo. Learn more at brushchamberofcommerce.org.

Photo:

1. Backing up on an interstate outside of Brush, CO.

119 Montague, MI

We coasted to a stop at the end of the exit ramp. The truck's engine had stumbled, then died. It wouldn't restart. I killed the battery trying.

So here we sat.

All fifty-five feet of us.

Blocking traffic.

Needing a tow truck.

Scratch that.

Needing two tow trucks.

One to get the truck to a shop. And another to get the RV somewhere more appropriate than a right-hand turn lane.

MsBoyink used her cell phone to call our insurance agency.

I used my phone to start researching campgrounds.

It didn't go well for either of us.

On MsBoyink's call, the insurance agency couldn't find us. They said the exit didn't exist. She felt she had a reasonably good argument, being able to see the exit sign from where she stood.

On my part, the nearest open campsites were 20 miles away.

We were in a bind.

Then the first road angel showed up. His name was John.

John parked behind us, then walked up to the truck to see if we needed a jump. I told him I didn't think it would help, but we tried anyway.

The truck didn't start, but John had a tow chain. He pulled us out of the busy intersection, around the corner, and onto the shoulder. He unhooked and went on his way.

I found a street sign. MsBoyink passed the street name to the insurance company and suddenly we existed again. One tow truck was finally on the way.

Then the second road angel showed up. His name was Mike.

Mike lived in the house that we were now parked in front of. He walked out carrying ice-cold water bottles and offered to let us park the RV in his yard.

That solved the campground issue. We took him up on the offer - provided we could somehow get the RV moved there.

Then the third road angel showed up. His name was Chad.

Chad drove a bright red diesel dually pickup. He asked if we had help on the way. We said yes - at least for the truck.

Chad got a funny look. "I wonder if that's my buddy?" A quick cell call confirmed that it was.

He asked his buddy if he had a fifth-wheel hitch on the tow truck. He didn't.

"That's OK," Chad said. "I'll run home and get mine." And he was off in a cloud of diesel smoke.

Then the fourth road angel showed up. His name was Dan.

Dan was the tow truck driver. He hooked onto our truck and headed for a repair shop.

Chad came back, hitched up to our RV, and parked it in Mike's yard.

We chatted a bit, then Chad headed for home.

We had just fallen into bed for a nap.

"WHO SAID YOU COULD PARK THERE!?"

Our fifth road angel had shown up. His name was Jim.

Jim wasn't angelic at first. He had a business behind Mike's house. People had often abandoned dead vehicles in his way.

I introduced myself and outlined the situation. Jim calmed down, and by the end of the conversation had offered us power and water from his business.

We spent the night in Mike's yard. The truck was repaired the next day. The repair shop was close enough to walk to. We paid, hitched up, and went on our way.

Fear is a funny thing. The fear of getting stranded on the side of the road had been on our minds ever since hitting the road.

God sent five road angels to help us that day. And, in the Bible, what's the first thing angels usually say?

"Fear not."

Montague, MI sits on the Lake Michigan shoreline. Learn more at cityofmontague.org.

Photos:

1. John pulled us out of traffic to the shoulder.

2. Dan tows our truck after a fuel pump failure in Montague, MI.

3. Chad placed our RV in the shade of a tree in Mike's yard. We spent the night there while the truck was repaired.

120 Benton Harbor, MI

A traveling sports team. Taking on pro teams in much-hyped exhibition games.

The "real game" interspersed with comedy routines based on extreme dexterity with the ball.

Sometimes hiding a thinly disguised professional player in their ranks.

Are you humming *Sweet Georgia Brown* and looking for your basketball?

Hold up.

The Harlem Globetrotters weren't the first group to blend sports and rehearsed routines into a blend of live entertainment.

No, that honor goes to a bunch of unshaven, celibate, vegetarian, teetotaling, non-smoking, communal-living cult members from Benton Harbor, Michigan.

Who played baseball.

Not kidding.

The House of David is an Adventist sect started in Benton Harbor, Michigan in *1903*.

Many aspects of the sect are unsurprising. Communal living. Assigning ownership of all personal possessions and income to the group. Ingestion of alcohol, tobacco, and meat was forbidden. All members were required to maintain celibacy.

And the men were forbidden to shave or cut their hair.

You'd think those rules would make for an unhappy bunch hiding out in some remote woods, just wanting to be left alone until the end times.

And to be sure, the House of David was nothing if not self-sufficient.

As the group grew, they were able to purchase *1,000* acres of land on which they grew their own fruit and grains.

They also built their own cannery, carpenter shop, bakery, laundry, coach factory, zoological garden, and tailor shop. All the buildings were lit by electrical lighting powered by their own electricity plant.

But they didn't just keep to themselves.

Quite the contrary.

In an effort to both spread their beliefs and generate an income, the House of David created an amusement park known as Eden Springs.

Eden Springs had a hotel, restaurant, bowling alley, billiard room, amphitheater, zoo, beer garden, and a miniature railroad.

It also had a baseball stadium. The leader of the House of David loved base-

ball, believing it taught "discipline of the mind, body and soul."

The games in Benton Harbor became popular. The House of David team got more organized. Leagues were entered. Matches with local semi-professional teams were booked.

The ball players became missionaries.

Sent out as "barnstormers" to travel the country, make an income for the sect and distribute religious literature for the House.

Due to their long hair and beards, the team was mostly shunned by mainstream baseball. Instead, they played against teams from the Negro league, often being the first time spectators saw black and white players on the field at the same time.

The House of David players added some rehearsed routines, tricks and stunts as a pre-game show called "pepper." They hid the ball in their beards. Juggled bats. Rode donkeys in the outfield.

And no mistake, these guys were good. Reports have them playing *200* games per season with a winning percentage around *.700*.

At the height of their popularity the House of David had three teams on the road full-time.

An internet search will turn up photos of Babe Ruth posing in a fake beard after meeting some of the players (the team even attempted to sign Ruth until realizing his lifestyle would be at odds with the beliefs of the rest of the team).

It was all good while it lasted. In the late *1920s*, a leadership scandal divided the House. By the *1950s* the baseball teams were gone.

These days?

The group claims a handful of remaining members.

Eden Springs was reopened in *2011* under new ownership. It now sports an RV park and campground. The miniature trains run again on the weekends.

And the sounds of a baseball game are still heard in the summer. The original House of David baseball diamond - now sprouting full-grown trees in the middle of the outfield - is used for vintage baseball games, played by the *1860* rules.

Which allow shaving.

Or not.

The House of David Christian community remains active. Learn more at israelitehouseofdavid.com.

Photos:

1. A team photo of the bearded House of David baseball team (source: Wikipedia.com).
2. A building on the grounds of the House of David property in Benton Harbor, MI.
3. Vintage baseball players on the original ballfield.
4. The park offers rides on a vintage mini-railroad.

121 Rantoul, IL

A vaguely industrial multi-floor building. Loading docks here, single-story office wings there. A locked up entryway hidden behind overgrown trees, broken branches, knee-high weeds, and piles of leaves.

Broken appliances outdoors on cracked pavement. Trailers full of tires and trash parked behind tall fences. The dirty outline of where the letters spelling "Hospital" used to be.

Coughwheezecough years ago MsBoyink was born in the hospital on Chanute Airforce Base in Rantoul, Illinois. The base closed in 1993. The hospital is now used as makeshift housing for migrant workers.

It's a bit of her story.

It's a bit of her parents' story.

There's nothing like being there. A cliche, yes. But true.

Being able to travel and visit a specific location can bring the history of that spot to life in a way that reading about it can't.

Walking from the hospital through the rest of what used to be the Air Force Base - we could better imagine what military life was like for MsBoyink's parents at ages 16 and 18.

And then adding a newborn daughter.

Visiting places important to our national history - like Gettysburg - has helped us more deeply and completely understand what led up to the event that happened there. We could then more easily see how it influenced the direction of our country afterwards.

There are more stories here than just our own.

To get to the former hospital we walked down Tuskegee Drive.

Our family's first real encounter with the Tuskegee Airmen was in the movie *Night at the Museum: Battle of the Smithsonian*. We met up with them again during a visit to the National Air and Space Museum in Washington, D.C.

We caught another piece of their story in Tillamook, Oregon. Later we visited the Tuskegee Airmen National Historic Site in Tuskegee, Alabama for the most complete telling of their story.

Now we learn that some of the Tuskegee ground support crew trained here before shipping off to Alabama.

When we can connect the dots of the same story across multiple loca-

tions, travel starts to feel like being in a *National Treasure* movie. We visit multiple locations, get little clues from each place, with a goal to figure out the mystery, solve the big picture, and save the world.

We connected Gettysburg, Pennsylvania to Picacho Peak, Arizona - location of the west-most battle during the Civil War.

We connected Johnny Cash from his boyhood home in Dyess, Arkansas, to a radio show he performed on in Helena, Arkansas, to a studio he recorded at in Memphis, Tennessee.

We've connected pieces of the Lewis & Clark Expedition in West Virginia and Montana.

And we could connect Rantoul, Illinois, to Animas Forks, Colorado.

Both towns are examples of what happens when a main reason for the town being there disappears. In Colorado it was the mines. In Rantoul, it was the Air Force.

The Air Force left Rantoul in *1993*.

They abandoned White Hall, all *500,000* square feet of it. It was the largest pre-Pentagon government building with enough space to house and train *2,200* residents and contain a post office, barber, and bowling alley. Soldiers called it "Buckingham Palace."

After the Air Force, different developers bought White Hall with various schemes in mind. A private college. A shopping mall. Residential and commercial units.

Ultimately, structural concerns, lead paint, and asbestos made any new use for the old building impossible.

By *2016*, the Air Force had completely demolished White Hall.

Every last brick had been removed before we got there.

Maybe it was better that way.

Sometimes when you revisit a place from your childhood, the reality of it doesn't match your memory of it.

With large parts of the former Air Force Base gone, it left space.

Space to begin again. Space to reinvent.

Space to finish off old stories.

Or write new ones.

Rantoul, IL is approximately two hours south of Chicago. Interior photos of the now-demolished White Hall can be viewed at atlasobscura.com/articles/haunting-photos-of-an-abandoned-air-force-base.

Photos:

1. MsBoyink poses at the sign of her birthplace.
1. A former Air Force hangar remains standing in Rantoul, IL.

122 Destin, FL

Nine months. From deciding to travel full-time to hitting the road it took us nine months.

It's an appropriate length of time to conceive, grow, and birth an idea that changed every aspect of our lives.

Many prayers were sent up during that time. For direction. For wisdom. For safety. For income.

And for purpose.

There were questions. We had them. Family and friends had them.

Why would you do this?

Give up comfort? Give up toys and hobbies? Give up a safe neighborhood?

And why as a family?

I'm not a big fan of mission statements, but I wrote one for our travels:

This trip is...

...not a field trip, but we want to be educated.

...not a business trip, but we need to work.

...not a family reunion, but we want to visit friends and family.

...not a vacation, but we want to be recreated.

...not a mission trip, but we want to be missional.

Looking back, I'm not sure how successful we were in living that out. A lot of our travels were simply because we wanted to see new places or reconnect with old friends.

But we had our moments.

One of them was in Destin, Florida.

The truck needed a new radiator.

Usually when we needed a truck repair we'd just park the RV in a campground and drive the truck to the shop.

But this was Destin. In the winter. A popular place at the height of tourist season. We had lucked into a couple of open nights at the beachfront state park. Those nights were now up.

We had to leave. With the RV.

No biggie. We'd just tow the RV to the

The foreman was a younger man, shorter than me, a face full of beard, and a carpenters pencil tucked into his ear.

I explained our situation.

He frowned and let out a deep breath. "You literally couldn't have picked a worse time," he said. "We're having a big parking lot sale to clear this place out. There's going to be a lot of traffic in and out of that lot. We'll need all the space."

I looked around. There was more work than workers.

Maybe this was a missional moment.

"We're stuck until the truck repair is done anyway. Put us to work while we wait."

I don't know if he was a pastor or hired help.

Or if it was a Holy Spirit moment.

But his entire mood flipped. Gratefulness replaced annoyance.

mechanics and unhitch it in their parking lot. They could fix the truck while we were "at home" outside the shop.

Then we drove past the shop.

The lot wasn't even big enough to turn around in.

I drove on, hoping to find RV parking nearby.

There was a church at the end of the street.

It was a weekday. Usually a quiet time for churches.

This one was busy with people and cars. Yellow tape surrounded tables, stacks of boxes, and rows of furniture.

But the corner parking lot was big. Easy in and out.

I went in to ask permission to park the RV in their lot for the day.

Inside, the building had seedy black walls, sticky floors, a DJ booth, and beer signs on the wall.

It used to be a nightclub. The transformation into a church had just started.

Asking for whoever was in charge, multiple workers relayed me deeper into the building where walls were being studded in.

DESTIN, FL

It was a deal. We had a parking spot and they had extra labor.

I went back to the truck and let the girls know I had just conscripted them into sweaty work. They walked inside while I got the truck to the mechanic.

For the rest of the morning and into the late afternoon, we did grunt work. We carried seasonal decorations, unused beer glasses, bar stools, tables, signs and who knows what-all outside for the sale.

We connected with other volunteers. They asked us where we were from. It was fun watching their reactions as we recounted the journey that led us to their door.

Late in the afternoon, the shop let us know the truck repair was done. I walked over, paid, and drove it back to the church.

A BBQ dinner had just arrived. The other volunteers invited us to eat with them. We loaded up styrofoam plates, found shady spots on the ground, and perched the plates on our knees. I think people were passing our story around to other volunteers that had been working deeper inside.

With our bellies full, we wished them well with their new building and said our goodbyes. We hitched up the truck and RV and pulled out.

"Missional" is a word that can trigger big visions. Quitting jobs. Traveling to other countries. Building wells, orphanages, or schools.

Some callings are all-in like that.

This was just one day. I've probably made too much of it in the retelling. We didn't go back to visit the church. We didn't friend all the volunteers on Facebook to stay connected.

We were there. We helped each other. And we were gone.

In our time on the road, we could have been better at being mission-minded. But at least for this one day, I felt like we had answered that call.

And for that, I remember Destin.

Henderson Beach State Park in Destin was one of our favorite campgrounds in the USA. Learn more at floridastateparks. org/parks-and-trails/henderson-beach-state-park.

Photos:

1. View of the Gulf of Mexico from Destin, FL.
2. The Boyink girls schlep parking-lot sale items.
3. The RV parking spot we earned.
4. The nightclub-turned-church had an unbelievable amount of stuff to sort through.

123 Valdosta, GA

Homesteading. There was a time when MsBoyink and I thought about it.

Living off the land.

Growing our own food.

Being self-sufficient.

Knowing that, even if work dried up, or the internet crashed for good, or our truck blew up we'd have a place to live and be able to put food on the table.

But MsBoyink and I?

Suburban kids.

We wondered. Might there be a way to dip our toes into the homesteading world without committing to a chunk of land?

In today's parlance: is there an app for that?

Kinda, yea.

Maybe you've heard of it.

WWOOFing.

The longer version: WorldWide Opportunities on Organic Farms.

In the US, WWOOFing centers around its website: wwoof.net.

Call it a dating service for farms that need help and people that want to learn farming skills.

The basic idea is that a host farm provides room and board in exchange for labor provided by a "WWOOFer."

WWOOFing is a thing in over 100 countries. People - mostly young singles - use it to learn farming skills. Or to experience other countries. Or take a different sort of vacation.

We signed up, created a profile, uploaded photos, described our skillset and what we were looking for.

We were not typical WWOOFers.

We were a family.

And we brought our housing with us.

But our kids weren't little. And many farms have plenty of space to park RVs. We just had to make sure the spots were accessible and there were hookups for the RV.

We had a couple of WWOOFing experiences.

One was in southern Georgia.

It had horses, cows, chickens, dogs, cats, and goats.

The farm made goat products including cheese, milk, and soap.

We proposed a deal. In return for

RV parking and laundry facilities, we'd provide approximately 1.6 employees.

Miranda full-time. MsBoyink half-time. And me a few hours a week.

They agreed. We headed their way, happy to have found somewhere to be in the south for the winter.

The farm had dedicated housing for its WWOOFers. We parked the RV next to it and sorted out water, sewer, and electric hookups.

Our daughter decided to get a bit of independence from her parents and moved into the WWOOFer housing.

We settled into a new routine.

The girls headed out at first light. Miranda joined the main crew tending to the animals out in the pens.

MsBoyink began an internship in the dairy.

While I worked from the RV wrangling code into websites, she herded goats into the building and learned the process of milking them. She learned how to make goat yogurt, goat cheese, and goat soap. She learned to deworm goats.

And when it came time, we all learned about the goat birthing process. We learned there are few days not able to be improved by watching young goats find the springs in their legs.

We got to know the farm owners. And we met the other WWOOFers. We made meals together. Played games. Watched movies.

I'd like to say it was one big happy learning experience.

One issue we've experienced with

these sorts of "work exchanges" - be it camp hosting or WWOOFing - is that, no matter how carefully worded the initial agreement, once you are on-site the expectations slowly creep up.

One campground waited until we arrived to let us know another host couple had left so everyone was going to have to work more hours.

Another didn't mention that we'd have to be on-call every third weekend.

The WWOOFing website suggested that *20* hours per week was the norm for WWOOFers to work for their host farm.

That's not what we experienced.

Miranda was putting in *12*-hour days six days a week. MsBoyink went from "mornings-only" to also working most afternoons. We started to hear rumblings that they wanted me to put in volunteer hours on their website.

And then there was the other thing.

That housing provided to the WWOOFers? Segregation by gender was not enforced. The farm owners let the mixed lot of single *20*-somethings figure it out on their own.

To a predictable result.

Miranda moved back into the RV.

We lasted about seven weeks before moving on.

Drama aside, we were successful in one thing.

We learned that we were not cut out to be homesteaders. Maybe with younger (and additional) kids to share the workload with the lifestyle would have been feasible.

But for our empty nest years?

Call us lazy city folk, but it all seemed like too much work for us.

Learn more about WWOOFing at wwoof.net.

Photos:

1. Miranda has company while distributing hay around the goat pens.
2. MsBoyink brushes off the goats before they are allowed into the dairy.
3. Nothing puts a smile on your face quicker than a newborn goat.
4. A Nubian goat possibly looking at the camera.
5. Goat milk ready for the market.
6. This baby goat is just finding the springs in its legs.

124 Ava, MO

A body at rest tends to stay at rest, and a body in motion tends to stay in motion, unless acted on by a net external force.

-Newton's First Law of Motion

Applicable in physics, yes. But also life. The easiest thing to do is what you've always done. But for external forces, we'd never change.

External forces got us on the road.

Some men flew a plane into a building in New York and I lost my comfy corporate job.

Our kids were growing up too fast. We wanted to do something special as a family before they aged out of our home.

We put our bodies in motion. For roughly eight years. We stayed in campgrounds, Walmart parking lots, and on goat farms. We visited 40-some states. Put 110,000 miles on the truck.

One kid eventually jumped ship, then the other.

But MsBoyink and I stayed in motion.

We sold the truck and fifth-wheel and kept going in a Class B motorhome.

Until a external force hit me.

For the last few years I had been running a business. While also trying to become an "RV influencer." I was blogging. Instagramming. Facebooking. Podcasting. Being interviewed on other podcasts. Designing t-shirts. Creating downloadable freebees. I was also doing interviews and research for a book.

I was burned out.

And an unexpected reality set in. We had built up an entire identity around a "do this before the kids are gone" lifestyle.

And now the kids were gone.

We were just another run of the mill, empty-nest RV couple.

I needed a break. From work, from empire-building, and from traveling.

I took a sabbatical. I went on a technology and media fast. I went completely without internet access, a cell phone, or laptop. I didn't listen to the radio, watch

TV, or read newspapers. I even went without talking for entire weeks.

Giving up my phone was like lopping off a hand. Countless times I'd reach for it before remembering it wasn't there. I worried about missing a big world event. Or a good photo opportunity.

Sabbatical. The word has the same root as *Sabbath*. This period became a long Sabbath. All of the space created in my day by not consuming media I filled with Bible study, prayer, and worship.

I don't mean to sound preachy or holier-than-thou. Quite the opposite. It was incredibly humbling. I had to face a fact about myself that I'm not proud of.

I was born and raised in the church. Made confession of faith when I was nine. Got married in the church. Had both kids baptized. At times I volunteered on the church sound board.

But the truth?

I'd hardly ever read the Bible. I'd rarely prayed for more than a minute or two. I wasn't comfortable talking about my faith. Church was a to-do item that I checked off most weekends.

Over the course of my sabbatical I went from missing my phone and the constant presence of mass media to enjoying the slower pace of a life without them.

To this day I still don't carry a cell phone.

While I was sabbatical-ing, MsBoyink traveled solo in the campervan. She visited old friends and made new ones.

One of those new friends - Lynn - was from Ava, Missouri. Lynn lived on a hippie commune.

Well, not really.

But that's what I thought when I heard about it.

Take a big chunk of land. Put a church building in the middle with a bunch of homes around it. Put a dozen families in those homes. Have worship services twice a week. Eat together three times a week. Run a school for the kids. Grow a community garden and raise community cows and chickens. Work together to put an addition on the church building.

Some planned communities also share their finances. Here, members of "the farm" own their homes, have off-site jobs, and manage their own finances.

Travel had challenged our thoughts about church. About community. And about how we wanted to live going forward.

The farm offered us a rent-free place to live while we figured life out. We felt it was God calling us to get off the road. Lynn's community offered an attractive alternative to the anonymous suburban life we lived before traveling.

We accepted their offer. Miranda - who had been living back in Michigan - decided to join us in our restart as Missourians.

Over the next few months we bought a cheap car, sold the campervan, and found jobs. MsBoyink - a registered nurse - went to work in a nursing home. I started as the News Editor of the local newspaper. Miranda found a fast-food job.

But we needed permanent housing. The church offered us free land on the

farm - but the costs of prepping it and then either building a house or bringing in a manufactured home were higher than we wanted to spend.

The alternative was buying in town. Ava had a number of small houses selling for reasonable prices. We put together our wish-list (under 1,000 square foot, small lot, bath and a half, at least one garage space) and started looking.

I didn't want a project. I wanted to move in and hang pictures.

We put an offer in on a three-bedroom ranch that looked great with recent flooring updates and new paint throughout. But a home inspection revealed issues with the HVAC system that we didn't want to address. We backed out.

The realtor took us to a listing so new he hadn't yet put it on the market. It was rough. Overgrown. Junk everywhere. Dirty paint. Popcorn ceilings. Smelly carpets. A half-bath was awkwardly placed in the corner of a small bedroom with only a curtain to block it off.

Of architectural value, it had little.

It was not move-in ready. And wouldn't be even after the cleanup work the realtor intended to do.

But it checked all the boxes. 950 square feet, combined kitchen and living room, two bedrooms, a bath and a half, and a nice two-stall garage. All on a tiny lot on a quiet street in a good part of town.

The kicker? The asking price was 45% less than the first house - and it included appliances. The inspection came back

with only minor issues. Under all that junk and dirt the house had good bones.

I wasn't thrilled about taking on a large house project, but our mortgage would be laughably small. We could live cheap and pay down some naggling debt.

So, after eight years of saying we'd never buy another house...we bought another house.

We were no longer full-time RVers. We were Missourians.

Photos:
1. Redbud trees bloom in the spring in Missouri.
2. Mailboxes after an ice storm in Ava.
3. Be it ever so humble - our house in Ava, MO.
4. Living room before.
5. Living room after.
6. Bedroom/bathroom before.
7. Bedroom/bathroom after.
8. Front room before.
9. Front room after.

125 How Travel Changed Us

So, was it all worth it?

In between working and house projects and doctor appointments and jury duty and oil changes, life offers quiet times when we can reflect on our years of travel.

And ask ourselves.

Was it worth doing? Did the experience leave us with anything more than a nice scrapbook? Did full-time travel change us?

Yes. Yes. And Yes.

We changed the very moment we made the decision to travel.

Up to that point, we had been following the script for the classic American Dream. Graduate high school. Go to college. Get a good job. Get married. Buy a house. Start a family.

Selling it all to hit the road may not seem radical now, but at the time there weren't nearly as many RVing TV shows, YouTube channels, and membership groups where we could talk to others who had gone down this path.

The decision was all on us.

For the first time in our marriage, we stopped living on autopilot, questioned what we were doing, dreamed up alternatives, looked at budgets, took brutal stock of our physical abilities, and ultimately, deliberately, and intentionally chose how we wanted to live.

The longer we were on the road the more attention our counter-cultural lifestyle attracted. Bloggers, podcasters, even reality TV show producers all wanted to know why we traveled. I boiled our goals down to:

Simpler living. Closer family. Richer education. Uncommon adventures.

It took time. But somewhere, in and around all the experiences captured in these pages, we accomplished all of those goals. And more.

We're More Willing to Try New Things

I wrote about spending two entire summers in Fremont, Michigan.

Fremont has a tavern that serves several specialty hamburgers. Options include burgers:

- Served between grilled cheese sandwiches.
- Topped with a hot dog, ham, and bacon.
- Topped with peanut butter, bacon, grape jelly, and crumbled potato chips.

On Monday nights, when the burgers were half price, MsBoyink and I would walk into town and split a new one.

With drinks and a tip, the cost of a little adventure was like *$12*.

The ladies in the RV park thought those burger ingredients were absurd.

"Peanut butter and jelly on a hamburger? Gross!"

"Have you tried it?"

"No. Gross!"

Travel forced us out of the big routines of life. It opened us up to new experiences including ordering weird things on restaurant menus. To a point. No tongues, feet, or eyeballs for us, thanks.

(I actually thought the PBJ burger was pretty good.)

We Overcame Fear

You've already read stories where we dealt with fear.

There are more.

Harrison sang an original song at an open-mic night in Austin, Texas, accompanying himself on guitar.

Miranda got up on stage at a poetry slam in Durango, Colorado and read some of her work.

MsBoyink and I spoke at an RV conference in Fredericksburg, Texas.

Our ultimate experience with fear?

Being driven down I-10 in Phoenix by a kid with only a learner's permit and a belief in his own immortality.

Successfully overcoming those fears gives us the courage to take on others.

We View Space Differently

RVs are small.

Yet, we were comfortable. We were organized. We even had space for non-essentials like instruments and kayaks.

In a country where the average home is 2,400 square feet for 2.5 people, that's absurd.

The house we bought isn't technically a tiny house, but it's rightsized for our life. It's small enough that we use every room every day and large enough to entertain guests and have hobbies.

Traveling also taught us that the idea of a "forever home" is short-sighted. We treat this house as a future rental rather than our retirement home.

Because who knows what the future will bring?

We Have More in Common with People

We left the road and settled into a new church, new community, and new jobs.

Which means lots of introductions to new people.

Which is usually when conversations get awkward for us adult male non-sports fans:

Them: *You're from Michigan!? I can't believe you guys let Birkenstocker go! We're gonna cream you this year...roll chalk tide hook 'em gopher nation YEA!*

Me: *blank look.*

We haven't been to every state (yet), but can usually find conversational common ground in their home state, favorite camping spot, or somewhere they used to live.

We View Church Differently

While on the road we learned to let church find us.

A local church here in Missouri gave us a place to live while we got off the road. We still call that church our home.

But we didn't completely revert back to our pre-travel habits. We mostly attend

on Wednesday nights. This leaves our weekend free for antiquing, camping, and other projects (like writing this book).

Traveling also opened us up to different ways of worshiping and experiencing God's presence. This new church practices things that the old us would have been uncomfortable with like ad-hoc open-mic sermons, speaking in tongues, prophecy, etc.

"We'll Figure It Out"

"We'll figure it out" became one of the most common things we said during our travels.

We appreciated how RV travel lowered the risk of adventure.

Miss a turn? Book the wrong campground? Noisy neighbors? Wake up with a cold? Run out of gas?

Don't worry. We're home.

Even if home happens to be parked in the nearest Walmart parking lot.

Knowing we had a place to sleep and eat gave us the security to explore new places, try new things, and "figure it out" on the fly.

As we successfully figured things out, the more comfortable we got with the process. Building on success, we expanded past campgrounds and figured out large cities, public transit systems, WWOOFing farms, etc.

I watch our now-adult children navigate solo travel and other new experiences and I know where their confidence comes from.

What Do the Kids Think?

Traveling families like to talk about how valuable we think the experience is for our kids.

But you rarely hear from the now-adult kids who grew up traveling.

So I asked Miranda and Harrison what they thought about our years on the road.

Miranda says:

Growing up is hard.

Growing up while traveling is no less hard. I might say it's harder, as your mental, emotional, and spiritual parts are growing many times faster than the physical part.

But if I hadn't traveled, I would've grown up into a much different person than I am now.

Traveling taught me:

- How to make friends with the right people.
- The importance of adventure, especially risky adventure.
- How to be lonely.
- How to love both the beach and the desert.

When I began traveling, I hated it. I was lonely and trapped and going through puberty.

But after I played games with the ocean and made friends with saguaros, I started to like it.

While our wheels were chocked, my heart was still in motion.

Harrison says:

Looking back at my five years of travel, I have a lot of positive memories.

I had unparalleled experiences that gave me a taste for adventure.

I learned to change how to interact with people based on their culture and beliefs. This directly translates to adult life and being in the workforce.

I also learned flexibility and adaptability. Life in an RV can be unpredictable and I had to be okay with anything that popped up.

These traits have proven handy while navigating the world - especially when unexpected events like a global pandemic occur.

But full-time travel also had grey spots.

Sometimes I feel like I missed out on typical teenager things like being dumb with my friends and getting to learn who I wanted to be as a person.

When I wanted to explore a new place I had to take my sister with me (safety in numbers). This precaution didn't allow me to learn who I was or wanted to be. I never got to be "Harrison" - I was always half of "Harrison and Miranda."

I didn't have the ability to connect with people in the way I would've liked. These days, I'm able to start a conversation with just about anyone, but it stays at surface level. Traveling never gave me the chance to learn to make lasting connections with people, which I'm still learning to do.

The experiences I had and the chance to see everything that I did was incredible. It instilled a love of traveling that I still have, and gave me the confidence to do so.

If we hadn't spent the time we did on the road, I don't think I would've moved to Australia or worked at different camps.

But I struggle to stay in one place. I'm trying to put down roots and I've never learned how. Before we started traveling, I was too young to learn it.

After I moved out on my own all I knew how to do was travel, so I kept doing it. Now, at the age of 25, I'm learning how to make friends, how to watch over and be watched over by neighbors, and how to build a home for myself. I know most people my age are still learning all of these things, but it's in a different way.

I don't have friends I've known for years and if I do they're across the country or the world, not across town.

I don't really know how to be a good neighbor, since I got used to being a neighbor to someone for short periods of time. I didn't have to remember to check on them if I hadn't seen them in a couple days.

In the end, I've gotten pretty good at being flexible and adaptable. I know with the patience and acceptance of my community, in time this will be just another step on my journey.

Photos:

1. Harrison and Miranda swim in Austin, TX.
2. Harrison and MsBoyink look at the Lake Michigan shoreline.
3. The Boyink kids play with friends in Kalaloch, WA.
4. Michael, Miranda, and Harrison eat supper on the Yellowstone River in Wyoming.

126 Epilogue

What happens if you play a country song backwards?

You know the old joke, right? The singer gets his truck back, his dog back, his job back, and his wife back.

There are times where our post-travel life feels like we filmed ourselves getting on the road and are now playing it backwards.

We move back into a house. The RV goes away. All of the stuff we worked so hard to get rid of starts trickling in again. And sofa by food processor by exercise bike, we get deeper and deeper entrenched back into a stationary life.

We used to brag (arrogantly, in retrospect) that we "owned our days." Between self-employment, homeschooling, and travel, on a daily basis we chose when and where we worked, schooled, and explored.

It's now been a few years since we got off the road. We're back working for the man, living for the weekend, and counting the days until we get a whole week of vacation.

You might detect a bit of angst in those words.

You're right.

It's not a daily thing. But most weeks there's a moment where we'd like to be somewhere warmer, cooler, more scenic, or closer to friends.

For a while there wasn't much we could do about it. Our jobs required our presence and allowed little time away.

MsBoyink had some health issues pop up that kept us even more rooted.

The angst isn't overwhelming. There are advantages to being stationary.

I felt called to my work at the newspaper - like God put me in this place at this time because this community needed the writing and photography skills I have. I got (mostly) good feedback from readers. I even won a couple of journalism awards.

MsBoyink left her stressful, off-shift nursing job and joined me at the newspaper. We bought a minivan and converted it into a camper for weekend trips. We outfitted our spare room as a craft studio and started exploring our artistic sides.

We created an idyllic small town life - working together just a couple blocks from home, out of adjoining offices,

co-creating the paper each week. On weekends we'd go on long drives, explore antique shops, take wine tasting tours, or work on creative projects.

Then the third-generation local owner we loved working for decided to retire. She sold the paper to a regional chain with an out-of-town owner.

It didn't take long to see that we weren't a good match. We saw the business through the transition, then I started job searching.

One upside of COVID was a job market more receptive to hiring a fifty-something white male. Another upside was many of those jobs were fully remote.

It took a few months, dozens of applications, and several interviews, but I found a remote position as Managing Editor with a global software implementation company based in Connecticut.

The benefits and pay are drastically better than what the newspaper provided. Our financial health hasn't looked this good in a long time. We are paying off debt and can think about a retirement plan.

But the biggest upside?

We are location-independent again. Not with quite the same flexibility we used to have. The new job is remote but it's still a full-time, Monday-Friday, 40-hour-a-week gig. We can't move whenever we want.

We met RVing families with similar jobs who adapted by staying in each location at least a week, then moving on the weekend. But, while I'll never say we'll never buy another RV, we're ready for something different.

The campervan gives us some short term RV-ish freedom, but we're considering other options. Do we rent the house out and go somewhere long-term? Do we take house sitting gigs? Caretaker jobs? Sublease student housing for the summer?

Not sure yet. With some larger house projects remaining, life may not look different for a while.

But the remote job means that's a choice, rather than a requirement.

That's already freedom.

And the kids?

Miranda was with us for a while here in Ava, but didn't enjoy it. She moved to the other side of Missouri and got married soon after. She and her new husband are in that early marriage phase of negotiating a couple out of two independent singles.

Harrison remains in West Michigan. He stayed with the same employer for a number of years, then moved to a smaller company where he's running the shipping department.

His life may look more traditional now than when he was with us, but he hasn't stayed completely stationary either. He went on a mission trip to Australia and has also traveled to Germany, Los Angeles, New York City, Toronto, and Mobile, Alabama.

And there's a girl.

But Harrison's story, like all of our stories, isn't done yet.

Which brings us back to wonder.

Our trip had its genesis in wonder.

After we got life mobilized and rolling down the road, wonder sustained us.

Here we are again. We have the means, motive, and opportunity to live in a different way.

We wonder where life will take us next.

And we are driven to find out.

Photos:

1. From a campervan day trip to the Buffalo National River in Arkansas.
2. Harrison and his girlfriend Helen.
3. Miranda with her new husband Keith.
4. Handcrafted greeting cards by MsBoyink.
5. This 60s era clamshell record player now houses our DVD player and collection.
6. All the supplies for this custom clock came from our local Walmart.
7. We collected fridge magnets while traveling, then turned them into Christmas ornaments.
8. I gave this 1940s box fan a mid-century modern twist.
9. Our campervan's anonymous exterior.
10. We removed all the seats and made a raised platform bed.
11. A drawer holds a camp stove, wash bin, and utensils. Under the hinged platform is a cooler and food storage.

Acknowledgments

First, the thank yous. As much as I might like to think I did everything it took to create this book, the reality is anything but.

I have to thank the good Lord for setting us up to travel full-time, keeping us safe, and for giving us memories we'll hold onto forever.

We met many husbands and wives who said "I'd love to travel fulltime but there's no way my spouse would do it." Thank you, MsBoyink, for being a willing partner in this uncommon adventure. And for enduring "book-widowship" while I wrote.

Harrison and Miranda. I know the experience had high points and low points for each of you. I hope you choose to savor the highs and learn from the lows. Thank you for not mutinying.

At different times our extended families would host us or meet us on the road. Thank you for your hospitality and support.

We met dozens of other families rebellious enough to do the same thing we were. Thank you for the laughter, the conversations, the shared understandings, the meals, and the ad-hoc church services.

Our early days of travel were funded in one way or another by the community around the ExpressionEngine® content management system. Thank you former employees of EllisLab, and my clients, students, readers, and fellow developers.

Members of "Mike's Irregular Newsletter" provided feedback and encouragement while I wrote this book. A quick scour of my email folders turns up Leslie Camacho, Kevin Banonis, Zack Flodeen, Jenni Keiter, Jamie Feinberg, Tom Brownsword, David Monsour, Margaret Zhang, Megan Mallonee, Troy Arnold, Susan Sherrouse, Renee Clark, Jenise Cook, Norm & Julie Harebottle, kellybellygolf, Gary Bex, Karen Riley, Rob Wilcox, Cheryl Beatty, Mike Corless, David Madsen, Jessica Connell, Patti Shelton, Sonia Martin, Donna Maukonen, Sallie Draper, Karis, Susan Beyers, Matthew Davison, Jane Timmons, Kelly Longgrear, Heather Gebbia, Matt Recupito, Jimmie McGhee, Rebecca Brasier, Philip Zaengle, Kevin S., Don Boggs, Jenny Keavy Olson, Jeremy Latham, Bob Watts, De'Etta, Bill Jewell, Doug Schaefer, Andrea Elkins, Holli Bradish-Lane, Jen Charrette, and Susan Kotello (my apologies for anyone I may have missed). Thank you all.

Thanks to Fiona Raven and Glenna Collett, authors of *Book Design Made Simple*. I won't agree that book design is simple, but your book enabled me to create this one.

Thanks to Paul Burton of OddBurton.com for the cover illustration.

Thanks to MsBoyink and Miranda for patient, persistent, and persnickety editing.

And lastly, thank you, reader, for reading.

All photos taken and © copyrighted by Michael or Crissa Boyink unless otherwise noted.

Photos of Sun Studio used by permission of Sun Studios in Memphis, TN.

Photos of the Peabody Hotel used by permission of the Peabody Hotel in Memphis, TN.

Photos of Christopher Blackwell and the Basin Range Volcanics Geolapidary Museum in Deming, New Mexico used by permission of Christopher Blackwell.

Photos of the National Eagle Center and its resident eagles used by permission of the National Eagle Center, Wabasha, Minnesota.

Photos of the Stennis Space Center and the NASA logo used by permission of NASA Headquarters, Washington, DC.

Photo of Colonel Glenn Frazier used with permission of his wife, Terri Frazier in Daphne, AL.

Photo of Willie's Wee-Nee Wagon used by permission of D. Lynne Howell, President, Willies Wee-Nee Wagon Inc, Brunswick, GA.

Photo of the D.B.A. Club used by permission of the D.B.A. Club, New Orleans, LA.

Photo of Tuba Skinny performing at the D.B.A. Club used by permission of Tuba Skinny.
Excerpt(s) from TRAVELS WITH CHARLEY: IN SEARCH OF AMERICA by John Steinbeck, copyright © 1961, 1962 by The Curtis Publishing Co.; copyright © 1962 by John Steinbeck; copyright renewed © 1989, 1990 by Elaine Steinbeck, Thom Steinbeck, and John Steinbeck IV. Used by permission of Viking Books, an imprint of Penguin Publishing Group, a division of Penguin Random House LLC. All rights reserved.

Jeep®, the seven-slot grill design, and "CJ5" are registered trademarks of FCA US LLC. The Author has no affiliation with Daimler/Chrysler, FCA US LLC, Fiat Chrysler or any other company or corporation that may be affiliated with any Jeep-related trademarks or logos. Throughout this publication any references to the terms "Jeep, "Jeeping", "Willys", "CJ", "TJ", "YJ", "Wrangler" are used nominally and for identification purposes only.

The ExpressionEngine® mark is owned and may be registered by Packet Tide. Author has not been authorized, sponsored, or otherwise approved by Packet Tide.

Gerber® is a trademark of the Nestlé company. Author has not been authorized, sponsored, or otherwise approved by Nestlé.

Photos:

1. Our first RV at Picacho Peak State Park in AZ.
2. Michael and MsBoyink with our third RV, photo by Joe Hendricks of joehendricks.com.

State/City Index

Photos:
1. Snorkeling in Key West, FL.
2. Miranda at the Cathedral of Junk in Austin, TX.

Keyword Index

About the Author

Michael Boyink is an award-winning writer and photographer who works as Managing Editor for a global software consulting and implementation company.

Michael, his wife Crissa (aka MsBoyink), and their two children spent eight years traveling the USA in an RV while continuing to work and homeschool.

While on the road, Michael and Crissa ran DitchingSuburbia.com, a popular website that provided resources, guides, and community for traveling families. Their story was covered by the Huffington Post, the Seattle Times, the Las Vegas Guardian, the Art of Noncomformity, Tiny House Magazine, and many other travel-related blogs and podcasts.

Michael and Crissa are now homeowners in rural Missouri where they continue to look for new ways to scratch the incurable condition known as hitch-itch.

Connect with Michael:
LinkedIn: linkedin.com/in/michael-boyink
Instagram: instagram.com/boyink
Website: boyink.com